T0247543

Marlon Brando

Marlon Brando

Hollywood Rebel

Burt Kearns

APPLAUSE
THEATRE & CINEMA BOOKS
Essex, Connecticut

APPLAUSE

THEATRE & CINEMA BOOKS

An imprint of Globe Pequot, the trade division of
The Rowman & Littlefield Publishing Group, Inc.
4501 Forbes Blvd., Ste. 200
Lanham, MD 20706
www.rowman.com

Distributed by NATIONAL BOOK NETWORK

British Library Cataloguing in Publication Information Available

Library of Congress Cataloging-in-Publication Data

Names: Kearns, Burt, author.
Title: Marlon Brando : Hollywood rebel / Burt Kearns.
Description: Essex, Connecticut : Applause, 2024. | Includes bibliographical
    references and index.
Identifiers: LCCN 2023037066 (print) | LCCN 2023037067 (ebook) |
    ISBN 9781493072507 (cloth) | ISBN 9781493072514 (ebook)
Subjects: LCSH: Brando, Marlon. | Motion picture actors and actresses—
    United StatesBiography.
Classification: LCC PN2287.B683 K43 2024 (print) | LCC PN2287.B683 (ebook)
    | DDC 791.4302/8092 [B]—dc23/eng/20231124
LC record available at https://lccn.loc.gov/2023037066
LC ebook record available at https://lccn.loc.gov/2023037067

♾️™ The paper used in this publication meets the minimum requirements of
American National Standard for Information Sciences—Permanence of Paper
for Printed Library Materials, ANSI/NISO Z39.48-1992.

For Alison, Sam, and Sally Jade.
And in memory of Gray Frederickson.

Contents

Contents

Prologue

We hear Marlon Brando before we see him in *The Wild One,* after the movie has faded in from black to a long, empty two-lane highway, stretching from the horizon through rolling hills and farmland. The camera has been placed in the middle of the road, atop the unbroken white line that extends to the grove of trees far off in the distance. The portentous music kicks in over the Columbia Pictures torch lady logo, even before the fade-in to the black-and-white scene and the imprimatur of importance, "Columbia Pictures Corporation Presents a Stanley Kramer Company Production"—Stanley Kramer being a producer known for tackling controversial issues in films of great social significance—followed by a disclaimer.

> THIS IS A SHOCKING STORY.
> IT COULD NEVER TAKE PLACE
> IN MOST AMERICAN TOWNS—
> BUT IT DID IN THIS ONE.
> IT IS A PUBLIC CHALLENGE
> NOT TO LET IT HAPPEN AGAIN.

And now the music segues into a generic, sultry, jazzy film score, dipping under the sound of Brando's unmistakable voice, in 1953 already in the arsenal of comedians and impressionists in nightclubs and on television. Brando speaks softly, with a slight lisp and a touch of Southern accent straight out of a honey-dripping Tennessee Williams play, as he adds additional context, explaining that "it begins here, for me, on this road.

"How the whole mess happened, I don't know. But I know it couldn't happen again in a million years. Maybe I could've stopped it early, but once the trouble was on its way, I was just goin' with it. Mostly, I remember the girl. I—I can't explain it, sad chick like that. But something changed in me. She got to me. Well, that's later, anyway. This is where it begins for me. Right on this road."

This is definitely not a narration from a stolid screen hero like John Wayne, Randolph Scott, or Gary Cooper, but by this point the words don't matter so much, because when Brando stops speaking, that cool, romantic jazz score is overtaken by an urgent "Flight of the Bumblebee" frenzy of strings that signals something appearing on the horizon, some kind of swarm approaching on that two-lane blacktop. A distant hum can be detected as it builds to thunder, and a brigade of motorcycles comes into view. Twenty of them, spread out across both lanes, roar over and past the camera. One of the last of the bikers fishtails in front of the lens, the last bike speeds by, and—*Cut!*—to Marlon Brando, leading the pack on a 1950 6T Triumph Thunderbird. It's a startling image, because it's obvious that Brando and the two bikers flanking slightly behind are no longer on the road but in a studio. They're sitting on stationary motorcycles in front of a rear projection screen, on which slightly blurred cyclists follow a camera truck through the twists and turns of a mountain road outside Los Angeles. The setup is deliberate. Within five seconds, the camera pushes in on Brando, past the rocking bike and Levi jeans to a medium close-up so the viewer can behold and soak in the image of the rebel.

Brando's wearing an eight-panel mariner's cap with leather visor, Bausch and Lomb aviator sunglasses—and sideburns. His hands, gripping the cruiser handlebars, are covered in black leather gloves and he wears a Schott Perfecto-style black leather motorcycle jacket, zipped to the neck, and personalized with a star on each of the epaulets, indicating his status as leader of the pack. The name "Johnny" is stitched over his heart—the name of his character, Johnny Strabler.

Then Marlon Brando's name fills the screen: *"Marlon Brando as"*—not "Marlon Brando *in*," but Marlon Brando *as* The Wild One. The camera sticks with the star for more than a minute as the credits roll over him. He and the other bikers in front of the screen lean right and left, almost in sync with the riders on film behind them. By the time the picture cuts back to that two-lane road and Brando eventually rolls into scene, viewers have had time to admire, and in fact, lust after the hero—make that the *anti*-hero. The stage has been set, and the image is indelible.

The plot of *The Wild One* is simple enough: Johnny Strabler and his gang of outlaw motorcyclists roll into a town and, acting like reckless teenagers, disrupt a proper motorcycle track race, are chased out by the law, and wind up in Wrightsville, a town with a less aggressive police presence. They cause a ruckus on Main Street, take over the local café, and raise a little hell before a rival gang led by Johnny's former riding buddy Chino arrives and all hell really breaks loose and rains down on Johnny. Johnny will show interest in a local girl, maybe even fall for her, be wrongly accused of attempted rape and beaten mercilessly by vigilantes, then framed for a killing, while the "squares" of polite society will turn out to be as contemptuous of the law as the rebel cyclists.

This was, in many ways, an unlikely role for an actor of Brando's stature. Already regarded as a transformative figure when he arrived in Hollywood from Broadway in 1949, twice nominated for Academy Awards for Best Actor, and most recently onscreen as Mark Antony in *William Shakespeare's Julius Caesar* (which would soon lead to his third

Brando as Johnny Strabler in *The Wild One*. The look that launched a thousand subcultures. Columbia Pictures/Photofest © Columbia

Best Actor nomination), he was playing what in effect was a grown-up juvenile delinquent. And though the music in *The Wild One* is jazz and the language is rebop, he would become the archetype for a rock 'n' roll generation just waiting to be unloosed, and more: actors, activists, fashion designers, artists, hipsters, and politicians will all follow because of the image of an actor pretending to ride a motorcycle in front of a rear projection screen.

With this role more than any other, Marlon Brando becomes more than a movie star. He is James Dean. He is Steve McQueen. He is Dennis Hopper and Peter Fonda in *Easy Rider*. He is Jack Nicholson in *One Flew Over the Cuckoo's Nest*. He is Robert De Niro in *Taxi Driver*, John Travolta in *Grease*, Johnny Depp in *Cry-Baby*, Ryan Gosling in *Drive*. He is John Lennon, Johnny Hallyday, Bruce Springsteen, Lou Reed, Freddie Mercury, Robert Mapplethorpe. He is the Ramones. He is Prince in *Purple Rain*. He is Austin Butler in *Elvis*. *He is Elvis.* Hey, he's Suzi Quatro, Chrissie Hynde, Cherie Currie, Madonna, Lady Gaga, and Rihanna, too. Or they are him. Marlon Brando was the rebel before any of them. He is the one they want to be.

There have been many biographies written about Marlon Brando. His life has been examined. His work has been deconstructed. His affairs have been chronicled. His embarrassments and tragedies have been rehashed, often with glee. Great writers, including Bob Thomas, Peter Manso, Patricia Bosworth, William J. Mann—and Brando himself—have claimed the biographical territory. What else, even this author asked at first, can be written about Marlon Brando?

Not a biography. What follows is not "another Marlon Brando biography"—nor a hagiography—but a study of how one man's artistic and personal decisions affected not only those around him, but all of Western society and popular culture. Specific instances and periods of his life will be recounted and reexamined in some detail, as will the stories and trajectories of some of those on whom Brando left a lasting impression. The reader will find that Marlon Brando's mark on the modern world has been indisputable and pervasive in the seventy-seven years since he walked onstage at Broadway's Ethel Barrymore Theatre, twenty years after his death, and one hundred years after his birth. What may be surprising is how widespread his influence extends—and how much of it can be traced to *The Wild One*.

One

Young Rebel

It's late summer. 1947. New York City at night. Marlon Brando and his lifelong buddy Wally Cox are riding their motorcycles up Eighth Avenue in Manhattan. They are, both would admit, an odd couple. In his black leather jacket, T-shirt, and jeans, straddling the used Indian bike he'd recently purchased, Brando is already the living embodiment of the American rebel. He's classically handsome, with a strong jaw, broad forehead, and a sensuous mouth. Cox, though athletically inclined and an Army veteran, appears to be a slight, bookish type. His jacket is brown. He wears a necktie and spectacles. Some of their colleagues and acquaintances whisper that these two might be more than friends. They *are* more than friends, that's for sure. Brando would make it clear. "He was more than a friend; he was my brother." Sex? Brando would shrug at the notion. Sex is sexless. Sex is natural. Sex is beside the point. Wally Cox is his oldest friend, the kid he rescued from bullies on the playground in the fourth grade back in Evanston, Illinois. Wally's family moved away, and Brando hadn't seen his little buddy in nine years when they bumped into each other on Sixth Avenue in the Village back in 1944. It was as if the years hadn't passed at all. Their friendship would last a lifetime, beyond both their lifetimes, and in some ways into eternity.

The friends ride on, entering Center Drive in Central Park, racing each other, but carefully; Brando can't afford to mess up that face. Truth be told, he's not that great a motorcyclist, and he rides cautiously, looking out for the droppings from the hansom carriage horses that, if encountered unexpectedly, could lead to a painful spill. But he looks good on a motorcycle and stands out because not too many of his colleagues and acquaintances are brave enough to chance the rocket rides through the concrete canyons. Then again, Marlon Brando has stood out since he arrived in Manhattan four years earlier, and now, at twenty-three, all the elements that will make him the most influential figure of his generation are already falling into place: artistically, politically, socially, and

1

sexually. By the final weeks of 1947, Marlon Brando will be on his way to becoming the most influential actor of his generation and generations to follow. But now, in the second half of this crucial year, as he powers his Indian under the sugar maple and green ash trees of the park, he's more than willing to take his greatest gift and throw it away.

First, the backstory, the biography part of this book that is not a biography at all: Marlon Brando's story, the information and context that help make sense of all that's to follow and be reflected in his life and in its wake. The story of the rebel begins on April 3, 1924, when Marlon Brando Jr. is born to a pair of alcoholics in Omaha, Nebraska. One of his earliest memories was of his early childhood, when he was three, maybe four years old, and sleeping with his governess, Ermi. "She was eighteen years old. . . . She was Danish, but a touch of Indonesian blood gave her skin a slightly dusky, smoky patina. She was nude, and so was I, and it was a lovely experience. . . . I sat there looking at her body and fondling her breasts, and arranged myself on her and crawled over her. She was all mine." The reader can see where this is going. Ermi *was* all his, that is until one day, when Marlon—or "Bud," everyone called him "Bud"—was seven, and Ermi left Bud's bed and the Brando home and went off to get married. "I felt abandoned," Brando told Robert Lindsey in long, freewheeling discussions that would become the book *Songs My Mother Taught Me*. "My mother had long ago deserted me for her bottle; now Ermi was gone, too. That's why in life I would always find women who were going to desert me; I had to repeat the process. From that day forward, I became estranged from this world."

Marlon Brando Sr. worked in the manufacturing business. He was a salesman, often on the road, a philandering womanizer who neglected his wife and was distant and unaffectionate with his son. Brando's mother, the former Dorothy Pennebaker, known as "Dodie," was a sensitive beauty who'd found her passion as an actress with the Omaha Community Playhouse—she recruited twenty-one-year-old Henry Fonda and got him interested in acting—only to have her dreams dashed in 1930 when her husband took a job in Chicago and moved the family, which included Marlon's older sisters Jocelyn and Frances, to Evanston, Illinois.

In Evanston, his parents' troubles only intensified. Young Bud was often truant from school. He developed a stammer, which would affect his performances as an adult. When he was twelve, his parents separated, and Dodie took Bud and his sisters to live with her mother in Santa Ana, California. There would be a reconciliation a couple of years later and the family would reconvene in a rambling farmhouse on the edge of Libertyville, Illinois, a small town north of Chicago. Dodie's drinking worsened and led to many embarrassing public scenes. Too many times,

Bud got the call and had to carry his mother home, dead drunk, from a bar or the side of a road.

Drama, acting, theater—those were what Bud Brando could grab onto and excel in without really trying. Everyone was aware of his talent, ever since he attended summer camp in Wisconsin when he was ten years old and showed a knack for calling attention to himself and a talent for mimicry. Acting seemed easy enough. At Liberty High School, he joined the Dramatics Club, but clashed with the teacher, who wasn't equipped to notice that Bud had something special.

Acting wasn't something in which Bud took particular pride. To him, acting was just something everybody did. "We developed the technique of acting very, very early, even from the time when we're a kid, throwing our oatmeal on the floor, just to get attention from our mothers," he'd say in later years. "Acting is surviving." His true passion was music—jazz music, and if he was going to be on stage, he'd prefer to be sitting behind a drum kit. Bud had a Slingerland set in his room that he beat away at and he carried sticks wherever he went. He tried out for the school marching band, but every time they'd go into a routine, he'd start riffing with Gene Krupa licks and fills. Bud had girlfriends—no one steady—and he made it clear to the other boys that he was experienced. He said he'd "done it" more than once and they believed him.

Bud Brando was also angry and edgy, and he played pranks that could be mean. He was, as he'd describe himself later, "a bad student, chronic truant and all-round incorrigible forever being sent to the principal's office to be disciplined." He had a "contempt for authority," and "didn't try hard because I was bored and irritated."

He was, from an early age, a rebel.

After it was ruled that Bud had failed or dropped enough classes that he'd have to repeat his sophomore year of high school, his father finally noticed him, stepped in, and made a drastic decision. He enrolled the teen at the Shattuck Military Academy in Faribault, Minnesota. Marlon Sr. had attended the school and believed the discipline would do his son good.

"My tenure at Shattuck was probably fated from the beginning to be short," Brando told Lindsey. "By then I was rebelling against any authority and against conformity in general with every ounce of energy in my body."

The military life was not one to which Bud Brando was suited. He resisted the philosophy that "it is only through order, submission to discipline, and the exorcising of individuality that you make a good soldier." Yet, from the time he entered the academy at sixteen, he was not unpopular. Brando made friends, played sports, joined the drill team. He also engaged in pranks and acts of vandalism, bragged of having sex with the local girls who worked as maids in the all-boys institution, and wasn't shy about his sexual relationship with a younger male cadet. He didn't do well in class.

"Because I flunked or dropped out of so many classes, I ended up spending a lot of time in study hall, which is where you were sent if you were kicked out of a class. And in study hall, I also liked to riffle through the pages of the *National Geographic*, where I made another wonderful discovery, Tahiti. . . . To a captive on what seemed like Devil's Island, Tahiti appeared to me at least a sanctuary, and at best nirvana."

Tahiti dreams would stay with him (and ultimately be fulfilled). Meanwhile, the one subject in which he did do well was English, in a class taught by a man named Earle Wagner. Known to all as "Duke," Wagner was in his early forties, an affected bachelor with a pencil mustache who'd sashay around campus wearing a battered hat and trench coat, often with a flowing cape draped across his shoulders, and sporting colorful ties and handkerchiefs. Duke was considered to be sophisticated and witty, drove a Packard convertible, and had as a companion an English bulldog. Duke lived on campus in Whipple Hall and was known to invite his students inside his apartment to loll on the Oriental rugs, marvel at his lithographs, and peruse his volumes of classics. He was, it was written, "Shattuck's answer to Mr. Chips," and a strange cat to be prowling around an all-boys military school, but at least for a time, he inspired Bud Brando. Duke led the Dramatic Association, so in addition to helping Bud appreciate the language and relevance of Shakespeare, he convinced the teen to act in his first Shattuck production, a short play called *A Message from Khufu*.

There were rumors on campus that Bud and Duke were engaged in a sexual relationship. Whatever the case, by the following year, there would be a break between them. After two years at Shattuck, Brando's pranks, resistance to authority, and most important, failing grades, had led to a breaking point. He was placed on probation, violated probation, and in May 1943, expelled. Duke Wagner was among his antagonists. He'd caught Bud smoking and offered testimony against the boy. (Four years later, Duke was kicked off campus, allegedly over his relationship with a faculty adviser's wife, but according to contemporaries, because he was caught having sex with a cadet.)

So in May 1943, nineteen-year-old Bud Brando was back in Libertyville, facing his disapproving and angry parents and an uncertain future. In an unprecedented move, his fellow cadets at Shattuck responded to his expulsion by rebelling and threatening "to go on strike" if he was not reinstated. The school administration compromised and invited Bud to return in the summer to complete his grades. He turned down the offer but did not abandon the idea of returning to a uniform. There was a war on. Many kids his age in Libertyville were being drafted, others were volunteering, and with his military school background, broken though it was, he could be commissioned as an officer. Shattuck, however, worked against him. A knee injury from a football scrimmage at the school got him classified "4-F."

Bud's father insisted he get a summer job, so he spent the next couple of months digging ditches and laying tile. By the end of July, emotions had cooled, and the family saw a direction for young Bud to take. His two older sisters had moved to New York City. Jocelyn, whom the family called "Tiddy," was taking classes at the American Academy of Dramatic Arts. Frannie was studying painting at the Art Students League in Greenwich Village. Money was not an issue. Marlon Sr. would pay for his son to attend the New School for Social Research. Bud Brando would study acting at the school's Dramatic Workshop.

That fall, Marlon "Bud" Brando was living with Frannie in Greenwich Village and signing up for classes at the New School at 66 West Twelfth Street. The New School was a progressive institution, dedicated to free thinking, and a haven for many Jewish intellectuals from Europe who'd fled the Fascists or Hitler. The Dramatic Workshop was run by Erwin Piscator, an influential theater director and innovator in epic, leftist theatrical productions, who'd left Germany in 1931. Students at the Workshop felt the same rush of freedom, on the loose in Greenwich Village among such creativity. Walter Matthau, who studied under Piscator, referred to the place as the "Neurotic Workshop of Sexual Research."

Brando, it is said, stood apart from the well-dressed crowd from the start. Legend has it he was already wearing jeans, T-shirts, and engineer's boots. A recent biographer says he actually wore nice clean shirts, khakis, and sneakers, but attracted attention as some kind of bohemian because he was the one male student who didn't wear a tie. Brando made friends, made women, made men, and was lucky enough to fall under the wing of instructor Stella Adler.

Adler was a striking presence, forty-two years old and a member of a Jewish acting dynasty. Her father was the great Yiddish stage actor Jacob P. Adler, her brother the actor and director Luther Adler. In the early 1930s, she'd studied under Konstantin Stanislavski of the Moscow Art Theater and brought his techniques to the Group Theatre, a company of New York actors, writers, and directors who'd banded together to challenge the light entertainment of American popular theater with cutting-edge, left-wing realism that reflected their times.

Brando remembered Stella Alder as "quite tall and very beautiful, with blue eyes, stunning blond hair and a leonine presence . . . a marvelous actress who unfortunately never got a chance to become a great star." Brando blamed her lack of stage and screen success on anti-Semitism. "Producers in New York and especially in Hollywood," he said, "wouldn't hire actors if they 'looked Jewish,' no matter how good they were." He gave Stella Adler full credit for the acting techniques he developed and would use to revolutionize the craft. He was not, he pointed out many times, to the point of exasperation, a proponent of "method acting," the technique that would be championed by and identified with former Group Theatre member Lee Strasberg in the 1950s. It was a fine distinction, though. Strasberg relied on the theory developed by Russian actor and director Konstantin Stanislavski that actors should use emotional recall, their own memories, to inhabit a character. When Adler studied with Stanislavski, she learned that he'd evolved in his method, urging actors to use not their memories, but imaginations. Brando would say that Adler taught her students "how to discover the nature of their own emotional mechanics and therefore those of others." She taught him, he said, "to be real and not to try to act out an emotion I didn't personally experience during a performance."

Marlon Brando was Stella Adler's star student. He possessed an ability to be natural onstage in a way that actors of the time were not. He first appeared on Broadway on April 6, 1944, as a giraffe in thirteen matinee performances of *Bobino* at the Adelphi Theatre on West Fifty-Fourth Street. The children's play by author Stanley Kauffman had debuted at The New School auditorium on Christmas Day 1943, and was revived by The American Theatre for Young Folks.

In the summer, it was Shattuck all over again. After one too many run-ins with Piscator, Brando was expelled from the New School—but, as luck would have it, he "simply stepped off one lily pad for another." Within weeks, he had his first real acting job. His "official" Broadway debut was recorded on October 19, 1944, in *I Remember Mama* at the Music Box Theatre. It was a heartwarming play about a family of working-class Norwegian immigrants chasing the American dream. Brando had a small role and an extended contract. *Mama* was a hit, but fifteen months of reciting the same lines, night after night and twice on Wednesday and Sundays, drove him crazy and almost out of acting for good.

Brando left the successful play and eventually was cast in *Truckline Café*, a controversial work by Maxwell Anderson, produced by Elia Kazan, another Group Theatre alum. When the play opened on February 27, 1946, at the Belasco Theatre, the critics tore it apart. John Chapman in the *Daily News* called *Truckline Café* "the worst play I have seen since I have been in the reviewing business." The play limped through ten performances—but it put Brando on the map. More than a year before he'd stop the theater world with a cry of "*Stella!*," he caught audiences and reviewers off-guard in a scene in which he let out a raw, primal howl that could be heard out on the sidewalk.

Howl: Brando's breakthrough performance in *Truckline Café*. Photofest

Truckline Café led Brando to Broadway roles in *Antigone* and *Candida*, produced by and starring stage legend Katherine Cornell. When *Candida* opened in April, Chapman of the *Daily News* said Brando again stood out, and "managed to make something different, something a little more understandable, out of the trying role of Marchbanks the baby poet. I thought that his intensity was within him where it should be and not spread all around the outside. For the second time this season—the first was in *Truckline Café*—the young man has shown himself a player of promise."

That Broadway season of 1945–1946 was when Brando first made his mark on the greater world of theater. Already, he was labeled a "mumbler" because his Adler-taught version of The Method conflicted with the traditional vocal projections of the stage actor of the time, but he was voted best supporting actor and most promising young actor of the Broadway season in *Variety*'s annual poll. ("When I mumbled my lines in some parts, it puzzled theater critics," he later said. "I played many roles in which I didn't mumble a single syllable, but in others I did it because it is the way people speak in ordinary life.") The jury consisted of the same merciless New York drama critics who'd savaged *Truckline Café*. Those critics also voted Laurence Olivier as Best Actor for his roles in the Old Vic's productions of Sophocles, Shakespeare, and Chekhov at the New Century Theatre on West Fifty-Eighth Street. That Broadway season was, Claudia Roth Pierpont wrote in *The New Yorker*, "the first sign of a momentous transition in the art, if not the business, of acting."

That same year, Brando was offered a role in Eugene O'Neill's latest play. O'Neill was a Pulitzer Prize winner, a giant of letters and the theater. A role in his new work would be historic, sure to take the young actor to a new level. Brando shrugged. He'd read a few of O'Neill's plays, including *Desire Under the Elms*. He found the playwright to be "dour, negative and too dark, and I couldn't understand the philosophical import of what he was trying to say." Brando tried to read O'Neill's latest offering but found it to be a bore. The speeches were too long. He didn't make it through the first act before falling asleep. He turned down the role. The play had its premiere at the Martin Beck Theatre on October 9, 1946. "Of course when it opened," Brando said, "*The Iceman Cometh* was called O'Neill's masterpiece."

The play that Brando signed onto instead of *Iceman* was a blatant political screed created in order to raise money, at least in Brando's mind, for terrorists ("terrorists" was the word Brando would use to describe them), and it signaled the activist path he would take in years ahead. *A Flag Is Born* was written by Ben Hecht, the former journalist who cowrote the Broadway hit *The Front Page* and went on to a career as a Hollywood screenwriter. Kurt Weill provided the music. The play was produced by the American League for a Free Palestine, a group formed to campaign for the creation of a homeland in Palestine for the thousands of European Jews displaced during World War II. The British government, which administered the region, was blocking the immigration drive. The play, Brando admitted, was "essentially a piece of political propaganda . . . indirectly condemning the British for stopping the Jewish refugees en route from Europe to colonize Palestine."

Brando's politics, like his acting, were visceral and personal. He was surely influenced by Stella and Luther Adler, who were on the ALFP board. Stella Adler had taken him into her family. He dated her daughter. Most of his friends in New York City were Jewish, really the first Jews he got know, and he was intrigued by them. "They introduced me to a world of books and ideas that I didn't know existed," he recalled. "I stayed up all night with them—asking questions, arguing, probing, discovering how little I knew, learning how inarticulate I was and how abysmal my education was." He'd seen newsreel footage of the liberation of the concentration camps. He was appalled by the images and outraged that the British Army was stopping shiploads of concentration camp survivors and placing them in detention centers on Cypress.

Sympathy and support for the displaced Jews might not seem controversial in 1946, especially not in the United States. But when the ALFP sponsored lectures, rallies and events, there were picketers, fights, and arrests. The protesters were not American Fascists or Nazis, but fellow Jews. The community was divided over how to bend the will of the British. Many backed David Ben-Gurion, who appeased the British publicly, while smuggling Jews into Palestine. The ALFP backed the Irgun Zvai Leumi, a paramilitary group led by Menachem Begin. The Irgun "believed that terrorism and military action were necessary to wear down British resistance and lead to the early creation of Israel," Brando explained. "I sided with the militants."

A Flag Is Born, directed by Luther Adler, opened at the Alvin Theatre on September 5, 1946, for what was to be a limited run. Academy Award-winning actor Paul Muni, a Jew born Frederick Meshilem Meier Weisenfreund and one of the few actors Brando held in awe, was the star. "Everyone in *A Flag Is Born* was Jewish except me," Brando said. Yet every night, the *goy* was the one who stole the show with another loud, impassioned cry.

The cry came during a speech in the second act in which he challenged the audience—and most in the audience were supportive or concerned Jews—on whether they'd done enough to help the ones victimized by the Nazis. "Where were you?" Brando asked. Staring beyond the stage lights, he asked again, and then shouted, "Where were you Jews when six million Jews were being burned to death in the ovens? *Where were you?!*"

That was not boring! "It sent chills through the audience," Brando recalled. "At some performances, Jewish girls got out of their seats and screamed and cried from the aisles in sadness." At one show, a woman rose from her seat and shouted back, "Vere were *you*?"

The run was extended to a hundred and twenty performances, and in January 1947, the play moved on to Chicago, Detroit, Philadelphia, and Boston, with Jacob Ben-Ami in the lead role. (Ultimately, *A Flag Is Born* raised more than a million dollars in ticket sales and donations. Some of the money was used to purchase a ship, renamed the S.S. *Hecht*, to carry Holocaust survivors to Palestine, some to support Israel fighters there. Equally important, the play roused support in the United States for the Zionists and helped persuade the British to withdraw from Palestine. *A Flag Is Born* has been called "the play that helped create Israel.")

Brando left the production before it hit the road (Sidney Lumet took his place). He couldn't afford to stay any longer. Like the others in the cast, he'd agreed to be paid the Actors' Equity minimum of sixty dollars a week, and that wasn't enough to even cover the rent on his small apartment. He was convinced—make that *forced*—to take another Broadway play. *The Eagle Has Two Heads* was a showcase for the outrageous, heavy-drinking, raspy-voiced actress Tallulah Bankhead. Brando was cast as the young lover of the forty-four-year-old star. The problem for him was that the oversexed Bankhead had one hand on the script and the other reaching down his jeans. She expected Brando to play the role off stage, as well. Brando had been with older women. He'd had a long affair with a married woman in New York. More than one biographer claimed he'd been intimate with Stella Adler. Bankhead, though, was "despicable."

On its tryout tour on the way to Broadway, the play was renamed *Angel of Death* and then *Eagle Rampant*. Brando didn't think he was right for the role, and the critics on the road agreed. His difficulty in mastering the required accent was only one reason. "When I was supposed to kiss her, I couldn't bear it," he said. "For some reason, she had a cool mouth and her tongue was especially cold. Onstage, she was forever plunging it into my mouth without so much as a how-do-you-do. It was like an eel trying to slide backward into a hole."

Brando managed to get himself fired before the new year, long before the play made it to Broadway in March and closed after twenty-nine performances. He could have chosen another Broadway show. Instead, he ran back to the terrorists. After a crash course in atrocities against the Jews, he joined one of about twenty two-man teams, and set off across the country on behalf of the American League for a Free Palestine, raising money for the Irgun.

It was on this trip that an actor whose greatness was about to become apparent confirmed his split allegiances. Anyone who'd be surprised in the years to come when Brando took on controversial causes or let activism take precedence over his screen career, would not be had they known him in 1947. "I am now an active and integral part of a political organization," he wrote to his parents from the train, as he and fellow actor Jerry Solars chugged toward Kenosha, Wisconsin, to speak on "The Palestine Situation" at the Beth Hillel Temple. "I am not slighting my career nor am I slacking on my job. The work that we'll be doing won't be easy by any matter of means. It is a tougher and vastly more responsible job than anything the theater could offer. I'm going to do my best to add my little bit."

Never had Bud Brando felt he had done something so important. Speaking in synagogues and schools and to Jewish groups, he used all his stage skills to convince audiences of the inhumane conditions their fellow Jews were suffering—not under the Nazis, but the British. "There was always a lot of yelling at the temples we visited between the Jews who favored Ben-Gurion's approach and those favoring the terrorists whom I supported and who at the time were called 'Freedom Fighters.'"

On the road that spring, Brando's eyes were opened even wider to the injustices he would fight for the rest of his career. "Washington is strongly anti-Negro and I'm getting awfully mad," he wrote to his parents from the nation's capital. "Saw in the newsreel that the Ku Klux Klan is beginning to function en masse again. It makes you gape in awe to think about it. . . . No definite plans for this summer yet."

Two

Cyclists' Raid

Looking back, it really wasn't much of a riot, after all. But while Marlon "Bud" Brando was chasing his alternative dreams of acting and activism that summer of 1947, what took place over Fourth of July weekend in the city of Hollister, California, has gone down in history as one of the most influential public disturbances since the Boston Massacre. Thanks to Marlon Brando, it would have an equally revolutionary legacy.

In those first days of July, folks in the community about forty miles northeast of Monterey had reason to be excited about the All-American celebration scheduled for the three-day weekend. The Veterans' Memorial Park Association and the Ramblers Motorcycle Club from nearby Salinas were sponsoring a motorcycle rally and gypsy tour, reviving a Hollister tradition that had been put on hold during World War II. A "rally" is a gathering of motorcyclists. A "gypsy tour" is an overnight event in which many participants would sleep in tents, around campfires—except for the headscarves and tambourines, just like the Romani people were depicted in the movies. The "gypsy" tourists would stay the weekend, clean up after themselves, and roll off in time for work on Monday.

Hollister, with its twenty-one bars and taverns and seven-man police force, was ready for a weekend that was bound to be profitable as well as fun for the entire family. The area around Hollister, with rolling hills, farmland, and vineyards, was already popular among motorcycle riders and clubs in the region. The event was sanctioned by the American Motorcycle Association and expected to attract as many as twenty-five hundred motorcyclists and clubs from across the West.

Events would kick off on the afternoon of Friday, July Fourth, at Lavagnion Ranch, about three miles outside town, with a "motorcycle hill climb" (admission $1 plus tax, fifty cents for the kids). On Saturday, the ranch would host a field meet—open to less experienced riders—which included slow rides, dig-outs and plank races, followed by a dance in the evening. The festivities would wrap up on Sunday with motorcycle races on a half-mile dirt track at Veterans Memorial Park ($1.50; children

13

seventy-five cents, tax included). Trophies and a purse of twelve-hundred dollars would be distributed.

All this, on the patriotic weekend, was a great way to get back to "normal" after the war. Motorcycling as a sport had spread widely as the country crawled out of the Depression in the 1930s. Motorcycling events and conventions had attracted cycling enthusiasts and clubs, which at the time were respectable organizations of outdoorsmen who obeyed speed limits and proper dress codes as they tooled along the highways, over mountains, and through valleys of the region. In fact, the Salinas Ramblers club—which boasted twenty-eight members "and ten female members"—was founded in 1934 "to promote the cause of private motorcycling through greater public acceptance and understanding, and to enjoy all the rewards of gentlemanly comradeship."

There was one minor—no, make that *major*—factor that the Hollister town fathers and Salinas cyclists either ignored or did not consider in July 1947: *Times had changed.* Since the end of World War II, a new breed of motorcyclist and new brand of motorcycle club had taken to American roads and highways. Many war veterans who'd roared through Europe on Army-issued Harley-Davidson motorcycles were recreating the excitement on facsimiles now that the manufacturer had returned to civilian production. These veterans were not "gentlemanly," and not necessarily law-abiding. Many were bitter and having a difficult time readjusting to polite society, and that is why they took to the road on their heavy metal machines.

The previous summer, a group of those veterans had gathered at the All-American Bar, a dive in South Central Los Angeles. At the center was William Clyde Forkner, whom everyone knew as "Wino Willie." Wino Willie had served in the war in the Pacific Theater as a gunner on a B-24 Liberator bomber crew. Before the war, he, like many of the others in the bar, had been a member of one of those law-abiding, socializing motorcycle clubs. Now, belligerent, more than a little drunk, but still very funny, Wino Willie had the idea of starting a new club, with new rules— maybe *no rules* at all—and certainly no concerns about public acceptance. Riding drunk. Breaking laws. Raising hell. Those were good enough reasons to head out on the road. That's the type of motorcycle club Wino Willie and his gang decided to assemble. Now what would they call this club? Somebody down the bar had a suggestion. "You might as well call yourselves the Boozefighters, 'cause all you ever do is sit around the bar and fight that booze." Wino Willie let that sink in, then shrugged. Yeah, that sounded good. They'd be the Boozefighters—"a drinking club with a motorcycle problem."

The Boozefighters were among the first post–World War II "outlaw biker" clubs—pissed off and bucking authority, but not anything close to the violent, deadly version of the outlaw biker gangs that would form in the decades to follow, the ones associated with indictments on federal RICO charges, including racketeering, drug-dealing, robbery, kidnapping, and murder. "The term *outlaw* referred to the fact that these bikers were those who did not race at AMA-sanctioned field meets. Simple as that," according to Dave Nichols, longtime editor of *Easyriders*, the preeminent bikers' magazine. "They were outside the convention of the AMA's rules and regulations and, therefore, 'bad boys.'"

Nichols explained, "Returning WW II servicemen didn't talk much about the horrors they had witnessed in Europe. . . . It was easy for a Vet to feel like he didn't fit into the sanitary, Disneyesque world of post-war America. Many felt a lot more at home in the company of other 'like-minded' brothers. . . . These were fun-loving guys who were out to taste a little of the freedom they had fought so hard to win during the war. Riding and racing motorcycles and raising a little hell was fun, and fun was what they were about."

In *The Original Wild Ones: The History of the Boozefighters Motorcycle Club*, motorcycle culture historian Bill Hayes places the average Boozefighter as "somewhere in between Brando's 'Johnny,' Marvin's 'Chino,' and the brilliant 1940s/1950s abandon of, oh maybe, a Red Skelton or a Jackie Gleason." As if to prove the bikers' relative harmlessness, he quoted records of a 1946 initiation test for club prospects that included, "get drunk at a race meet or cycle dance," "eat live goldfish," and "bring out a douche bag where it would embarrass all the women (then drink wine from it, etc.)." All that mattered, Hayes concluded—in fact, insisted—was "fun."

But it is a fact that for all the "fun" they were after, many of these cyclists were veterans who had been through incredible trauma and seen and done things they could not talk about. Unlike the majority of their fighting brothers, they were unable to come home, marry the girl next door, start a family, and blend back into "normal" society. They either wanted to recreate the rush of war, relive the adventure, and continue the thrill, or ride as fast they could and seek escape with like-minded outcasts on the open road. By July 4, 1947, the Boozefighters had expanded to three chapters in California, spawned imitators across the West, and were leading the charge of a new kind of rider toward Hollister. If they were looking for fun, they were going to find it. They would find trouble, too. On this ride, on this weekend, the era of the outlaw biker would make its official debut and the seeds of *The Wild One*, the movie featuring Marlon Brando's Johnny and Lee Marvin's Chino, would be scattered.

The bikers began thundering into Hollister early on Friday morning. As the first of these motorcycle clubs came blasting and skidding into the center of the city, anyone standing on the sidewalks, waving small

American flags and cheering their arrival were soon ducking for cover. Soon there were hundreds, and then there were thousands: rough, unshaven, disrespectful outlaws, many of them drunk and rowdy. Far too many were "straight pipers," riding bikes without mufflers, making them sound even louder. Most of the outlaws ignored the hill-climb races and headed straight downtown to San Benito Street, the city's "main drag," where they revved their engines, performed wheelies and burn-outs, smashed bottles, and whooped it up. Hundreds joined the "dig-out" races, with bikes lined up at a dead stop, then "digging" from zero miles an hour to finish lines in the middle of the streets. According to one news-paper report, "these wild, unscheduled races, with the motors roaring unrestrained by mufflers, turned the city into bedlam."

Along with the Boozefighters came the Pissed-Off Bastards of Bloom-ington, the Market Street Commandos, Galloping Gooses, Jackrabbits, Thirteen Rebels, and other fresh outlaw cycle clubs. Bikers rolled in from Los Angeles and Nevada, Arizona, Oregon, and Washington, and from as far away as Florida and Connecticut. Hollister's seven-man police force set up barriers at either end of San Benito Street and began writing tickets. The bikers tore them up. The owners of the city's twenty-one bars and taverns appreciated the business at first and might even have found it amusing when bikers rolled their hogs straight through the doors and inside their establishments. But as furniture was destroyed, mirrors bro-ken, and bottles smashed against walls and hurled from second-story windows, the novelty wore off. By 4 p.m. Friday, the barkeeps agreed to shut down early—or at least stop selling beer, on the assumption that these bums couldn't afford anything more expensive. But the wilding continued into the night. Many of the invaders slept on the courthouse lawn or on hay bales on the outskirts of the city.

Reinforcements from the state highway patrol were called in, arrests stacked up, and Police Judge Frank Buchter convened a special night court.

The motorcyclists doubled the population of Hollister that weekend: four thousand drunk, unruly, disorderly, fun-seeking outlaw bikers. On Sunday, thirty-three highway patrolmen lined up with tear gas and threats of force, and the bikers began to head back home. They left behind fifty of their brothers in the hospital, three seriously injured, another sixty arrested, a few still awaiting court appearances, and piles of litter and broken bottles in the streets. They also left behind two thousand dollars from the fines levied by Judge Buchter.

The story was picked up by papers around the country, and the reports were frightening. The city of Hollister, really not much more than a small farm town, had been trashed in what would be described as the first outlaw biker riot. This "forty hours of terror" in the farming belt of

"The forty hours that shook Hollister": The *Life* magazine photo that shook the nation
. . . and led to *The Wild One.* Photo by Barney Peterson/San Francisco Chronicle via
Getty Images

the Monterey peninsula was an outrage that was only compounded and
made into a national scandal when *Life* magazine ran a feature in its July
21 issue, including a full-page photo of a drunken cyclist, leaning back
on a parked Harley roadster, with a beer bottle in each hand and more
beer bottles scattered and piled on the street beneath him. The headline

read: "Cyclist's Holiday: He and Friends Terrorize a Town." According to the accompanying story, "Police arrested many for drunkenness and indecent exposure but could not restore order. Finally, after two days, the cyclists left with a brazen explanation. 'We like to show off. It's just a lot of fun.' But Hollister's police chief took a different view. Wailed he, 'It's just one hell of a mess.'"

"What happened in Hollister lives in the annals of motorcycling history, like some festering sore," Dave Nichols admitted. The weekend "single-handedly created an unwholesome image for both Harley-Davidson and motorcyclists in general." The only catch, he wrote, is that "little that the media of the day reported . . . was actually true. The misdemeanors that supposedly took place over the course of the weekend were pretty much of the 'public intoxication' or 'drunk and disorderly' variety, with one guy cited for trying to urinate into the radiator of his truck."

Revisionism isn't uncommon in interpretations of history, but for all his excuses in defense of the outlaws, Nichols has history on his side. That photo of the beer-swilling biker in *Life* magazine had allegedly been staged—and it wasn't even his motorcycle. And after the bottles and trash were swept up, mirrors replaced, streets cleaned, and ticket and arrest revenues totaled, Hollister city leaders assessed the damage from the "forty hours that shook Hollister" and concluded that no serious harm had been done to anyone but the bikers. Most of the arrests had indeed been for misdemeanors, and there were only a few serious injuries—to bikers, not Hollister residents. No one had been raped; no one had been killed. And the reason those four thousand bikers had cleared out by late Sunday: Most of them had to be back at work on Monday morning.

Hollister was so untroubled by this historic, uninhibited "weekend of terror" that the city invited the cyclists to return for races three months later. This time, its seven-man police force was backed by eight highway patrolmen and other special law enforcement officers, and there were roadblocks at all entrances leading to the city. This time, the two thousand cyclists who came to play were far more subdued. The races went on at the Veterans Memorial Park dirt track on Sunday, October 19, without incident. Police chief Roy McPhail said that cool weather, and the start of the work week on Monday, kept the cyclists from getting too drunk or passing out on lawns and hay bales. Had the outlaws gotten out of hand, the chief was ready to close all twenty-one bars and taverns. Ultimately, there was no need.

Life went on in Hollister and the *Life* magazine exposé had two lasting effects: a debate among journalists over staging news photos, and a resulting letter to the editor, claiming that only a "small percentage" of cyclists caused trouble in Hollister, a letter that led to the term *one percenter*.

Outlaw bikers began to refer to their gangs as "one percenter motorcycle clubs." The term is still used today to describe the baddest of the lawless motorcycle organizations.

The *Life* article, and indeed Hollister's July Fourth weekend, may both have faded from memory and been overshadowed by other events, had not a writer named Frank Rooney been inspired by the reports and stories about the outlaw bikers. He turned the holiday weekend into a work of fiction entitled *Cyclists' Raid* that would be published in the January 1951 issue of *Harper's* magazine. In 1953, the short story became the basis for a movie called *The Wild One*.

But we're getting ahead of ourselves.

Three

Meat

In the wake of his experience with Tallulah Bankhead and energized by his activities as an activist, Marlon Brando in 1947 confounded many of the giants of theater who saw him as an actor with great potential. Elia Kazan had offered him a chance to break out from Broadway and head straight to Hollywood in his new movie, *Gentleman's Agreement*. Brando turned him down. He said he preferred to continue working to help the Jews. Kazan didn't bother to tell the young man that *Gentleman's Agreement* was a movie about anti-Semitism. The role went to John Garfield. (In need of money and pressured by his agent, Brando did take his first steps toward a film career that year: he submitted to a screen test for a picture called *Rebel Without a Cause*. It was an early adaption of the book, *Rebel Without a Cause: The Story of a Criminal Psychopath*, nothing like the 1955 film that made a "new Brando" out of Brando idolizer James Dean.)

A second opportunity to work with Kazan, this time onstage, was one that Brando did not reject out of hand that summer. He was not supposed to play the role of Stanley Kowalski in Tennessee Williams's *A Streetcar Named Desire*. The director and producer did not have him in mind. He was too young, too pretty, too sensitive . . . too *poetic* . . . to portray the working-class Polish American husband and brutal rapist. The role had been tailored to John Garfield, the movie star, but Garfield wanted too much money to make the trek from Hollywood. After Garfield turned down the role, it was offered to Burt Lancaster, who could not get out of his studio contract.

Harold Clurman, the Group Theatre member who'd directed Brando in *Truckline Café*—and Stella Adler's husband—put the idea into Kazan's head that the actor would make a perfect Kowalski. Kazan knew of Brando's naturalism and power. Yes, he agreed. Of course. But he wasn't sure. He was too young. Maybe too soft. Irene Selznick, the play's producer, was more practical. She wasn't confident that the play could go forward without a major star. So they punted and decided to leave it up to the playwright. Kazan arranged for Brando to meet Tennessee Williams at his beach house in Provincetown on Cape Cod, Massachusetts.

Provincetown was an arts colony and also a mecca for homosexuals. Williams lived in a shack at the far edge of town with his lover, Pancho Rodriguez y Gonzalez. That posed no issue for Brando. He had a reputation as a womanizer, but he also had sex with men and had recently gotten into group sex. "Let's say sex has no sex," he said, confident and comfortable in his bisexuality. He'd been to Provincetown before. The previous year, he'd arrived, made it with several women, made it with the male bartender he was staying with, and decades before Matthew McConaughey was arrested for playing bongos in the nude, had been busted and convicted of disturbing the peace for playing his bongo drums too loudly after midnight.

Now, as was often the case, Brando was broke, so after Kazan slipped him the bus fare to Provincetown, he spent the money on food. It wasn't until late August that he got around to sticking out a thumb and hitchhiking out to the Cape. He arrived to find that Williams's house contained guests, a clogged toilet, and no electricity. That's where he came in handy. Brando stuck his arm down into the toilet bowl, got it unstuck and flushing again, went around back, soldered some wires, got the lights on, and after he got cleaned up, took a long quiet walk on the beach with the playwright.

Brando later read for him. Williams delivered his reaction in a letter to his agent, Audrey Wood:

> I can't tell you what a relief it is that we have found such a God-sent Stanley in the person of Brando. It had not occurred to me before what an excellent value would come through casting a very young actor in this part. It humanizes the character of Stanley in that it becomes the brutality or callousness of youth rather than a vicious older man. . . . A new value came out of Brando's reading, which was by far the best reading I have ever heard.

The decision was soon official.

> Marlon Brando signed yesterday to take over the leading role in Tennessee Williams' *A Streetcar Named Desire*, which was to have been played by John Garfield. (*New York Daily News*, September 3, 1947)

While many of the Hollister cyclists were back at their workaday jobs with beer hangovers on Monday, October 20, Marlon Brando was at the Amsterdam Roof Theatre in Times Square. He was beginning the third of three-and-a-half weeks of rehearsals for *A Streetcar Named Desire*. The sessions that had begun on October 6 were not the typical script reads and stage blocking that many actors may have been accustomed to. Director

Kazan was going deeper. From the start, he'd led many discussions to help the actors find personal connections between the script and their own experiences. He pushed them, using techniques borrowed from his brother, a psychoanalyst. Brando had already taken and used what Stella Adler had taught him. He'd even bulked up for the role. During these rehearsals, he was transforming into something different, something greater.

> I caught a glimpse of young Marlon Brando, star of *Streetcar Named Desire* in the rain after his show. He gets $500 a week, and wore a necktieless shirt and cheap corduroy jacket. Sometimes he shows up at the theater in a T-shirt or sweatshirt. Shades of John Barrymore! (Over the Coffee by Harlan Miller, *Des Moines Register*)

A Streetcar Named Desire, summarized simply, is the story of Blanche DuBois, a neurotic, aging, fallen southern belle who, after a series of devastating losses (including the suicide of her gay husband) and public shaming, leaves her town in Mississippi and moves in with her pregnant sister, Stella Kowalski, and her husband, Stanley, in their modest apartment in a working-class neighborhood of New Orleans. The delicate, aristocratic Blanche, and the brutish, macho Stanley clash immediately. Their antagonism, fueled by Blanche's disdain for Stanley's common vulgarity and his suspicion that she's holding out on family money, ultimately leads to violence when Stanley rapes Blanche (offstage, of course). Blanche is left in a catatonic state and carted off to a mental hospital while life in New Orleans goes on.

When *Streetcar* opened on December 3, 1947, at the Ethel Barrymore Theatre on West Forty-Seventh Street, the critics were as one in their praise and astonishment at the depth and beauty of Tennessee Williams's work. "Out of poetic imagination and ordinary compassion he has a spun a poignant and luminous story," *New York Times* critic Brooks Atkinson wrote. "It almost seems not to have been written but to be happening." Most of the performance reviews focused on the star, Jessica Tandy, in the role of Blanche DuBois, the fragile, tragic heroine (a role that Williams had written with Tallulah Bankhead in mind). "Her performance is almost incredibly true," Atkinson raved. "For it does seem almost incredible that she could understand such an elusive part so thoroughly and that she can convey it with so many shades and impulses that are accurate, revealing and true." The acting of the other main players—Brando, Karl Malden, and Kim Hunter, "is also of very high quality indeed." The three actors may have received less attention in the *Times*, but John Chapman in the *New York Daily News*, the people's tabloid, saw something that overshadowed Tandy on the Barrymore stage. "Mr. Brando is magnificent as the forthright husband, in his simple rages, his simple affections and his blunt humor." It was Brando's photograph featured in the *Daily News* review, and soon it was apparent that it was Brando, the muscular, pretty young man in the tight, white T-shirt, whom audiences were lining up to see. His performance—well, it seemed to be something other than a performance. He was reciting Tennessee Williams's lines, of course—he wasn't going off script, but it didn't seem like he was acting, either. Everything Stella Adler had taught her student had come together. Brando was *being* on stage. He *was* Stanley Kowalski. Brando was—

Let's drop the pretense. There was much more than fine acting on display. There was sex. Raw sex. Brando had been transformed, not into a character but a force of nature. His stocky frame was now rippling with muscles—an image that would come to define masculinity in his and future generations. His pecs and biceps strained against the T-shirt that was deliberately created a size too small and the scent of the sweat that glistened on his skin and fine facial features and darkened that T-shirt could almost be detected from the first few rows. Brando's thigh muscles pushed against the denim of his tight blue jeans and the bulge in his crotch was just as evident, even to those who did not bring opera glasses. Brando was offering Stella, and every woman and man in the audience, *his meat.* Literally. This is not a metaphor or a subtext. Brando first did so, literally, in Act One, when he made his entrance with Karl Malden as Stanley's friend, Mitch, stopping at the steps of his apartment house. According to the stage directions, Brando walks onstage carrying his bowling jacket and "a red-stained package from a butcher's."

STANLEY [bellowing]: Hey, there! Stella, Baby!
[*Stella comes out on the first-floor landing, a gentle young woman, about twenty-five, and of a background obviously quite different from her husband's.*]
STELLA [mildly]: Don't holler at me like that. Hi, Mitch.
STANLEY: Catch!
STELLA: What?
STANLEY: Meat!
[*He heaves the package at her. She cries out in protest but manages to catch it; then she laughs breathlessly.*]

A red-stained package from a butcher's. "*Meat!*" "Meat" was a popular euphemism for male genitalia, in "street talk" and the "dirty blues" records popular before World War II, in songs like Bessie Smith's "You've Got to Give Me Some" ("Said Miss Jones to old Butcher Pete, 'I want a piece of your good old meat'") and Lil Johnson's "Take it Easy, Greasy" ("I'm goin' downtown to old Butcher Pete, cause I wanna piece of his good old meat"). In 1948, Norman Mailer would make use of the term in his World War II novel, *The Naked and the Dead*, in the words of Sgt. William

Brando and Jessica Tandy on Broadway in *A Streetcar Named Desire*. Brando had been transformed, not into a character, but a force of nature. Photofest

Brown ("We're just a bunch of GIs. Okay, while we're home and slipping a little meat to them every night, they're all lovey-dovey. Oh, they can't do enough for ya. But the minute you go away they start thinking.") and Cpl. Stanley ("I was president of my junior high school class, I don't mean that that's anything to beat my meat about.")

In *Streetcar's* final scene, Stanley and his friends are playing cards in the apartment. Blanche has been taken away to an insane asylum. Stella, who's pregnant with Stanley's child and doesn't want to believe that her husband is a rapist, sobs. Brando had stunned the audience earlier, as he howled Stella's name into the New Orleans sky. Now, he is gentle and seductive, comforting her. "Now, honey. Now, love. Now, now, love," he whispers while, in Williams's words, "he kneels beside her and his fingers find the opening of her blouse." She sobs. He feels. The "blue piano" and muted trumpet play. The card game goes on. One of the players says, "This game is seven-card stud."

And the audience is silent for a moment. What have they just witnessed? The women are not sure how to react. They may have been repulsed by Brando's animalistic behavior, but they are, just the same, aroused. The men may feel a twinge of shame yet are somehow vitalized by the expression of brutal urges they may have repressed. The stirrings of a sexual revolution could be documented by the dampness on every seat in the Ethel Barrymore Theatre that opening night. Brando had thrown them raw meat. His meat.

As the engagement continued and ticket sales soared, Brando riffed on the Kowalski role, never quite playing it the same, fighting the boredom that had almost made him walk away during the long run of *I Remember Mama*. If Brando didn't feel well, neither did Stanley Kowalski. If he was energized, so was Stanley. If his belly itched, he scratched it. If his pants rode up into the crack of his ass, Stanley would adjust. Jessica Tandy was infuriated. He threw her off with his "line readings." He added a natural comedy to the role. He was *too good*. "The audiences adored Brando," Kazan recalled. "When he derided Blanche, they responded with approving laughter. Was the play becoming The Marlon Brando Show? What would I say to Brando? Be less good?"

As the play's run extended through 1948 and into 1949, Brando continued to vary his performance, such a star presence that despite the intentions of the playwright, he was winning over the audience to Stanley's side. When he was offstage, he often sparred with stagehands to keep his energy up. One night in April 1949, Brando was boxing with a young crew member, who threw a haymaker and split open his nose. Brando went onstage with his face dripping blood. Tandy adlibbed, "You bloody fool." Mercifully, before Brando's boredom did lasting damage, contracts, and his commitment to the play, were soon up. The original cast would leave the show at the end of May.

By June 1, when he was replaced by Ralph Meeker after more than five hundred performances, Brando had been overwhelmed with offers from Hollywood. He'd even taken a trek out west in February, with Kazan.

The director had convinced the actor to do a screen test for a movie he was planning to direct about Emiliano Zapata, the Mexican revolutionary and leader of the peasant uprising against wealthy landowners in 1910 that widened into the Mexican Revolution. Brando was, as might be expected, ambivalent about playing the charismatic hero, and when the time came to decide, he ran off in the opposite direction. "How much is Clift getting in the movies?" he joked to a friend about Montgomery Clift, a naturalistic, sensitive Broadway actor who'd already made the transition to Academy Award-nominated movie star. "I want a dollar more." Then he left New York City and left the country to hide out in Paris for a while.

Hedda Hopper, queen bee of Hollywood's judgmental gossip columnists, the woman before whom screenland newcomers were expected to bow, already had Brando in her sights. Weeks earlier, she had the exclusive scoop on where he would land once he headed west. "Marlon Brando was wooed by every studio in town, but the Nassour Brothers will likely get him for *St. Benny the Dip*, which is described as a Protestant *Going My Way*."

Hedda Hopper got it wrong. The official word came in late August: Brando had accepted an offer from producer Stanley Kramer to star in a film called *The Men*. Brando would portray a hospitalized former GI who'd been shot in the spine and paralyzed from the waist down. Kramer was known for his liberal "message movies," and Brando was impressed by his two most recent pictures: *Champion*, a film noir focused on a ruthless prizefighter, and *Home of the Brave*, in which a Black GI is literally paralyzed by racism. Brando accepted the offer via transatlantic phone call and agreed to begin rehearsals in September.

> This talented Brando won extra fame by zipping up and down Broadway on a motorcycle with a passenger jouncing behind him. On Broadway this isn't done, & NY's Finest took after him. Soon he'll be riding his motorcycle to Hollywood, where 3 on a cycle's okay. (Over the Coffee by Harlan Miller, *Des Moines Register*)

When Marlon Brando arrived in California, he did not alight from a plane at Los Angeles Airport, greeted by a frenzy of fans and flashbulbs, or at Union Station, the grand rail terminal downtown. Brando stepped off a train at the Southern Pacific station in Alhambra, a small city about fifteen miles east of Hollywood. He was not driven to the Beverly Hills Hotel or a rented compound in the Hollywood Hills, but to the home of his mother's sister in the working-class neighborhood of Eagle Rock. While he was making his first movie, he'd be "Bud" again, living with Aunt Betty Lindemeyer and her husband, Oliver, in their two-bedroom bungalow. According to reports, his grandmother was visiting at the time, so Brando slept on the couch in the living room.

He didn't spend his entire stay in the humble abode. As part of his preparation for filming *The Men*, Brando moved into Birmingham General Hospital, a US Army facility in Van Nuys, about thirteen miles north of Hollywood. For four weeks, he lived in a thirty-two-bed ward with paraplegic veterans, wheelchair-bound and practicing life without the use of his lower extremities. When the other patients realized that he was serious, and living as they were, they accepted him. Some of the hospital staff members were fooled into believing he really was a paraplegic.

This was Brando's unique introduction to Hollywood—and Hollywood's introduction to him. When Bob Thomas, the Associated Press entertainment reporter, arrived to interview Brando in October, he found the actor asleep in bed in the hospital ward. "He crawled out of bed and lowered himself by his arms into a wheelchair."

"You can't understand what it's like to be a paraplegic unless you have lived as one," Brando told the reporter, after he was wheeled into a refreshment room. "For instance, if you or I drop a pack of cigarettes, it's a simple matter to pick them up. It isn't to a paraplegic."

This was Brando's Method in full bloom; this was why Robert De Niro would fight several boxing matches against real professional pugilists and gain sixty pounds to play Jake La Motta in *Raging Bull*, why Daniel Day Lewis would lock himself in solitary confinement to prepare for *In the Name of the Father* and live in the woods for *The Last of the Mohicans*. From Nicolas Cage to Joaquin Phoenix, Michelle Williams to Nicole Kidman, actors who immersed themselves deeply in preparation for screen roles could point to Brando as the model.

Meanwhile, the twenty-five-year-old actor in the wheelchair already had Hollywood sussed out. "The film offers I get are from the major studios," he told Thomas. "I would never sign with one of them. They dress you up in a tuxedo and tell you to go to this party and do that. I would never end up like—" He named a veteran character actor. "—Waiting by the phone until the studio calls up and says I get a part playing a cannibal in a Johnny Weissmuller picture. That's not for me. I value my independence too much."

"Brando is husky, with a sharp face that becomes good looking as you watch him," Thomas wrote. "He could probably become a movie star if he wanted to. But he appears to be unwilling to be tied down to the bother that film fame brings. . . . When he finishes the picture, he'll return to New York, but not for a play. He plans to attend the New School for Social Research."

"I got kicked out of school when I was a sophomore, and I always wanted to go back to school," Brando said. On the cusp of movie stardom, he was making it clear just how little it meant to him. When shooting wrapped on *The Men*, he would return to New York City, but not permanently. He wouldn't go back to school, and he'd never again appear on a Broadway stage. He would start making movies, and it was Hollywood that was about to be taken to school.

Four

Welcome to Hollywood

Once Marlon Brando arrived in Hollywood in the fall of 1949, Hollywood wasn't sure what to make of him. There were, of course, other actors who were surly with the press, who had their feuds with the big town gossip writers, but not so many who really didn't seem to give a hoot, one way or another, about their image or Hollywood in general.

Principal photography on *The Men* had begun at the end of October, and by December Brando had already wrapped most of his work and split for New York. "Marlon Brando packed up his T-shirts and blew out of Hollywood today," Virginia MacPherson, the United Press's woman in Hollywood, reported. "The movie queens he left behind still are scratching their peroxided locks. They can't figure this lad out. His football build . . . His Greek god profile . . . His lady-killer look . . . had many a local female a-twitter and hopeful. But Brando couldn't be bothered."

It wasn't only the movie queens who were left wondering what hit them in December 1949. Virginia MacPherson was actually speaking for herself and her colleagues in the press. "He was here two months, but he refused to play the 'Hollywood game' every movie newcomer is told he must follow religiously if he wants to get any place in the Hollywood sideshow." MacPherson explained that the game could be condensed into "five rigid rules"—and alleged that Brando broke each one. He didn't lease a big Bel-Air mansion. He didn't buy a fancy car. He didn't "do" the nightclub circuit with a "name actress" on his arm so he'd get in the columns ("Brando didn't once stick his nose inside Ciro's, Mocambo, or any other nightclub 'must'"), and he didn't buy himself an expensive wardrobe (legend already had it that he'd come to town with three T-shirts, and maybe an old suit). But most important, he broke Rule Number Five: "Be nice to the 'big-name' syndicated columnists."

"He snubbed them all."

(Actually, Brando had done more than "snub" the columnists, even before he headed west. Back in New York, during the run of *Streetcar*, Jessica Tandy walked into his dressing room with top Hollywood gossip

Sheilah Graham. "Marlon," Tandy said by way of introduction, "I want you to meet—" "Your mother?" he interrupted. Graham was but five years older than Tandy, who was thirty-eight.)

Brando has "the distressing habit of yawning in the face of movie producers and gentlemen of the press who interview him," syndicated writer Louis Berg observed. "Ladies of the press, too." Brando laughed at the questions lobbed at him in "a mass interview to some fan magazine ladies," and actually dozed during an interview on *The Wendy Barrie Show* (one of the first television talk shows.).

"Only had two hours sleep," Brando mumbled on camera. "Went motorcycling with Wally Cox up to the Palisades."

When Barrie asked when his first movie would open, he opened an eye, and called out past the cameras to his press agent. "Hey Mike! When's *The Men* opening?"

That just wasn't done then (and in tightly controlled movie rollouts, it's rarely done today), but Brando was an oddity. To Hollywood studio bosses and entertainment writers alike, there was suspicion about his character, mainly because he'd turned down so many inviting contracts the studios had offered at a time that the "studio system" was still intact. Brando wasn't interested in being tied down. If he was going to play the Hollywood game, he'd play by his own rules, as a free agent.

Reluctantly, perhaps surprisingly, Hollywood shrugged and said, "Okay." Brando's behavior, lies, and the myths surrounding him, were accepted and traded because the jaded ladies and gentlemen of the press sensed someone special was among them. "Brando eats when he is hungry, sleeps when he is sleepy—even in fancy company—talks only when he has something to say and only to people he likes," Berg wrote.

At this early stage, the myths were taking hold. It was written that Brando gave his hefty paychecks to his father to handle and lived on a hundred and fifty dollars a week. Sometimes that money lasted him two weeks. His apartment was spartan. "His costume, for formal and informal wear, consists of blue jeans and T-shirt."

"This town and everything in it is overrated," Brando told MacPherson. He was playing the game, all right, but it was a different game. This was a game that rebellious Hollywood stars would pick up on, and the game would be followed for decades.

It appears that even Hedda Hopper, whose power had not yet run its course, realized that even she must adapt, as she ate it all up and regurgitated the contents all over an entire newspaper page in her first big splash on Brando. Her syndicated feature story that ran in May 1950 relied on quotes from Tandy—"Oh, boy, he's dynamite!" Brando's *Streetcar* costar said, probably happy to have him on the West Coast as often as possible—and expanded, embroidered versions of the official anecdotes that had been dished out since the actor first showed up in town. Earlier, it had been reported that Brando had arrived in Los Angeles with "three changes of T-shirts and jeans and an old blue suit that's full of holes." Hopper edited his belongings to a small canvas bag containing "two pairs of blue jeans, four T-shirts, two pairs of socks and a copy of the philosophy of Spinoza." Brando had told MacPherson that he'd once gone swimming in the Pacific at 3 a.m. Now, ocean swimming in the nude at 2 a.m. was "one of his favorite forms of diversions." Hopper was slotting him into the same old Hollywood publicity mill, or at last trying to, because when she finally got a sit-down with the actor, he responded to her inane questions mostly with grunts and monosyllabic replies.

"He loves to shock people," Hopper shrugged. "While making *The Men* here, I was assured that he was never late and was always letter perfect in his lines. In fact, he concentrates so hard it's impossible to talk to him. I was telling him a story once and only at the end did I realize that he hadn't heard a word I said. He was off on another planet."

The columnist did get an answer out of Brando when she asked what he thought of acting "as a profession." He chewed it over, took his time, before finally replying. "If you're successful at it," he said, "it's a fine way to make a living. If you're unsuccessful, it's worse than having a skin disease."

Another actor might have been cast off planet Hollywood for insulting the gossip queen. But Brando was different. "When it was announced that he was coming here to make a picture, people wondered what Hollywood would do to him. Before he left, they wondered what he'd done to Hollywood," Hopper admitted. "Marlon's not only a great character, but he's a great actor. And if he chooses, he'll continue to set Hollywood on its ear."

"It seemed less like animosity than he was playful with them," says pop and gay culture writer Stephen Rutledge. "He would just fuck around with them, as opposed to, 'No, I'm not talking to you,' or saying anything. It's that meeting of old and new Hollywood. It was very different than how, let's say, Cary Grant got on with the media. He wasn't kowtowing at all, and I think they didn't know what to do with him. They didn't know what to do with somebody who was in one way incredibly open and in another way very, very closed. And I think a lot of that had to do with his humor and his nonchalance about anything that could be considered controversial. It's like, 'I don't care. I'm just gonna ride out in the desert.'"

When Brando first left Hollywood after *The Men*, he claimed he was headed back to the legitimate stage, "as far from Hollywood as possible." That would not be the case. He never again appeared on Broadway, but for his second picture, he signed on to the screen adaptation of the Tennessee

Williams play that put him on the map. Production on *A Streetcar Named Desire* began in August 1950 on the Warner Bros. lot in Burbank. A few months later, Brando was explaining in a United Press story that was syndicated in newspapers across the country, that he really didn't hate movies. "It's been said that I held back from pictures because I didn't like them. Nothing could be further from the truth," he was quoted.

> Actually, I am a big movie fan. The only reason I delayed so long before coming to Hollywood was that I was offered contracts and not individual pictures that excited me. I want to grow to develop as an actor and to keep growing. I think the only way to do that is to stay away from any binding deals. Then I can choose what I please. Whether I'm right or wrong in my choices I'll be gaining experience. You can't learn anything when others are doing the selecting for you. That's why I want to avoid contracts.
>
> Since I've been working in front of cameras I actually have enormous respect for Hollywood actors. It's a tough job and hard on the nerves. I find that conserving energy is a real problem when you're working in movies, what with doing scenes over and over again until they are right, technically and histrionically. In the theater, an actor has a chance to build up to the emotion demanded by the role. In Hollywood an actor must depend on a fine technique to create that emotion on a few minutes' notice.

Brando was, it seemed, having it both ways. Even as he was pledging allegiance to the motion picture industry, he was declaring his independence from it. The journalists played along. They'd bite back soon enough, and when they did, before the end of the decade, their teeth would leave scars, but by then Brando would have changed the game for coverage of celebrities once again.

For now, in the early 1950s, it was the trade papers, the entertainment industry's house organs (where bottom-line box office prospects mattered most and whose reviewers' names were most often abbreviated), that looked askance at this brat from Broadway. When *The Men* was released in June 1950, *Variety* saw in Brando's debut "overtones" of his "roughneck" role in *Streetcar* on Broadway and claimed that the actor lacked "the necessary sensitivity and inner warmth which would transform an adequate portrayal into an expert one." The reviewer also commented that Brando's stutter, a "slight speech impediment, which sharply enhanced his *Streetcar* role, jars here," and made him appear less convincing as a supposed college graduate.

The views from the major metropolitan critics, who had a far wider readership and influence on mainstream moviegoers, were far more enthusiastic. Edwin Schallert at the *Los Angeles Times* wrote that Brando "is easily the center of this picture's appeal. . . . The growth of character that he achieves, the setbacks he endures . . . are quickly registered by him through smoldering eyes. The rough resentful accents of his voice give tremendous impact to the portrayal." Brando was, Schallert asserted, "a new and fascinating personality" who "is unquestionably destined for much attention in the future."

Bosley Crowther, as the *New York Times* film critic and with a somewhat scholarly approach, had an even greater cultural impact. He agreed that Brando as a paraplegic "is so vividly real, dynamic and sensitive that his illusion is complete. His face, the whole rhythm of his body and especially the strange timbre of his voice, often broken and plaintive and boyish, are articulate in every way. Out of stiff and frozen silences he can lash into a passionate rage with the fearful and flailing frenzy of a taut cable suddenly cut. Or he can show the poignant tenderness of doctor with a child."

After wrapping his role on *The Men*, Brando had gone his own way, back and forth from New York on his own adventures before returning to Hollywood with Kazan for the screen version of *A Streetcar Named Desire*. This time, Blanche DuBois was portrayed by Vivien Leigh. She'd played the role in the West End production that had premiered the previous October, coached and directed by her husband, Laurence Olivier, and had as colorful a history of mental fragility as the Tennessee Williams creation. Brando was of the opinion that Leigh was much better suited to the role than Jessica Tandy, with whom he had problems from the start. When the film opened in September 1951, *Variety* resumed its quibbles—Brando "occasionally . . . performs unevenly in a portrayal marked by frequent garbling of his dialog"—yet the view from the *Times*es on both coasts reflected the general consensus: "The film is in all major respects a finer achievement than the original." It was, Schallert continued, "a momentous event to be lauded long and emphatically for both its acting and direction as well as the inherent power of its story. . . . Starting in a high-keyed vein of robust humor, Brando gradually becomes a sinister, powerful figure of old-time justice."

Brando was "brilliant," Crowther decreed in New York, "and he carries over all the energy and the steel spring characteristics that made him vivid on the stage. But here, where we're so much closer to him, he seems that much more highly charged, his despair seems that much more pathetic and his comic moments that much more slyly enjoyed."

Wrote Jane Corby in the Brooklyn *Daily Eagle*: "Marlon Brando's Stanley Kowalski is as earthy a character, probably, as the screen has ever seen." That earthiness, in a torn tight T-shirt, muscles bulging, garbled words and all, made him a bona fide sex symbol onscreen, just as it had on Broadway.

Brando as the Mexican revolutionary in Kazan's long-gestating *Viva Zapata!*, written by John Steinbeck, followed in February 1952. *Variety* groused that Brando's "trenchant moodiness in delivery, and a makeup that tends to the Oriental rather than the Latin, makes for a character strangeness that will do little to warm an audience towards it." But Schallert insisted that the actor "comes through with punchful moments that will unquestionably evoke popular plaudits. He shows the ability to individualize this new character. . . . It shines by contrast with his Kowalski." Crowther agreed that "when this dynamic young performer is speaking his anger or his love for a fellow revolutionary, or when he is charging through the land at the head of his rebel-soldiers or walking bravely into the trap of his doom, there is power enough in his portrayal to cause the screen to throb. And throb it does."

By now, with his third film, the Hollywood establishment accepted that for all his eccentricities and rebellion against the "system," Brando was worth the trouble. Hedda Hopper said as much in March 1952.

> He's done only three pictures, but his salary has tripled, placing him in the wage brackets of far older and more famous film stars. What is the secret behind the spectacular rise of this fellow who has been appropriately called "the brilliant brat from Broadway"? I liked him in *The Men*, but failed to share the enthusiasm of a lot of critics. . . . In *A Streetcar Named Desire*, he played the part of the brutish husband so realistically that I confess he revolted me. . . . I can see why his performance in *Streetcar* was considered by some to be one of the finest of last year. But it hardly afforded a basis of judging him as a screen actor. He played the role so often on the stage that he should have been perfect in the movie. . . .
>
> Not until I saw *Viva Zapata!* was I sold on Brando as an actor. As the Indian peasant who became a great revolutionary Mexican general, Marlon . . . succeeded in conceiving and sustaining an original characterization, a feat for which most Hollywood stars are not noted. That's why Marlon's electrifying talent should be cultivated.

Hopper ran down the usual Hollywood list of screwball stories about Marlon Brando, some of which she said upset him, but that he did little to contradict. "If a star of his caliber roams around wearing dungarees, T-shirts and canvas sneakers with a pet coon perched on his shoulders, as Marlon does, he's naturally regarded as being a bit on the abnormal side even in Hollywood. He has stated the only thing an actor owes his public is not to bore them.

"This he never does."

Two-and-a-half years since he'd touched down in Hollywood, Brando was already mythologized as the star who hated the limelight, made up stories about his past, got by on a hundred and fifty dollars a week, turned down studio limousines, and showed up for a three-week shoot in Texas with his entire wardrobe in a small canvas bag.

"I don't think Marlon can be explained in terms of either the uninhibited brat or the sensitive artist," Hopper opined. "He's a combination of both seeing through sham and defying it, yet a bit guilty of sham himself. . . . Brando, being an extremely positive character, will continue to be controversial, but he won't be ignored. And as far as I'm concerned, he's arrived as a new type of movie actor."

When Hopper's feature story appeared, Brando had already been nominated for, and lost out on, an Academy Award as Best Actor for *A Streetcar Named Desire*. Ten days earlier, on March 20, 1952, *Streetcar* had made history as the first motion picture to score three awards for acting—Vivien Leigh for Best Actress, Kim Hunter for Best Supporting Actress, and Karl Malden for Best Supporting Actor. Brando was the only one left out. Humphrey Bogart took home the Best Actor Oscar for *The African Queen*. Brando would be nominated again in 1953 for his role as Emiliano Zapata. He'd lose that year to Gary Cooper in *High Noon*, while Anthony Quinn, who played Brando's brother in *Viva Zapata!*, would win the award for Best Supporting Actor.

For his fourth film, Brando took a real chance, and possibly did so on a dare. The mumbling Method actor, the one whose style and "realness" defied centuries of stage acting and precise enunciation, took on Shakespeare. It could have been his way to transcend the "slob" label the gossips had bestowed on him, but by taking on Mark Antony, the leading role in *Julius Caesar*, he was risking ridicule. Producer John Houseman and director Joseph L. Mankiewicz were well aware that his hiring was "stunt casting," In case Brando wasn't up to handling the soliloquies, they had British Shakespearean actor Paul Scofield on stand-by. But when filming began in August 1952 on the MGM lot in Culver City, Brando more than held his own alongside British stage veterans including James Mason and John Gielgud. Brando befriended Gielgud, who played Cassius, and sought out guidance with his phrasing and delivery.

"The first day we were there, he took me up to his bungalow and said, 'You must do a speech for me,'" Gielgud told Dick Cavett in 1971. "And I found that he had tapes of Maurice Evans, John Barrymore, all the people he admired—Olivier—and he wanted me to do a bit, too. And he was studying all the ways people spoke Shakespeare. And one day he did ask me to help him with his speech and I made some suggestions, and the next morning he came down and he mugged them up and got them exactly."

According to gay culture historian Rutledge, Brando expressed his thanks graciously. "He said that he slept with John Gielgud because Gielgud helped him with his lines. He said it was the least he could do. That was one of my favorite things that (author and Academy Award-winning screenwriter) Gavin Lambert told me."

"A new and possibly great Shakespearean actor has been born." MGM/Photofest
© MGM

Louis Berg was back on the Brando beat in early 1953, and had been on the MGM lot to witness Brando deliver the film's crucial speech, the one that begins: "Friends, Romans, countrymen, lend me your ears."

"Generations of schoolboys have mouthed those words mechanically, but as Brando delivered them, they emerged as a compelling roar, commanding attention above the clamor of the mob of extras," Berg wrote. "The next 34 lines—probably the longest uninterrupted speech of the history of Hollywood—were delivered with no change in lighting or any shifting of equipment. . . . Movie sequences are usually chopped up affairs—a minute or two of action, a line or two of speech and then hours of waiting for lights to be changed and equipment moved. The only break in Brando speech, however, came when the playwright himself had originally ordered it. At the close of his oration, extras, prop men and grips joined in the applause—a rare thing on a movie set. A new and possibly great Shakespearean actor has been born."

Was it merely PR puffery? Or had Brando rewritten the rules once again, opening the gates for future movie stars—and unlikely Shakespeareans—including Al Pacino, Mel Gibson, Mekhi Phifer, Keanu Reeves, Claire Danes, and Leonardo DiCaprio, to take on the Bard on-screen? The latter seemed to be the case. Popular culture historian Gary Shapiro, a lifelong "Brandophile," says the secret is actually quite clear, in comparison to the world of great British stage actors. "When you look at Laurence Olivier's *Hamlet*, which is a great movie—the Academy Award for Best Picture and Best Actor (in 1949)—Olivier is very good. He's Olivier, and you totally believe him. But at the same time, you're always aware that you're watching Shakespeare. With that and his *Henry V*, you're thinking, 'Well, I can almost understand what he's saying.' But Brando, in his 'Lend me your ears,' which is one of the most-quoted Shakespeare scenes, you understand every word and you're as mesmerized as the people who are listening to him. That is an unbelievable, great performance, just that monologue, which is a long monologue. He delivers it with passion, and he is that guy as much as he's ever been any guy."

(Andrew Dickson wrote in *The Guardian* in 2019 that "Brando's blazing turn as Antony ['Lend me your ears'] is so riveting that you almost forget Roland Barthes wrote an entire essay mocking the wigs.")

Julius Caesar received a very positive reception at its world premiere at the Liberty Theatre in Sydney, Australia, on May 10, 1953 (the first Hollywood major motion picture to open in Australia), and word spread quickly. When the film had its "official" world premiere on June 4 at the Booth Theatre on West Forty-Fifth Street in New York's Theater District, Brando had, in a way, returned to Broadway, after all. The Booth was, and remains, a legitimate theater. With the installation of a large, curved screen and stereophonic sound system, the *Caesar* engagement—only two showings a day—was the first time anything other than a live play had been presented there. After the premiere, Bosley Crowther, a couple of blocks away at the *New York Times*, came to praise Brando, announcing that he was "the delight and surprise of the film . . . something memorable to see. Athletic and bullet-headed, he looks the realest Roman of them all and possesses the fire of hot convictions in the firm elasticity of steel. Happily, Mr. Brando's diction, which has been guttural and slurred in previous films, is clear and precise in this instance. In him, a major talent has emerged."

"He put great feeling and unexpected clarity into his 'Friends, Romans, countrymen' delivery," Philip K. Scheuer wrote in the *Los Angeles Times*, "and to the extent that he moves us it is possible he could have moved the mob."

This time, even *Variety* was swayed. "Every performance is a tour de force. . . . Any fears about Brando appearing in Shakespeare are dispelled by his compelling portrayal as the revengeful Mark Antony, in which he turns in the performance of his career. His interpretation of the famous funeral oration will be a conversation piece. The entire speech takes on a new light as voiced by Brando."

Variety sealed it. Now Brando was deemed, officially, as great and game-changing an actor on film as he had been on stage.

Mark Antony in *Julius Caesar* would lead to his third Academy Award nomination in the category of Best Actor.

What would be Brando's next move? What genre would he conquer next? Ultimately, he would choose a project that seemed to be the most logical step in his quest to make films that not only mattered to him but would make a difference in the world. The project would not be the cudgel he had originally envisioned, but it would touch off a revolution he never imagined or would comprehend. The role would be as historic as his Broadway breakthrough in *A Streetcar Named Desire*, not only introducing a new Hollywood leading man, but influencing a generation, and generations to come. Of all the work Brando had done, and would do in the next half-century, this next step would be the most significant.

He decided to make a biker flick.

Five

The Wild One

By the time Marlon Brando had shaken off his role as Mark Antony in *William Shakespeare's Julius Caesar* at Metro-Goldwyn-Meyer studios in the fall of 1952, he'd proven he could hold his own against British thespians schooled in the classics. He was also, after four pictures, fed up with Hollywood, and determined that if he was going to make any more movies, they'd be ones that "mattered." So when Stanley Kramer came calling again, Brando listened. Kramer was the "social issues producer," a guy who didn't heed Sam Goldwyn's aphorism about leaving the delivery of "messages" to Western Union. Kramer had done pretty well with his left-leaning "message movies," and had done right by Brando when he cast him in *The Men*, the motion picture that focused on the struggles of paraplegic war veterans (there were said to be twenty-five hundred left by World War II). The picture had been praised for its documentary quality, and Brando, in his first movie role, for his acting.

Now, Kramer's independent production company had a deal with Columbia Pictures and a project based on *Cyclists' Raid*, the fictional short story written by Frank Rooney and based on the motorcycle gang rampage in Hollister, California, in 1947. The story had been published in the January 1951 issue of *Harper's Magazine*, and according to Kramer, "It touched my sense of social responsibility. I wanted Marlon to play Johnny, the leader of one of the gangs." The film would highlight issues that had been making the papers and catching the attention of civic leaders and politicians in recent years: group violence, highway lawlessness, the social pressures and difficulties war veterans faced in returning to civilian life (an echo of *The Men*), and most obviously—even though Brando would be twenty-eight years old when production began in late January 1953—juvenile delinquency, which, in the postwar era, was perceived as a widespread problem by local law enforcement agencies and church and civic groups. The teenage crime crisis also served as an easy, publicity-grabbing topic for politicians and future congressional committees.

Brando considered the project, agreed with the premise, and signed on to the film. But he demanded the script make it clear that the towns-folk—the straight, white bread, so-called "law-abiding" members of the community—would be equally culpable for the violence, and that by the end of the picture, they and the audience would understand the issues and stultifying social conditions that had caused the cyclists to rebel in the first place. He signed on to the picture called *The Cyclists' Raid*, convinced that even though the role of a motorcycle hood was quite a step down from Shakespeare, he was setting off on a socially-relevant project, a step in his crusade to "make a difference." Besides, Kramer promised Brando that he'd get to ride his own motorcycle.

To direct the picture, Kramer brought in Hungarian-born László Bene-dek. The pair had collaborated in 1951 on the film version of Arthur Miller's Pulitzer Prize-winning play, *Death of a Salesman* (which received five Academy Award nominations), Benedek shared Kramer's politi-cal views, and Kramer believed that the picture would benefit from a European's sensibility. (Brando biographer Charles Higham wrote that Benedek revealed a personal connection to the subject: "While he was at Malibu beach, his car had been surrounded by black-leather-clad motor-cyclists, in helmet and goggles, shouting menacingly as they circled the vehicle before Benedek was able to make his escape.") Ben Maddow, who with director John Huston had written Huston's film noir heist picture, *The Asphalt Jungle*, in 1950, typed out a first-draft screenplay. "Then," Maddow told Patrick McGilligan for his book *Backstory 2: Interviews with Screenwriters of the 1940s and 1950s*, "Kramer called me into his office. He said, 'I'm sorry, I have to fire you.'" Maddow was a victim of the Holly-wood blacklist, the practice of denying work to those in the entertainment industry who were suspected to have been or to be sympathetic to mem-bers of the Communist Party. "Well, so many people had already been fired that I didn't really need any further explanation. But I took my name off *The Wild One* because I saw a version of it that I disliked very much. It was partly mine and partly not." John Paxton, who'd been nominated for an Oscar in 1948 for writing the film noir *Crossfire*, took over.

Brando returned to Hollywood in early 1953, got a house in Pacific Pali-sades near the ocean, gave some notes on the script (which was still being written), and began his research. By night he would pilot his motorcycle around Los Angeles, cruising the city, stopping in at roadhouses and saloons patronized by the *pachucos*—Southern California's Mexican biker gangs. It's said that he would order straight whiskey at the bar and sur-reptitiously pour the shots onto the floor, as he studied those around him. In one joint, he got caught up in a police raid. The cops checked his arms for needle marks before letting him walk, not realizing they'd missed a chance at nabbing an autograph. There were also reports that he ran with L.A.'s first gay motorcycle gang. Darwin Porter writes in *Brando Unzipped* that the actor had been spotted patronizing gay-oriented shops, "dressed in black leather and silver chains, his face partially hidden by a cyclists' cap, which he wore at a jaunty angle some described as 'feminine.'" Other reports said he rode with the Hells Angels, the Harley-riding outlaw gang founded in 1948 in Fontana, about sixty miles east of Hollywood.

It's well-documented that Brando did not, in the end, use his own personal motorcycle for the filming, but was loaned a 1950 Triumph 6T Thunderbird—a British bike, at that—which he hopped on to make the three hundred-mile run from Hollywood to Hollister, where he met up with Kramer, Benedek, Paxton, and members of motorcycle clubs and gangs. The production team had been in the area for weeks, doing research and trying to find the motivation of the motorcycle gang members. Brando studied the cyclists. He listened to the way they spoke, tried to perfect the speech pattern and use the lingo, which wasn't that far from the rhythm of the jazz slang he was already familiar with. He saw how the men engaged in corny, adolescent games and rivalries, and watched the arm-wrestling and primitive fights for power. He, like his colleagues, was hearing lots of stories, and noted the colorful details, but although there was a lot of great action, there were not many satisfying answers. Legend has it that Kramer asked the group, "Well, what is it you're rebelling *against*?" and one of the bikers shouted back, "Well, what you got?"

Brando took note, as he did of comments from another cyclist, who came up to him to talk about that infamous July Fourth weekend. "Shit, man," he said. "Find another little town without a main highway and get that number of bikers together and it could happen again. Yes, sir, we treed Hollister."

"Treed" was an old expression used by trail-drive cowboys, for when they'd come into a town, drink, shoot their guns, ride their horses up and down Main Street and break things, causing the townspeople to hide until they left. That warning was foremost in Brando's mind when he contributed more notes to the script. It had to be made clear that what happened in Hollister was not an isolated incident, but one that could happen again and could happen anywhere. These "outlaws" didn't just fall out of the sky: they were American-made, products of a time of conformity and automation. They were rebelling against the status quo they'd fought a war to establish. They were rebels with a cause. The director and producer agreed that actual outlaw cyclists be cast as extras in the films (Wino Willie Forkner was among them, serving as an uncredited technical adviser). As the filming date neared, Brando, more than ever, was looking forward to making this picture.

He was not aware that the Breen office had rejected the script.

Joseph Breen ran the Production Code Administration, the board that enforced the Motion Picture Code, Hollywood's self-censoring guidelines which set the boundaries regarding profanity, violence, and indecency in films produced by the five major studios. Since 1934, no major studio film could be released without the PCA's approval, but by the 1950s, a more permissive postwar era, producers were pushing back at the restrictions on sex, language, and brutality.

Brando had experienced PCA censorship when he filmed *A Streetcar Named Desire* with Kazan. Before production began, Breen had announced that the play could never be filmed as it was staged on Broadway, especially not with references to homosexuality and a rape scene. Tennessee Williams, who collaborated with Kazan and screenwriter Oscar Saul in adapting his play for the screen, agreed to remove the overt gay references but wrote an impassioned letter to Breen in defense of the rape scene. "*Streetcar* is an extremely and peculiarly moral play in the deepest and truest sense of the term," he wrote. "The rape of Blanche by Stanley is a pivotal, integral truth in the play, without which the play loses its meaning, which is the ravishment of the tender, the sensitive, the delicate, by the savage and brutal forces of modern society. It is a poetic plea for comprehension." How could Hollywood argue with that? Williams got his rape, but in exchange, the ending was rewritten so that Kowalski is punished for the crime.

The Cyclists' Raid, the first draft of which had been submitted in December 1952, pushed more than most on the violence front, and despite their efforts, Kramer and Paxton did not get anywhere close to revealing the motivations of the cycling perpetrators. All that remained was the anarchy and violence, and the script readers of the PCA were said to have been shocked by the extent. "The idea of a bunch of roughnecks coming into a town and taking it over! You make them seem like heroes!" censor Jack Vizzard raged. "By God, if they tried to do that to a town where I lived, I'd shoot 'em first and ask questions later!" Jerold Simmons, professor of history at the University of Nebraska, Omaha, found in the PCA files that staffers had noted that the script "abounded" with "fury, violence, lawlessness, the destruction of property, brutality, drunkenness, callousness, and contempt for society." Breen himself spelled out the major concern in a memo to George Glass, the chief publicist for the Stanley Kramer Company: "The callousness of the young hoodlums in upsetting the normal tenor of life in a small town, the manner in which they panic the citizens, the ineffectiveness of law and order for the majority of the script, the brawling, drunkenness, vandalism and irresponsibility of the young men are, in our opinion, all very dangerous elements. They cannot help but suggest to younger members of the audience, it seems to us, the possibilities that lie in their power to get away with hoodlumism, if only they organize into bands."

The film that was meant to explore and explain the phenomenon of juvenile delinquency was seen as a potential *cause* of the problem. The PCA's rejection of *The Cyclists' Raid* script left Kramer in a difficult spot. His Stanley Kramer Company had already laid out $200,000 on the project and had a firm starting date for filming on the Columbia Ranch in Burbank. (Columbia Pictures had added another snag to Kramer's plans. The studio's tyrannical president and production chief Harry Cohn slashed Kramer's budget, refusing to let him film on location and shunting production to the rural backlot, on sets usually used for B-movie westerns. Cohn also eliminated rehearsal weeks, some scenes, and, to save more even money, decreed that the movie be filmed in black-and-white.)

Kramer had to get the schedule back on track. Four days after the script was rejected, he, Benedek, and Paxton met with Vizzard and longtime staffer Milton Hodenfield. While the filmmakers tried to sway the censors, Kramer began to tap dance before throwing the Hail Mary pass. The gang members don't pay for their crimes? Nothing is learned? Blame Paxton! The screenwriter had inadvertently, Kramer claimed, left out the very premise of the film: gang leader Johnny would be redeemed and set straight by the love of a woman! That's right! The waitress he fancies would save him from a life of crime. In order for that redemption to pay off, he said, the cyclists had to be violent to begin with. When the PCA censors didn't buy the explanation, Kramer changed tack. He promised to cut 60 percent of the "hoodlumism" from the script. He also agreed to make the police chief less of a milquetoast, and, significantly, to add a preface to the film condemning the violence: *"This is a shocking story. It could never take place in most American towns—but it did in this one. It is a public challenge not to let it happen again."* That should be enough, Kramer said, for the PCA to approve the script and allow production to get underway.

The shadow of the deadline was looming. The following day, Kramer instructed Paxton and Benedek to assemble an outline of the movie that addressed the concerns of the PCA, scene by scene. That seemed to work. The censors granted tentative approval and, making a rare exception, agreed to handle the script piece-by-piece while filming commenced. They were satisfied that Kramer was an experienced producer who knew how to deal with touchy subjects and would make sure that the finished product didn't go over the edge. "Over the next several weeks, Paxton forwarded sections of the script to the PCA, and the staff responded with detailed suggestions," Simmons wrote in his 2008 study of the censoring of *The Wild One*. "Nearly all focused on reducing the violence of the original. They warned against too much vigor in the rocking of the car by the youths in the street riot, against 'unnecessary brutality' in the fight scenes, and against 'kicking and gouging' throughout. Kramer and Benedek complied with the instructions, and the feature moved swiftly through the Code machinery without further snags."

After the cameras rolled, the PCA added one more, significant, demand. In addition to the written preface at the top of the film, there would be a second disclaimer. This one would not only be spoken, but spoken by the star, announcing that what was to follow was a singular incident that could never happen again. Brando was already in on the picture; he had invested too much of his own time and passion in the project, so he was forced to go along. That is why Marlon Brando, as Johnny Strabler, is heard before he is seen. "It begins here for me on this road," Brando says. "How the whole mess happened, I don't know, but I know it couldn't happen again in a million years." *Couldn't happen again in a million years?* That was the opposite of what Brando had heard directly from one of the cyclists in Hollister, the opposite of what he believed, and totally negated a major reason he'd agreed to do the picture. Brando was convinced that the breakdown in law and order depicted in Wrightsville could happen

Johnny Strabler and the Black Rebels Motorcycle Club Columbia Pictures/Photofest © Columbia

in any town, and that the monotonous, soul-crushing routine of life in the dishwater-dull postwar era (Dwight Eisenhower would be inaugurated for his first term as president ten days after the scheduled start of filming) had helped create these outlaws on wheels. Brando read the words. Talk about mumbling! He could barely bring himself to read the newly scripted lines, but he did, in a way that signaled his protest.

This is why, when Brando is first heard in *The Wild One*, he's speaking with the lisping Southern drawl. Witnesses, including director Benedek, claimed he used the voice deliberately in the recording studio, so he could say it wasn't him, but "someone else" reading the text, and that he made faces throughout the session. Said Benedek: "It was his own way of saying to the Breen office: 'Screw you.'"

It would turn out that the "screw you" was directed at a wider target than the Hollywood censors. Brando used that voice throughout, in a performance that was neither macho nor even necessarily heterosexual. In doing so, he was producing the template for a new Hollywood leading man—and a new kind of masculinity that would transform not only cinema, but society.

But time for a pause.

What about that final script? A quick sidestep to recap the events depicted in the film that began production as *The Cyclists' Raid*:

The movie opens on that empty country road, the written disclaimer at the top followed by Brando's monologue, assuring the audience that an incident like this could never happen again, not in a million years. (Like hell it couldn't.) The bikers of the Black Rebels Motorcycle Club thunder past the fixed camera in the middle of the road, and after the opening credits, during which moviegoers get to study and absorb the sensuous image of Brando as leader Johnny Strabler, roll into a town called Carbonville. The outlaws ignore a roadblock and drive straight onto the track of an officially sanctioned motorcycle race. These cyclists definitely stand out, as outsiders—and punks—in their blue jeans and black leather jackets with B•R•M•C and a skull-and-crossed-pistons logo stenciled on the backs. They walk across the track, disrupt the race, antagonize the participants, and act adolescently enough to attract the attention of a highway patrolman, who orders them to get out of town, like now. (The patrolman is much taller than the gang members, making the Black Rebels, who all appear to be in their mid- to late-twenties, seem even more like teenagers.) As they retreat to their bikes, one of the cyclists hands Johnny a second-place trophy he'd swiped from the awards table. ("So Johnny only won second place, huh?" "Whaddaya mean? First place was two feet high!") Johnny stuffs the prize in his jacket. As they ride off, he's got the trophy strapped to the handlebars of his Triumph.

The Black Rebels descend as a horde on the sleepy town of Wrightsville. The locals watch with worry from the sidewalks. Young boys' eyes widen in excitement. The cyclists begin drag racing on Main Street. The racers takes off just as old Art Kleiner comes driving into town—straight for them. Kleiner's car veers out of control. A

Black Rebel called "Crazy" slides his bike into it, and breaks an ankle in the collision. The old man blames the gang. The cyclists blame the old man. The police chief wades in but is too meek to take sides, let alone action. Johnny, meanwhile, notices Kathie, the pretty young waitress from Bleeker's Café-Bar. He unties the trophy from his bike and follows her inside the cafe. They flirt at the counter. Johnny offers to give her the trophy, but she won't accept it. Two Black Rebels enter to ask their leader if the gang will be leaving town or waiting until the local doctor treats Crazy. With an eye toward Kathie, Johnny tells them they'll stay until Crazy is patched up.

Through the window, the Black Rebels can be seen continuing their genial, obnoxious behavior in the street—chicken-fighting, slaloming cycles around beer bottles—even hopping on pogo sticks. Kathie's uncle, who owns Bleeker's, takes advantage of the potential customers and urges them inside for cold beer. The bikers gather at the bar while Johnny continues his conversation with Kathie on the café side. Their differences are clear. She's lived her life in a small town. Once, she almost went on a fishing trip to Canada with her dad. Almost. Johnny reveals that he and the Black Rebels are, like the Hollister invaders, weekend warriors. On the weekends, he says, "We go out and have a ball." "What do you do?" she asks innocently. "I mean, do you just ride around, or do you go on some sort of a picnic or something?" "Picnic! Man, you are too square." Johnny explains, "You don't go any one special place. That's cornball style. You just go. (snaps his fingers) The bunch gets together after all week. It builds up."

In the original script, Johnny goes deeper into his background: "After all week. You got to have a ball. Every day the same thing. Crawling around underneath. You shoot a Chevy." He makes the sound of a lube gun. "*Phhuuusp! Phhuuuusp!* Okay. You shoot a Study. *Phuuuusp! Phhuuuuuuuusp! Phhuuuuuuuuuusp!* Same thing. Grease. It builds up. You got to sing. You got to feel good. You got to really go."

Back to the movie:

The Black Rebels are drinking and carrying on in the bar. A pair of them dance with a couple of local girls to the swinging jazz on the jukebox. Kathie, who's working, won't dance with Johnny, so he stands by the jukebox tapping out a rhythm. One of the girls asks him what he's rebelling against. He replies: "Whaddaya got?" The police chief enters and tries to make peace with Johnny, but Johnny won't have it. He doesn't like cops. When Johnny finds out that the chief is Kathie's father, he's had enough of Wrightsville. Johnny's outside with a few of his boys, reattaching the trophy to his handlebars, when a Black Rebel, carrying a patched-up Crazy on his cycle, roars past and, in a nod to the events of Hollister, through the door of Bleeker's and up to the bar. Everyone's back inside celebrating his return when another gang comes riding into town.

This group is wilder, dirtier, drunker—in appearance a lot more similar to the actual outlaw motorcycle clubs of the era, dressed not in uniforms of black leather jackets but garish combinations of army surplus and thrift store duds. They're led by Chino (played by Lee Marvin), and when Johnny steps out of the bar, he sees that Chino has taken possession of his trophy. It turns out that the two men (boys) have a history. They once rode together. Now, they fight in the street. Johnny hurls Chino through a store window. The local citizens want it all to stop. One of them, Charlie Thomas, suggests that he and others should do what the sheriff won't. As the cyclists and spectators fill Main Street, Charlie drives his car slowly through the pack. Chino's boys pull him out of the car, then attempt to overturn it. Finally, the sheriff agrees to arrest Chino, and leads him off to the jail.

That night, the real trouble begins. The bikers are making noise with their motorcycle horns outside the Police Department jail, then move to take over the town. Chino's boys invade the Wrightsville switchboard office, send the operator home, and cut off communications. Black Rebels drag Charlie Thomas from his home to the jail and stuff him in the cell with Chino, who's sleeping off too many beers and whatever else he'd imbibed. Other cyclists are wreaking havoc in Bleeker's bar. Kathie is sent off to tell her father the police chief about the telephone problem. Outside, Johnny rejects the advances of one of Chino's female followers (called "Beetles") and returns to the bar in search of Kathie. Her uncle pleads with him to stop the bikers from "wrecking my place," but Johnny waves him off.

The lawlessness escalates. Some men from the town free Charlie (leaving the cell door open for Chino to stroll out), arm themselves, and head out as vigilantes. Bikers from both gangs have looted a beauty salon and are carousing outside. When Kathie walks by, they hop on their bikes and follow her, circle her, terrorize her—until Johnny comes to the rescue. He orders her to "get on" his Triumph and they ride off through the countryside, eventually stopping in the middle of the woods, where a love scene appears imminent. But after Johnny grabs Kathie in a rough embrace for a clumsy kiss, the more she seems willing—and the more he recoils. "You're afraid of me," she says. He acts offended. When she says she wishes they could take off together, he pushes her away, and she runs off in tears.

When Johnny follows, he's captured by the vigilantes. Kathie witnesses the abduction and runs to her father, who's hiding at his desk, downing shots of whiskey. She convinces him to leave his bottle and do something. Meanwhile, Johnny has been taken into a building, where he's taking a beating by Charlie and his neighbors. "My old man used to hit harder than that," Johnny taunts, after a particularly solid blow. More punches are to come when the police chief arrives to stop the violence and take Johnny into custody. While the townsfolk argue, Johnny escapes. He finds his bike, and after having a good cry, attempts to ride away. But the mob spots him and gives chase. Someone throws a tire iron and hits Johnny's motorcycle. He falls to the street. The riderless cycle speeds out of control and smashes into the old man who washes dishes at Bleeker's, killing him.

The next morning, sheriff's deputies are on the scene. They've rounded up the cyclists, are stuffing some into the back of patrol cars and impounding motorcycles. Johnny is inside the police station, where a large and imposing county sheriff has taken control of the situation. The sheriff and his deputies are about to haul Johnny away to face a manslaughter charge when Kathie and her father arrive. She insists that the sheriff has it all wrong and convinces her uncle and old Art Kleiner to tell the truth about what they saw the night before: Someone threw a tire iron at Johnny when he was trying to leave town; Johnny was the victim. The sheriff agrees to give Johnny a break and let him go, as long as he and his gang leave town and don't come back. Johnny can't bring himself to say "thank you," but before he leaves Wrightsville, he stops in at the cafe and leaves that trophy on the counter for Kathie. He smiles for one of the first times in the film. Consider him redeemed, if not punished.

So, in the end, the citizens of Wrightsville show themselves to be as violent and potentially anarchic as the cyclists, the weak-kneed police chief finds the strength to stand up against the vigilantes in the name of law and order, sheriff's deputies are introduced at the end to restore order and round up some of the miscreants, and the county sheriff (played by Jay C. Flippen, imposingly and authoritatively) steps into the police station with the intent of charging Johnny with manslaughter—but when the truth is revealed, settles for a stern lecture.

"I don't get you," the sheriff says to Johnny, who looks appropriately chastened. "I don't get your act at all. And I don't think you do, either. I don't think you know what you're trying to do or how to go about it. I think you're stupid, real stupid. And real lucky. Last night, you scraped by. Just barely. But a man's dead, on account of something you let get started, even though you didn't start it. I don't know if there's any good in you. I don't know if there's *anything* in you. But I'm going to take a big fat chance . . . and let you go." Even Johnny seems surprised to hear that.

When next seen, Johnny and the Black Rebels are on their bikes in the street outside the Police Department. Johnny is tucking the trophy back into his jacket when the sheriff sends them off with a Wild West-style warning: "Okay, hotshots, the fun's over! Every one a' you monkeys is down in my book. And every stick of damage around here'll be paid for. You've got ten minutes to clear out. Just stick your nose back in this county, any of ya, and you'll never see daylight again as long as you live. Now get!"

In February, *The Cyclists' Raid* underwent a title change to *The Wild One*, and the first reports of the producers' problems with the censors went public. The issues took a serious and potentially box office–threatening turn that month when word circulated that because of the film's depiction of violence and lawlessness, the PCA would recommend that the State Department not allow *The Wild One* to be distributed outside the United States. This censorship of cultural exports was not unusual during the Cold War, a period of tension and potential confrontation between the United States and Soviet Union in the wake of the nations' temporary alliance during World War II. The US State Department and especially the new Eisenhower administration determined that it was not in the nation's best interest to export any motion picture that might give allies and nonaligned countries a less-than-rosy impression of the American way of life. Despite its pruning and scrubbing by the PCA, *The Wild One*, which depicted roving gangs of disenfranchised war veterans, juvenile delinquency, the destruction of property, lawlessness, vigilantism, and lethal mob violence, would definitely fit the bill as undesirable advertising (in fact, after his first reading, Breen had decried the script as "antisocial, if not downright communistic.")

Stanley Kramer responded quickly to neutralize the threat, and knew to turn to a power more influential than any in Washington. Louella Parsons was Hedda Hopper's archrival in the Hollywood gossip business, equally vindictive but not as vehemently conservative. In her column of February 19, Parsons wrote that "Stanley Kramer tells me there is nothing damaging about *Cyclists' Raid*, now called *The Wild One*," and got an MPPA official to confirm that the office "has neither the authority nor the inclination to be concerned with the distribution of motion pictures outside of the United States. Says Joseph Breen, head of the censorship board, 'We would not presume to recommend to the State Department anything concerning the exhibiting of pictures.'"

For all the assistance she gave, Parsons couldn't help but reignite the fire the previous paragraph had extinguished by adding, "This is in answer to the widespread report that *The Wild One* might be fodder for the Soviet mill because it shows a group of American youths who are vandals in every sense of the word."

Few were as frustrated by the controversies as Brando. A few days after Parsons's scoop, Bob Thomas reported that Brando was more soured on Hollywood than ever, and planned to walk away after his next film. "I'm not saying I'll never see Hollywood again," Brando told him. "Nothing can foresee the future that well, but my present plan is to do *Pal Joey* this fall, and in the fall of 1954, I'll take an extended trip around the world that will last a year. After that, I'll confine my acting to the stage. This is the result of a long-term plan. I got what I wanted out of pictures. I was able to buy a ranch for my folks in Nebraska and provide a nest egg for myself. Now I can do the things I want to do."

The stage, Brando said, offered far more freedom from censorship. He used *The Wild One*, a film he was currently shooting, as an example. "There were fifteen different pressure groups that didn't want this picture made." he complained. "Everything from women's groups to motorcycle clubs came out against it. This sort of pressure has robbed the movies of their vitality."

Although Brando's depiction of Johnny Strabler would make him the iconic symbol of the rebel outlaw motorcyclist for decades to come, he couldn't resist sticking it to the studio publicists. He told Thomas he wasn't such a motorcycle enthusiast after all, and claimed that he rode for only a year and had given it up. "I had too many narrow scrapes in city traffic," Brando said. "I figured my number was getting too close on the lottery; I didn't want to take any more chances."

Along the way to its release, the film's title was changed again, from *The Wild One* to *Frenzy*, before Columbia settled on *Hot Blood*—until the marketing department tested *Hot Blood* for several women's groups and got a cold reaction. Weeks before the premiere, *Variety* reported it was back to *The Wild One*. "In mapping marketing plans, Columbia aims to stress the pic's value in the nationwide fight against juvenile delinquency. . . . It focuses on a band of motorcyclists who give free rein to brutality instincts in a small California town. The 'Blood' nomenclature might have attracted a similar element among theater audiences, Col felt."

The Wild One did not come close to offering motivations, a goal that was a major reason why Brando had taken the role. In the end, much of the shocking brutality in the original script was gone, but still included were depictions of street violence, mob violence, fighting, destruction of property, larceny, drunkenness, reckless driving, vigilantism, beatings, mob anarchy, manslaughter, terrorism, and potential rape (the censors dealt with that last situation by refusing to allow the cyclists to do anything more than circle Kathie before she's rescued by her knight in black leather). And in the end, the Black Rebels receive not much more than a threat of punishment for what transpired. They really did "get away with it."

Nevertheless, after the initial burst of notes and haggling in December and into January, the Production Code Administration didn't raise any more objections, and the censors' readers raised no red flags on the way to the film's release. The issue of screen violence didn't come up again. "Apparently," Simmons wrote, "they were persuaded that Johnny's transformation from Black Rebel to solid citizen at the end of the film offered sufficient compensating moral values to offset the violence and intimidation."

There was something that the censors couldn't see on the written page: Brando's narration at the top of the picture, the one he could barely get himself to mouth, wound up serving not as a sobering call to attention, but a tease—and with that "screw you" southern drawl he put on, it was an even more tingling, titillating come-on—because once he was done speaking, and that battalion of bikers roared past the camera in the middle of the country road, the picture cut to that beauty shot of Brando, swaying side to side in front of that rear-projection screen, with that big 650cc Triumph 6T Thunderbird motorcycle throbbing between his legs.

Brando's Johnny Strabler was so seductive, so alluring, and *so damn cool*, that the viewer had no choice but to identify with him and take the rebel side. The film may not have been marketed to teenagers, but Brando's biker was most certainly a figure that young people would want to emulate. Brando knew it.

"More than most parts I've played in the movies or onstage, I related to Johnny, and because of this, I believe I played him as more sensitive and sympathetic than the script envisioned," he later explained. "There's a line in the picture where he snarls, 'Nobody tells me what to do.' That's exactly how I've felt all my life . . . and have always thought that Johnny took refuge in his lifestyle because he was wounded—that he'd had little love as a kid and was trying to survive the emotional insecurity that his childhood had forced him to carry into adulthood. . . . He was a rebel, but a strong part of him was sensitive and tender."

"He was antisocial because he knew society was crap; he was a hero to youth because he was strong enough not to take the crap," according to film critic Pauline Kael. "There was a sense of excitement, of danger in his presence, but perhaps his special appeal was in a kind of simple conceit, the conceit of tough kids. . . . We in the audience felt protective: we knew how lonely he must be in his assertiveness. Who even in hell wants to be an outsider? And he was no intellectual who could rationalize it . . . he could only feel it, act it out, be 'The Wild One'—and God knows how many kids felt, 'That's the story of my life.'"

Brando was disappointed with the way *The Wild One* turned out, and how it was received. The picture did not express what he'd hoped it would, and this left him depressed. His sister Jocelyn, who'd been with him on the set, said this was when he began to eat to excess, and when he first began to show a tendency to put on weight. *The Wild One*, Brando said later, "was a failure. We started out to do something worthwhile, to explain the psychology of the hipster. But somewhere along the way we went off the track. The result was that instead of finding why young people tend to bunch into groups that seek expression in violence, all that we did was show the violence."

"Brando was disappointed because he wanted to make a movie that tackled social issues," says Hollywood historian and archivist David Del Valle. "His concept of *The Wild One* was not just about being anti-establishment. It's about recognizing fascism in small towns and the attitude toward violence, because one of the key points is that the violence comes from the townspeople, not the bikers. He was against what *The Twilight Zone* would later portray in *The Monsters Are Due on Maple Street*. But it still became a seminal movie."

The experience only made Brando more eager to move on and move away from Hollywood. He'd planned on heading to Paris, but instead traveled to New England with a group of friends to do some summer theater, just for fun. As he plotted his next move, he couldn't know (and he would later show that he didn't care) that the character he created would not only set the standard for a new kind of rebel, but that the film that disappointed him would spark a revolution more historically significant and far more widespread than the one led by Emiliano Zapata. This little biker movie that didn't accomplish what its star had hoped, would, in the end, accomplish much, much more.

"The emotional impact of Brando in that outfit, on that motorcycle, that's what people remember, not the narrative," Del Valle reminds us.

In the words of Pauline Kael, "God knows how many kids felt, 'That's the story of my life.'"

Six

Elvis

> I've made a study of Marlon Brando. And I know why girls go for us. We're sullen, we're broodin', we're something of a menace. I don't know anything about Hollywood. But I know that you can't be sexy if you smile. You can't be a rebel if you grin.
>
> —Elvis Presley, 1955

It's important to know that *The Wild One* was not being marketed to teenagers. Young people were not yet the prime demographic that movie studios were targeting. Counting on Stanley Kramer's credentials stretching back to *High Noon*, Brando's two Oscar nominations—with a third for his work in *Julius Caesar* on the horizon—the studio played up and publicized the movie's seriousness and social value. The release date was moved up to Christmas Day, 1953, with an exclusive engagement at the Orpheum Theatre in downtown Los Angeles in order that the movie and Brando be eligible for Academy Award nominations. Two days before the premiere, *The Hollywood Reporter*'s Milton Luban raved over Brando's "tremendously powerful performance" in "a splendid example of film craftsmanship from the viewpoint of production, acting, direction—in fact, everything but choice of subject."

Everything but.

The Wild One was "a frightening picture," Luban cautioned, "certainly not for the family trade, nor would parents want their youngsters to see it. Its main appeal would seem to be to those lawless juveniles who may well be inspired to go out and emulate the characters portrayed."

Variety warned that the film was "long on suspense, unmitigated brutality and rampant sadism," and would be "hard to sell. . . . Exhibitors will readily identify Brando's chums as spiritual kinsmen of seat-slashers and delinquents who like to throw ushers down from the balcony foyer. . . . What Columbia has on its hands is a small epic of human nastiness. . . . Exciting though the film is, many people are going to be offended by the unrelieved grimness."

Despite the forebodings, the Christmas Day premiere went off without a sliced seat or tossed usher. Philip K. Scheuer's review in the *Los Angeles Times* the following day called *The Wild One* "Stanley Kramer's hottest picture since *High Noon*. . . . As moviemaking *The Wild One* is a humdinger—tingling stuff. . . . Brando varies a deadpan spoiled-big-boy performance with glints of humor that in the end touch our feelings."

Scheuer was troubled, however, by "unanswered questions" about the invaders' backgrounds and motives, and the "muddled" impression of the townspeople. "The total effect, at any rate, is to split our sympathies. Neither side is villainous, but there are villains on both. We must settle for that."

That was a split Brando could live with. But damage had been done before the picture began to be released in theaters across the country in early 1954. When *The Wild One* opened in New York City on December 30, 1953, its controversial reputation preceded it, and because of that, one would be hard-pressed to find an advertisement for the picture's premiere in Times Square. The major metropolitan newspapers featured prominent display ads for *Miss Sadie Thompson*, the lusty, provocative film starring Rita Hayworth in 3D; *The Robe*, the biblical epic and first picture released in widescreen CinemaScope; and Alan Ladd's latest, *Paratrooper*. Burt Lancaster, Frank Sinatra, Deborah Kerr, and Montgomery Clift got big play for *From Here to Eternity*, as did *Easy to Love*, the "holiday gift" starring Esther Williams, Van Johnson, and Tony Martin at Radio City Music Hall. It may be hard to believe today, especially following the high-profile, Christmas Day, Academy Award–qualifying opening in Los Angeles, but only a small ad in the *New York Daily News* announced that *The Wild One* was screening at the RKO Palace Theatre on Broadway at Forty-Seventh Street. In the *New York Times*, a reader would have to squint to notice the announcement, tucked in the top of a large ad for the final showings of *The Robe* at other RKO theaters.

B'WAYS ONLY STAGE AND SCREEN SHOW!
8 BIG ACTS 8
VAUDEVILLE IN THE PALACE MANNER
plus ON SCREEN
MARLON BRANDO
THE 'STREETCAR' MAN HAS A NEW DESIRE
'The WILD ONE'

Intentions and kudos aside, *The Wild One* was being slipped into town, in a formerly grand New York City vaudeville house that had recently been upgraded in an attempt to revive a dead art form. In the 1910s and 1920s, the Palace was the country's most successful vaudeville venue. In 1949,

RKO brought back the old format, slating a stage show featuring vaudeville acts between movie screenings.

Bosley Crowther, the *Times* critic, noticed the insulting treatment of an important film. "A little bit of the surface of contemporary American life is scratched in Stanley Kramer's *The Wild One*. . . and underneath is opened an ugly, debauched and frightening view of a small but particularly significant and menacing element of modern youth. . . . It is a tough and engrossing motion picture, weird and cruel, while it stays on the beam."

"*The Wild One* is," Crowther concluded, "a picture of extraordinary candor and courage. . . . It is too bad that some mutterings in the industry have seemed to deprecate it and it should turn up as the passing feature on an eight-act vaudeville bill."

Then the real backlash hit.

> *The Wild One* is a percussion piece played on the moviegoer's nerves, a kind of audiovisual fugue in which the themes of boogie and terror heap up in alternations of juke-yowl and gear gnash to a climax of violence—and then fall patly silent, leaving the audience to console its disordered pulse and unsweat itself from the seat. . . . The effect of the movie is not to throw light on a public problem but to shoot adrenalin through the moviegoer's veins. . . . Its main purpose seems to be to shock.

The blast in the influential and usually dispassionate *Time* magazine wasn't tempered by praise for Brando, described here as "an actor whose sullen face, slurred accents and dream-drugged eye have made him a supreme portrayer of morose juvenility." Reviews like the one in *Time* opened the door for more extreme reactions for a film heralded in a *Philadelphia Inquirer* listing as "Jazzed-Up Hoods on a Bust-Up Binge." *The Wild One* may have received the Production Code Seal of Approval and been commended by groups including the PTA, American Association of University Women, and Daughters of the American Revolution, but that didn't stop local criticism. And it didn't stop Lloyd T. Binford from deciding that *The Wild One* shouldn't be screened at all.

Binford, who'd recently celebrated his eighty-eighth birthday, was chairman of the Memphis and Shelby County, Tennessee, Board of Censors. On January 16, 1954, he announced that the board had banned *The Wild One*. "That was the worst, the most lawless bunch I ever saw and the most lawless picture I ever saw," Binford told the Memphis *Commercial Appeal* newspaper. "There was nothing immoral in it; it was just rowdy and unlawful and raw. The leader of the bunch, a handsome man, might attract the average boy, six or eight or ten years old, to take him as a model. And his philosophy is, 'Nobody can tell me anything; I'll do as I please.'"

While Binford's ban meant that *The Wild One* would not be screened in Memphis theaters, *Commercial Appeal* reporter and film critic Ben S. Parker pointed out that the picture "presumably will soon enjoy a fat and profitable run across the river in West Memphis."

That did promise to be the case. A few weeks earlier, the Memphis censors had banned Columbia's Rita Hayworth 3D sex drama, *Miss Sadie Thompson* ("It is a raw, dirty picture," said Binford). Columbia responded by booking the movie at two theaters just over the bridge in West Memphis, Arkansas. Norman Colquhoun, Columbia's Memphis branch manager, said *Miss Sadie* was doing "sensational" business and shrugged at the ban of *The Wild One*. "We'll probably put it in West Memphis as soon as we can," Colquhoun said. "The film is trying to point out the evils of young adult delinquency. In view of the business *Miss Sadie Thompson* is doing over there, the Columbia New York office is beginning to regard West Memphis as a first-run outlet."

Columbia didn't bother fighting the Memphis ban. The marketing department anticipated that *The Wild One* was a hot one, and the publicity would add even more heat when the picture began an extended run at the Avon Theatre and Sunset Drive-In Theatre in West Memphis, Arkansas on April 1. When the film opened at the Holly Theatre in Holly Springs, Mississippi, about forty minutes away, the ads read, "Banned in Memphis."

Banned in Memphis, viewed easily just across the Mississippi River, *The Wild One* could look to be forbidden fruit to young folks. It was one thing to be steered away from Rita Hayworth's dirty dancing and provocative come-ons—but Marlon Brando as a handsome leader of young rebels whom kids might take as a role model? A leader whose philosophy is, "Nobody can tell me anything; I'll do as I please"? Publicity like this would certainly stir up youthful interest, make a kid want to cross the river and see a movie.

So it was a notable coincidence and a matter of historic timing that Memphis banned *The Wild One* just as one particular youth in Memphis, Tennessee, was striking out on his own in the entertainment field. This young man had just turned nineteen, and in April, right around the time *The Wild One* was projected under the nighttime sky at the Sunset Drive-In, had taken a job driving a truck, delivering appliances for the Crown Electric Company. He handed most of his pay to his dad, Vernon, to help with the bills, but held on to just enough to keep himself in sharp threads and take his girlfriend Dixie Locke to the movies.

Elvis Aron Presley had graduated from L.C. Humes High School the previous June 3. Forty-five days later, he paid $3.25 to record two songs on a ten-inch acetate at the Memphis Recording Service, which was also the office of Sun Records, at 706 Union Avenue. Marion Keisker, who recorded his voice that day, was impressed. She'd told her boss, Sam Phillips, about the young man who stopped by.

Elvis loved music. Music moved him. He wanted to be a singer—not a rebellious one, necessarily. He wanted to be a star like Dean Martin. Elvis also loved movies. Movies moved him, too. In fact, more than making it in the music business, Elvis Presley wanted to be a movie star. His high school buddy George Klein recalled that during his senior year at Humes High, Elvis worked as an usher at Loew's State Theatre, the grand movie house at 152 South Main Street in downtown Memphis. "He had the chance to watch the movies that played there over and over and became a real student of film," Klein wrote. "He watched James Dean and Monty Cliff and Marlon Brando and saw how they moved and spoke and got the greatest impact with the littlest gestures. He paid enough attention to pick up an intuitive knowledge of the medium that would later surprise the Hollywood folks when Elvis started making his own movies."

The gist of Klein's recollection is true, and so is the sentiment, although the only Brando film to play Loew's State during that period was *The Men*, back in 1950, when Elvis was a sophomore. *From Here to Eternity*, starring Montgomery Clift, was screened at Loew's State, but only after Elvis's graduation—and, according to Klein, after his firing from Loew's. *East of Eden*, James Dean's first starring role, didn't arrive in Memphis until 1955, at the Warner theater. But it is undeniable that the image of Marlon Brando, motorcycle rebel, surly and ready to rebel against anything, surely played a role in Elvis Presley's transformation from slightly girlie hillbilly singer to snarling, pompadoured, leg-shaking, hip-swiveling icon of the teenage generation.

In July 1954, while *The Wild One* was opening in more theaters across the South, Elvis signed a contract with Sun Records. His first single, "Blue Moon of Kentucky" and "That's All Right, Mama," became a local hit, and on Friday night, July 30, Elvis, sporting Johnny Strabler sideburns, was featured at a "folk music frolic" at the Overton Park Shell amphitheater, along with *Louisiana Hayride* stars Slim Whitman and "The Tall Texan," Billy Walker. When Elvis sang, he shook a leg in time with the music, and when he did, his pleated pants gyrated, causing the girls in the crowd to scream. When a new Brando picture, *On the Waterfront*, opened in Memphis at the Malco Theatre on September 17, the advertisement and Ben S. Parker's review appeared on the same page of the *Commercial Appeal* as the ad for Elvis's appearance, along with Tiny Dixon and "The Best Western Dance Band in Town," at Sleepy Eyed John's Eagle's Nest.

Elvis's regional hits began to make noise far beyond the region, and in the fall of 1955, Elvis's new manager, Colonel Tom Parker, convinced Sam Phillips to sell Elvis's contract to RCA Records. RCA paid $35,000 to

Phillips and tossed another $5,000 to the Colonel (who'd go on to take as much as 50 percent of his boy's earnings).

Elvis signed with RCA on November 20, 1955, three weeks after the release of *Rebel Without a Cause*—the second starring role and first post-humous picture for James Dean, who died when he crashed his Porsche on September 30. Brando's latest movie, which had premiered in New York City on November 3, was a sign of how far he'd moved beyond his own rebel image. He was starring as Sky Masterson—singing alongside Frank Sinatra—in *Guys and Dolls*, Sam Goldwyn's CinemaScope version of the Broadway musical. Brando had made peace with Hollywood, or at least seemed to be playing the game, after picking up a Best Actor Academy Award for *On the Waterfront* in March. His next stop would be Nara, Japan, for *Teahouse of the August Moon*, but Johnny Strabler, in his leather jacket, cap, and Levi jeans, straddling his Triumph, was still in theaters, influencing young minds who heard in the jazz soundtrack the makings of a rock 'n' roll revolution.

Elvis Presley, in those early days, was still an unknown to many. Weeks before his first recording sessions at RCA Studios and his first Number One record, he should have been concentrating on his music, maybe studying Dean Martin records. But Elvis had other priorities. Hollywood was already calling, and Elvis had taken that handsome man, the leader of the bunch, as his role model. He said so, out loud, and in print, in a room on the sixth floor of the Peabody Hotel in downtown Memphis. He was talking to Lloyd Shearer, who was following him around, asking questions and taking pictures for *Parade* magazine. Elvis was twenty, still the polite, deferential mama's boy, calling thirty-eight-year-old Shearer "suh," but ordering him to hold his horses as soon as the camera came out. "Suh," Elvis said, "you gotta promise not to snap me even if I'm just smilin' slightly, even if I'm just grinnin'.

"I've made a study of Marlon Brando," he explained. "I've made a study of poor Jimmy Dean. I've made a study of myself. And I know why girls, at least the young 'uns, go for us. We're sullen, we're broodin', we're something of a menace. I don't understand it exactly, but that's what girls like in men.

"I don't know anything about Hollywood. But I know that you can't be sexy if you smile. You can't be a rebel if you grin."

"And then," Shearer recalled, "he stripped off his shirt, flopped himself on the floor, edged up against the bed, lay his head on the mattress, and soulfully looked up at the ceiling. I pressed the shutter."

In 1956 it all came together for Elvis Presley, and it was clear by then that Brando had informed Elvis's image as a musician, singer, and star. Elvis made his first national television appearance in February on *Stage Show*, a half-hour variety series on CBS hosted by big band leaders and brothers Tommy and Jimmy Dorsey. He had a new single on RCA, "Heartbreak Hotel," but it was his look, not music, that got him the gig. Show producer Jack Philbin was handed a publicity photo of the singer and supposedly declared, "He's a guitar-playing Marlon Brando!" (That label got around; by April, columnist Erskine Johnson was referring to Presley as "Marlon Brando with a guitar.") Elvis performed "Blue Suede Shoes" and "Heartbreak Hotel." The show lost in the ratings to Perry Como on NBC, but Elvis's spot caught the attention of a Hollywood big shot. Hal Wallis, who'd produced films including *Casablanca* and *The Maltese Falcon* and who'd most recently succeeded with the team of Dean Martin and Jerry Lewis, arranged a screen test.

Elvis arrived at Paramount Studios on Melrose Avenue at the end of March. Director Frank Tashlin, who in a couple of weeks would start shooting *Hollywood or Bust*, the final Martin & Lewis comedy, ran the test in two parts. First, to determine if the heat he generated on television could be transferred to the big screen, Elvis was handed a prop guitar so he could lip-sync to "Blue Suede Shoes" in wide and close-up shots. Screenwriter Allan Weiss, who'd go on to write a half-dozen Elvis films, had the job of dropping the needle on the record Elvis would mime to. "The transformation was incredible," he said. "We knew instantly that we were in the presence of a phenomenon; electricity bounced off the walls of the sound stage. One felt it as an awesome thing—like an earthquake in progress, only without the implicit threat. Watching this insecure country boy, who apologized when he asked for a rehearsal as though he had done something wrong, turn into absolute dynamite when he stepped into the bright lights and started lip-syncing the words of his familiar hit. He believed in it, and he made you believe it, no matter how 'sophisticated' your musical tastes were."

Elvis next performed two scenes from *The Rainmaker*, a Burt Lancaster period drama that Paramount was still casting. Wallis had Elvis in mind for a supporting role as Katharine Hepburn's "simple" younger brother. Photos show Elvis in a work shirt and jeans, gesturing with a cigar, emoting, doing his best Brando. Even in the still frames, he can be seen to be over-acting. A second scene was filmed with twenty-one-year-old actress Cynthia Baxter. Weiss was more impressed with the lip-syncing. "Elvis played the rebellious younger brother with amateurish conviction—like the lead in a high school play," he recalled. "His performance was believable but lacked the polished subtleties of a professional."

Wallis, though, got very excited when the tests were screened for him. "I felt the same thrill I experienced when I first saw Errol Flynn on the screen. Elvis, in a very different, modern way, had exactly the same power of virility and sexual drive. The camera caressed him."

Within a week, Wallis had signed Elvis to a seven-year, three-picture contract. Elvis was back on the road, performing on April 9, when he was interviewed by Charlie Walker on KMAC Radio in San Antonio, Texas. The previous day, he'd been presented with a gold record for selling a million copies of "Heartbreak Hotel," but to Elvis, that was far less important than his movie deal. "I guess actually that's about the biggest thing," he said. "It's a dream come true, something that I'd never think would happen to me, of all people. I've had people ask me, was I gonna sing in the movies. I'm not. I mean, not as, as far as I know, 'cause I'd took a strictly—an acting test. And I wouldn't—actually, I wouldn't care too much about singin' in the movies, 'cause I did enough singin' around the country."

Elvis apparently forgot the "Blue Suede Shoes" portion of his audition. He didn't get the role in *The Rainmaker*, in part because he looked nothing like Katharine Hepburn, who would have played his big sister, but also—although Wallis didn't say it out loud in front of his new signing—because the producer knew that Elvis Presley was a music star whose fans would demand that he perform music in every one of his pictures. Wallis had no scripts on the shelf to tailor to Elvis, so he assigned Hal Kanter to come up with one.

In May, Elvis was back home, speaking to Robert Johnson of the Memphis *Press-Scimitar* about the movie deal that would make him, in Johnson's words, "enough to buy him three Cadillacs, a three-wheel Messerschmitt runabout and—the pride of his life—a motorcycle. There's a bit of bickering going on right now because the movie studio wants to write in a clause forbidding him to ride the motorcycle. 'I'd rather not make a movie,' said Elvis."

Elvis was sounding like Marlon Brando. "What I really want . . . is to be a good actor," he said, and claimed he'd turned down the role that would have been his debut. "It was a good part, but I just couldn't see it for me. A good-natured, happy teenager but with nothing up here. After I read the script, I just want to do another kind of part."

Elvis had already made it clear to his manager that he intended to be a "serious" actor like his hero, Marlon Brando. He wanted to take classes at the Actors Studio in New York and keep his movie career separate from his music. But Colonel Tom Parker knew there was more money to be made by merging the two.

While waiting for Hal Kanter to deliver his script, Hal Wallis loaned out Elvis to 20th Century-Fox for a Civil War drama, *The Reno Brothers*. He'd make his movie debut as Clint Reno, the youngest of four brothers, the one who doesn't go off to fight for the Confederacy and marries his eldest brother's girlfriend, believing that the long-gone soldier is dead. Richard Egan and Deborah Paget were the stars of *The Reno Brothers*. Elvis had a supporting role, but producers found a way to include four songs for him to sing. When one of those songs, "Love Me Tender," was released as a single and began climbing the charts, *The Reno Brothers* became *Love Me Tender*.

Egan, a leading man and World War II veteran fourteen years Elvis's senior, played the eldest brother. He said he was fine with Elvis's inexperience and "natural" way of talking. "Forget that 'reading lines' business. Just be natural, say what the script says to say, and do what director Robert Webb tells you," he said he told Elvis. "Anybody who can get up before thousands of screaming kids and sing isn't going to be bothered by a piece of glass and a camera.

"I studied drama for seven years before trying for a career as an actor and I taught speech at the University of San Francisco, but it would have been a crime to try to change Elvis. The boy's a natural and his great charm is just being himself. I hope nobody starts drumming Stanislavski into him."

Love Me Tender was shot in black and white, and so were the reviews after its premiere on November 15. *Variety* recognized that 20th Century-Fox had "whipped up a minor league oater (and oncer) in which to showcase one of the hottest showbiz properties around today. . . . Appraising Presley as an actor, he ain't. Not that it matters."

Among the harshest of the influential critics was Bosley Crowther of the *New York Times*. Crowther was no fan of this new rock 'n' roll fad. Nor did he appreciate—and was in fact offended by—"cultural accretions from other media," like the Andrews Sisters, Liberace, and "Slapsie" Maxie Rosenbloom, wedged into motion pictures because of their sizable circles of fans (not unlike the casting of YouTube and TikTok stars sixty years later). So even though the title song was a ballad, and young Elvis could match Jackie Wilson and Dean Martin note for note, Crowther described Elvis's singing as "grotesque . . . a sort of frenzied puffing of throaty and none too melodic tones that heave out of Mr. Presley's system while he beats his guitar and shakes his legs." His acting was "turgid, juicy and flamboyant, pretty much as he sings. With his childish face, puffy lips, and wild hair, he might be convincing as a kid with a load of resentment in his system. But he's not much more than a singing 'heavy' in this film."

Ironically, it was only in comparison to the other actors that Presley received any recognition from the *Times* critic. Richard Egan was "virtually lethargic," Debra Paget "bathed in melancholia." Elvis, however, "goes at it as though it were *Gone with the Wind*." That instinct, or naivete in not realizing how inconsequential this picture may have been, paid off for Elvis Presley. After all, it was his image, head-to-toe, wiggling, rocking with his guitar, that appeared in every newspaper ad and on every movie poster. It was his likeness, fifty feet tall, standing atop the marquee of the Paramount Theatre in Times Square as hundreds of teens filled the sidewalks and streets, screaming his name.

Elvis was a special added attraction in *Love Me Tender*, with musical numbers slotted amid the action, and callow in the role. But his movie debut did have added cultural significance, especially in the shadow of James Dean, and under the influence of Marlon Brando. In this and several roles to follow, Elvis did step in where James Dean had left off. In fact, Dean could have been Elvis's stillborn twin Jesse Garon. Onscreen, Elvis could be sullen, brooding, and unsmiling, and erupt unexpectedly in petulant, punk, Baby Brando anger—as he did in *Love Me Tender* and in *Loving You*, the musical drama that Hal Kanter conjured.

In *Love Me Tender*, directed by Robert D. Webb, Richard Egan was the square-jawed hero, who in the opening scene with two younger brothers pulls off a train robbery and rides away while his pursuer yells, "Fire at 'em, boys! They're rebels!" But it turns out the real rebel, the new anti-hero, was the youngest brother whom the three older Renos had left behind when they went off to fight the war. The soft-featured boy—and when he's not wielding a guitar, Elvis does come off as a boy—is first seen behind a plow pulled by a pair of horses. He's the one who stole his big brother's lover, married her, has sex with her, and sleeps with her in the same house to which his brothers have returned. He's the one who, after an extended, adolescent tantrum, winds up dead. In a twist that was becoming all too common in the Brando era, the character who might have once been the victim or a hapless sidekick, was "the new hero."

Drama critic Gerald Weales coined the term in an essay in the newsmagazine and literary journal, *The Reporter*. "Who is the new hero?" he asked. "His mannerisms, by Brando out of the Actors' Studio, have been perfected, imitated, parodied, done to death. First of all, he does not walk: He slouches, ambles, almost minces. His hand gestures are all tentative, incomplete, with arms out in front as though he were feeling his way along a wet-walled underground passageway, or folded back against the body as though he were warding off a blow. Although he is a tough guy, his face is excessively sensitive, almost effeminate. with full-lipped pout and large-eyed lostness. The new hero is an adolescent. Whether he is twenty or thirty or forty, he is fifteen and excessively sorry for himself. He is essentially a lone wolf who wants to belong, but even when he is the member of a gang or a group, he is still alone."

Brando in *The Wild One* was "the new hero at his most romantic . . . at once stronger and more sensitive than his followers. He might have been any age, since the cyclists seemed to range from sixteen to forty, but his orientation with the cyclists and against the town was part of the adolescent protest against the society in which it cannot yet take part."

And Elvis? He was "the new hero . . . in its latest, most grotesque form," in a role "particularly tailored to his appearance, for Presley resembles an obscene child, a too sensuous adolescent."

If Elvis was the latest "teenage" version of Brando in *The Wild One*, he'd play variations on the role in his next few films. *Loving You* was a traditional music biz success story in bright Technicolor and widescreen VistaVision, with eight songs and a strong supporting cast. When the film opened in July 1957, *Variety* wrote that the picture allowed Elvis to "do the kind of thing he does best, i.e., shout out his rhythms, bang away at his guitar and perform the strange, knee-bending, hip-swinging contortions that are his trademark. . . . Apart from this, Presley shows improvement as an actor."

It was in his third film that Elvis Presley went full Brando. *The Hard Way*, later retitled *Jailhouse Rock*, was a black-and-white picture in widescreen CinemaScope, a dark twist on *Loving You*, and a parody of Elvis's real-life rise to stardom—no, it was beyond that. It was if Elvis had taken *Time* magazine's review of *The Wild One*, the one describing Brando as "an actor whose sullen face, slurred accents and dream-drugged eye have made him a supreme portrayer of morose juvenility," taped it to his bathroom mirror and combed his greasy pompadour just right until he looked exactly like the guy in that review. Elvis told anyone listening that the character of Vince Everett was modeled on Brando, and it was true that the character was as close to Johnny Strabler as Elvis got.

When the movie opens, Vince is working construction, rolling onto the worksite atop a skeletal tractor to grab his paycheck, and crowing, "I'm gonna buy me a herd of some chorus girls and make 'em dance on my bed!" He winds up spending his check in a bar that looks more than a little like Bleeker's in Wrightsville, and gets into a brawl, defending a barfly who might be a hooker from a guy who could be her boyfriend or maybe even her pimp.

Elvis had a Technicolor fight scene in *Loving You*. Taunted into a punch-up with a blowhard in a steakhouse, he sends the galoot sprawling against a jukebox, then kicks the guy's leg out from under him, so he slides to the floor, comically. In the black-and-white *Jailhouse Rock* barfight, Vince keeps pounding his opponent, mercilessly, in the face, prompting the bartender to shout, "Vince! He's had enough! *He's had enough!*" But Elvis as Vince throws one more punch to the head that knocks the guy into another jukebox. Only this time, his opponent is dead.

In *The Wild One*, Brando's Johnny Strabler is accused of manslaughter, but cleared of the charge. Vince Everett is found guilty of manslaughter, and sent to prison, where he shares a cell with an older, second-rate country singer who teaches him few chords on the guitar, arranges for him to sing in a televised prison variety show and then tricks him into signing a fifty-fifty partnership for all his future earnings. (It's been said that the inclusion of the fifty-fifty split was evidence that the picture's "technical adviser" Colonel Tom Parker—who had a similar, outrageous agreement with Elvis—never read the script. It is, however, the same deal that Elvis's character had with his would-be agent, played by Lizabeth Scott, in *Loving You*, so perhaps Parker was trying to set precedent.)

Of course, Vince gets into a fight in prison, slugging a couple of guards during a mess hall melee. When he pays the price, he outdoes Johnny Strabler's beating by townsfolk in *The Wild One*. Elvis is stripped to the waist, wrists bound to a pipe over his head, and whipped by a guard, as the warden counts off each stroke. With each flaying, Elvis grimaces in expressions that could be mistaken for sexual ecstasy. (Brando, the master of eroticized beatings, would one-up Elvis a few years later, when he'd be lashed to a hitching post and flogged by Karl Malden in *One-Eyed Jacks*—a screenplay written, coincidentally, by Guy Trosper, who wrote *Jailhouse Rock*).

Vince leaves prison, bitter, cynical, sullen, angry, and determined to become a star, no matter what. After a series of misfires, tantrums, and confrontations, he scores a hit record, a Hollywood movie contract, and winds up surrounded by an entourage of yes-men, not unlike the "Memphis Mafia" posse of Southern-fried sycophants already gathering around Elvis in real life. After an unlikely plot twist, he finds his way to a happy ending.

In the end, the most memorable scene in *Jailhouse Rock* is one unlike any other in the picture: a production number for another big television show. It's no scene from *Guys and Dolls*—in fact, there are no dolls—but it is very Brandoesque, in the way Elvis moves, on a stylized two-story jail block set, with sixteen male dancers who are not, for the most part, chorus boy types, and in its casual intimation of homosexual prison sex. Elvis sings, *"Number Forty-Seven said to Number Three, 'You're the cutest jailbird I ever did see. I sure would be delighted with your company . . .'"* and a comic pair of older dancers, a sort of a Mutt and Jeff team, simulate some flirting before dancing off together, the shorter one suddenly leaping into the air in surprise when his partner knees him in the ass.

James Dean never lived to star in a fourth film. He was in line to play a Golden Gloves boxer dragged into a world of crime in *A Stone for Danny Fisher*, a dark drama based on a 1952 novel by Harold Robbins. When Dean died, the script collected dust on the shelf until Elvis came along. Danny Fisher became a singer, a rebel seeking the approval of his weak father, the setting was moved from Brooklyn to New Orleans, eleven songs were added to the mix, and the movie became *King Creole*.

Production began on January 20, 1958, on the Paramount lot. Marlon Brando's production company, Pennebaker, Inc., had offices there.

That week, Brando, whose latest film, *Sayonara*, had opened in December, stopped in for lunch at the Paramount commissary. Elvis and Jan Shepard, who was playing his older sister in *King Creole*, were already seated.

"We always ate together that first week, 'cause it was just the two of us," Shepard recalled. "Elvis is sitting with his back to the rest of the room, we're kind of in a corner and I'm facing out . . . then I see Brando coming in. And as he comes in, he knows damn well that that's Elvis sitting there, and so he pulls his chair out, the one right behind Elvis, and sits down. So I'm leaning over, saying, 'Marlon Brando's right behind you,' and Elvis is going—he almost wanted to climb under the table. I said, 'When you get up, the chairs are gonna bump.' And I said, 'Just talk to him,' because he went (whispers), 'Brando's back there!' I said, 'Yes, he's right behind you.' When we're ready to leave, he got up and they did bump chairs and Marlon stood up. And of course, they're face-to-face now, and they shake hands and just a little bit of a chit chat: 'Nice to meet you' and 'Good luck with your show,' and that sort of thing. He's very cool, did it very cool. I was very proud of him. And as we walk out, he walks out very cool, like nothing happened. We get outside, he jumped up at least five feet in the air. He could not believe that he shook hands with Marlon Brando!"

This could have been a sign, a sign of what was possible, for when *King Creole* was released in July, critics finally recognized, accepted, and even praised Elvis Presley as an actor. *Variety* acknowledged that "in all fairness Presley does show himself to be a surprisingly sympathetic and believable actor on occasion." *The Billboard* raved that "the star gives his best acting performance to date." And Howard Thompson exclaimed in the *New York Times*, "As the lad himself might say, cut my legs off and call me Shorty! Elvis Presley can act. . . . He does a good convincing walk-through as a downtrodden New Orleans youth who tangles with some gangsters (along with that blasted guitar). . . . As a surly, befuddled and basically decent musician, bloodied by some tough French Quarter denizens before seeing the light, he looks and behaves accordingly."

"Well, for heaven's sake. Elvis Presley is turning into an actor," Charles Stinson echoed in the *Los Angeles Times*. "Elvis is the surprise of the day. He delivers his lines with good comic timing, considerable intelligence and even flashes of sensitivity. If he's been studying, it's paying off handsomely."

Elvis was on his way to becoming the new hero in the Brando mold. His acting was beginning to catch up with his celebrity, his skills were meeting his ambitions, and his persona had been established at age twenty-three—the same age as James Dean when he made *East of Eden*, Brando's age when *Streetcar* opened on Broadway. There was talk that Elvis might even be nominated for an Academy Award—that's how surprisingly impressive he was.

But it was too late. Elvis was gone. He'd already left the building.

Elvis Presley had received his draft notice in December 1957. He was being called up for a two-year military stint at the peak of his career, during peacetime, yet under the guidance of Tom Parker, he did not challenge the call or come up with a medical excuse. He only requested and received a two-month extension so he could squeeze in one last movie before his induction. Elvis was going into the US Army. According to his manager, he'd rejected offers from the Navy and Air Force to join their special forces as an entertainer or recruiter, and even turned down the Army's plan that he be on hand only to perform concerts for the troops. Elvis said he preferred to be treated like a typical G.I. On March 24, 1958, two weeks after filming wrapped on *King Creole*, Elvis reported to the induction center in downtown Memphis and was sworn in as a regular Army recruit. Elvis spent three days at the Fort Chaffee, Arkansas, reception station before heading off to eight weeks of basic training at Fort Hood, Texas. He shipped off to Germany in September, where he spent two years, was first exposed to karate and amphetamines, and in 1959 met fourteen-year-old Priscilla Beaulieu, who became his girlfriend and later, his wife.

Elvis left active duty at Fort Dix, New Jersey, on March 5, 1960. A month later, he was back on the Paramount lot shooting *G.I. Blues*, a musical comedy based loosely on his military experience. When the film was released in November, it was a shock to anyone expecting a return of the 1950s rebel. "Whatever else the Army has done for Elvis Presley, it has taken that indecent swivel out of his hips and turned him into a good, clean, trustworthy upstanding American young man," Crowther enthused in the *Times*. "Gone is that rock 'n' roll wriggle, that ludicrously lecherous leer, that precocious country-bumpkin swagger, that unruly mop of oily hair. Almost gone are those droopy eyelids and that hillbilly manner of speech. Elvis has become sophisticated. He's a man of the world—almost."

The rebel, and the "serious" actor, had not been beaten out him completely. There was an attempt to keep Elvis in the game when he followed up *G.I Blues* with *Flaming Star*, a lean Western drama directed by Don Siegel and written by Nunnally Johnson. Elvis starred as Pacer Burton, a "half breed"—son of a Native American mother and white father—on the Texas frontier. The role had originally been written for Marlon Brando, with Frank Sinatra cast as his half-brother. The demand on Elvis, in a role intended for Brando, may have been beyond his abilities. "The film relies heavily on his reactions as an explanation for its dramatic maneuvers and thematic attitudes," Tube wrote in *Variety*. "But, at this stage of his career, Presley lacks the facial and thespic sensitivity and projection so desperately required here. . . . One other thing can be said for Presley's approach—he's never guilty of overacting." The film includes only one complete song performed by Elvis.

Another dramatic outing followed. *Wild in the Country*, directed by Philip Dunne and produced by Jerry Wald at 20th Century-Fox, was an attempt to turn Elvis back into the Brandoesque rebel, and had even more Brando connections. Back in 1948, Wald had attempted, unsuccessfully, to get studio boss Jack L. Warner to sign Brando to a Warner Bros. contract. Dunne had cowritten the screenplay to *The Egyptian*, the movie that Brando had signed to star in after he completed *On the Waterfront*, the film that followed *The Wild One*.

The script for *Wild in the Country* was written by Clifford Odets, the great playwright and, along with Elia Kazan, Stella Adler, and Lee Strasberg, a member of the Group Theatre in the 1930s. In Odets's story, Elvis was a rebellious country boy who coulda been a . . . great writer. When the movie was released in June 1961, *Variety*'s Tube said that Elvis was "subdued," and "uses what dramatic resources he has to best advantage," but that it was "difficult to accept the character as a potential literary genius." Crowther didn't bother with niceties. "Mr. Presley, who did appear to be improving as an actor in his last picture, is as callow as ever in this. . . . His appearance is waxy and flabby," he wrote. "Elvis has retrogressed."

"I think *King Creole* is the best performance Elvis ever put on. I think he had potential as an actor but the thing that did him in was drugs," Gary Shapiro, the pop historian, says. "When Elvis came back from the Army, he was addicted to pills and he never could concentrate again. He made some great records and he made some interesting movies, but his period of great influence is 1954 to 1958 and never again did he have that concentration as a performer, whether singing or acting. But *King Creole* shows that with the right director, he would have been a very, very good actor."

"Singers come and go, but if you're a good actor, you can last a long time," is one of Elvis' most repeated quotations. For him, it was the acting that carried him through most of the 1960s. After *Wild in the Country*, he was off to *Blue Hawaii* and the "travelogue pictures": movies that dropped him in exotic or exciting locales, paired him with starlets, were packed with enough disposable songs to sell on soundtrack albums, and continued to erase the legacy that once elevated him to the influential rebel trinity that included Brando and Dean. Elvis didn't wear a black leather motorcycle jacket often in these films, but when he did in *Roustabout*, he rode a motorcycle and the publicity insisted that his inspiration was Brando in *The Wild One*. When he made his "comeback" in the 1968 NBC television special, *Elvis*, his custom full-body leather suit was a direct

"I've made a study of Marlon Brando. What I really want to be is a good actor." Elvis Presley "coulda been a contender." Paramount Pictures/ Photofest © Paramount Pictures

tribute. From there, it was on to Las Vegas, concert tours in second-tier markets, more pills, more isolation, and that final ignoble tumble from the bathroom throne.

Brando, more than ten years older than Elvis, outlived him by almost thirty-seven years, and ultimately, like Mark Antony in *Julius Caesar*, came to bury Elvis, not to praise him. "It seems to me hilarious that our government put the face of Elvis Presley on a postage stamp after he died from an overdose of drugs," Brando says in *Songs My Mother Taught Me*. "His fans don't mention that because they don't want to give up their myths. They ignore the fact that he was a drug addict and claim he invented rock 'n' roll when in fact he took it from black culture; they had been singing that way for years before he came along, copied them and became a star."

He makes no mention of Elvis's acting.

Seven

Teenage Raceland

When *The Wild One* opened at the Hollywood Theatre in Fort Worth, Texas, on February 12, 1954, the display ad in the *Star-Telegram* left no mystery about what was in store. Taking up almost half a page and far larger than any other movie advertisement, the panel contained three photos of Marlon Brando under the standard tagline, *"JAZZED-UP HOODS ON A BUST-UP BINGE,"* pumped up with the addition of *". . . And They Don't Care Who Gets Hurt!"*

"Marlon Brando is the only man who could play The Wild One." Looking very Kowalski-like, Brando is pictured standing over Mary Murphy, who's on the ground, reaching up toward him—and the words: *"Once in a while a guy's got to let go . . . ."* There's a close-up photo of Brando's face and a depiction of his fight with Chino: *"Hot feelings hit terrifying heights in a story that really boils over!"*

Despite the "AN ADULT MOTION PICTURE" disclaimer to make it clear that the movie was being promoted as pulpy, sexy, violent exploitation for grown-ups, the ad was also undeniably attractive to a teenage, thrill-seeking audience the marketers hadn't yet tapped into with any serious thought. Teenagers, looking for entertainment on Friday night, might have skipped the article about *The Wild One* in the previous day's edition of the *Star-Telegram*, in which Eleanor Wilson focused on the more worthy attributes of what "promises to be one of the most controversial movies of the year." "First," she wrote, "we'd like to say that aside from its social implications, *The Wild One* is a bang-up movie—violent, disturbing and realistic. . . . It has been banned in Memphis and Alberta, Canada. It has been strongly recommended by a national reviewing board of educators as important and significant. It has been termed harmful for young moviegoers by a group of Fort Worth visiting teachers and representatives of the probation department who viewed the film at a special screening earlier this week."

Adults "in charge" in Fort Worth realized that its sociological significance aside, *The Wild One* was bound to further stoke youthful unrest that had so far been viewed as problematic, but not yet the powerful tide that would wash over and transform society as they knew it. Wilson wrote that "educators"—the ones who some might be described as working in ivory towers, at a distance from the staff in the trenches of public schools—saw the film as "a powerful instrument" with which teachers could "discuss and analyze with their classes one of today's most urgent problems, namely youthful delinquency," and would prompt students to "tell their teachers why it is that teenagers feel they gotta 'go-go-go.'" The Fort Worth teachers knew better, and "expressed the fear that teen-agers will tend to 'idolize' Brando, missing the significance of his bewildered restlessness." They insisted *The Wild One* was not for kids, but "strictly adult entertainment."

Their fears were well-grounded. In Texas and far beyond, *The Wild One* took on a life of its own, and without an explicit announcement, channeled and pushed forward social change, merging African-American subculture into the mainstream of postwar white society, and inspiring teenage, rock 'n' roll, and civil rights revolutions.

From a look at *The Billboard*'s pop chart in the first months of 1954, one might not notice the growing influence. As canisters containing reels of *The Wild One* were being dropped off at movie houses around the country, the best-selling and most-played records that winter and spring were Eddie Fisher's "Oh! My Papa" and Tony Bennett's "From Rags to Riches." It would take time for rock 'n' roll to make an impact on the charts. Bill Haley and His Comets didn't even enter the Pythian Temple Studios in Manhattan to record "(We're Gonna) Rock Around the Clock" until April 12 of that year; Elvis would record his first single, "That's All Right" (a song written and originally recorded in 1946 by Black Delta blues singer Arthur "Big Boy" Crudup), at Sun Studio in Memphis in July. But the pop chart didn't necessarily reflect all the music young people were taking in. The music business was segregated, and the chart that tracked the sales, deejay spins, and jukebox drops of records made by Black artists (and originally produced for a strictly Black audience) was called the "The Harlem Hit Parade" in the early 1940s, became the "Race Records Best Sellers," and ultimately *The Billboard*'s Rhythm & Blues chart. While Eddie Fisher was warbling about his papa on the pop side, R&B records often moved and rolled with a sensuality and beat that went straight to the groin. By 1954, white "kids" were listening to Guitar Slim grind out a fuzzy, electric sound in "The Things That I Used to Do." With its talk about a "one-eyed cat peeping in a seafood store," the jump blues "Shake, Rattle and Roll" by Big Joe Turner was all euphemism and sexual innuendo. "Work with Me, Annie" by Hank Ballard and the Midnighters was downright dirty. *"Please don't cheat, Give me all my meat! . . . Let's get it while the getting is good."* It was good, all right. So good that the song's sequel was "Annie Had a Baby"!

(Brando would have a tangential connection to the first recognized "rock 'n' roll" song to hit the Top Ten of the *Billboard* pop chart that year. "Sh-Boom (Life Could Be a Dream)" by the Black R&B group The Chords reached number 9 in the summer of 1954. A few weeks later, a cover version by The Crew-Cuts, a white group, went to number 1, while in October, a parody record by humorist Stan Freberg made the Top Twenty. Freberg's disc featured the "mumbling" Marlon Brando of *Streetcar.* "Hold it, you guys! This is a rhythm and blues number," Freberg, as Brando, says. "You gotta be careful or somebody liable to understand what you're singin' about. . . . You gotta talk unintelligible like me. Right, Stella?" Freberg's "Sh-Boom" reached number 14 in the United States— and number 15 in the United Kingdom.

The music, and the beat, were in the first stage of crossing over—and taking over. America's economy was expanding in a postwar boom—an economic boom and baby boom. Prosperity fed juvenile delinquency and defiance of authority. The civil rights movement was rising, buoyed in May by *Brown v. Board of Education of Topeka*, the landmark US Supreme Court ruling that racial segregation of children in public schools was unconstitutional. Marlon Brando rode into this perfect cultural storm. *The Wild One* revealed, as Crowther had written in the *New York Times*, "a small but particularly significant menacing element of modern youth. . . . Given to jive or be-bop lingo and the grotesque costumes and attitudes of the crazy cognoscenti, these 'wild ones' resent discipline and show an aggressive contempt for common decency and the police. Reckless and vandalistic, they live for sensations, nothing more—save perhaps a supreme sensation of defying the normal world."

The unspoken connection between *The Wild One* and Black Americans, at a time when white Americans, many with funding from the GI Bill, were leaving big cities for houses in the newly created suburbs, while the fight against segregation and a Black demand for equal rights were reaching a tipping point, could be read in Crowther's description of this "menacing element . . . given to jive or be-bop lingo and the grotesque costumes," who "resent discipline and show an aggressive contempt for common decency and the police." In *A Streetcar Named Desire*, Brando as Stanley Kowalski was the dark New Orleans savage who ultimately raped the tragic heroine Blanche DuBois—*Blanche* being the French word for "white." Here, his Johnny Strabler is leader of the *Black* Rebels Motorcycle Club, a group whose members talk in the daddy-o slang made popular by Black jazz artists and hipsters in the late 1940s. "Bebop" was jazz—Black jazz, invented by Thelonious Monk and picked up by Dizzy Gillespie, Charlie Parker, and Miles Davis, among

others. Bebop was complex, fast-moving music with key changes and
flights of improvisation that might only touch on the melody. It was not
music for dancing, and along with it came a culture of jive lingo, also
called bebop, or rebop, named perhaps for "Hey! Ba-Ba-Re-Bop," Lionel
Hampton's call-and-response R&B hit and rock 'n' roll harbinger from
1946.

The Black Rebels have their own bebop jive number in a Bleeker bar
scene. A cyclist played by jazz harmonicist Danny Welton blows a quick
Toots Thielemans break for the gang, moves to the bar with actor Charlie
Cirillo—neither is credited onscreen, but both are named "Bee Bop" on
the IMDb website—and the pair trade bebop lingo.

"Bop me, Dad!" Bee Bop Cirillo says. They slap palms.

"I bopped you, Dad," Welton responds, then turns to old Jimmy behind
the bar. "Hey Pops, thumb me, will you, Daddy-o?" He gives a "thumbs
up" and Jimmy warily does the same. "C'mon. That's it! Thumb me!"
Welton grabs Jimmy by that thumb for a modified handshake.

"Now give me some skin," says his pal, using the era's Black slang ter-
minology for a greeting in which palms are slapped or, in this case, slid.
"And ooo-ooze it out! Nice! Atta boy, ooze it out!"

As he rubs the other Bee Bop's hand, Jimmy looks confused as the
demands get crazier. "Now elbow us! Just elbow us."

"Pops, do you pick up on this jive, man?" Welton asks.

"What?"

"Do you pick up on this jive? This crazy music here, man. Did you dig
the rebop?"

"What?"

"The Rebop, Dad! The Rebop."

"He's a square, man," says his pal. "Don't you get this a-tall? 'Fore
you take the brew on the side on the time and you take the bottle, *brrrie
toopa do beedle toopa la bow!*" Soon both Bee Bops are scat-bopping to a
beat they're drumming on the bar—"*a doodle bop, doodle bop, a bop bop bop,
a reeba dabba doo a scabba dabba doo—*" They're groovin' high, and then a
platter drops on the jukebox and some of the Black Rebels are dancing
with a pair of white, blonde townie chicks. Johnny Strabler moseys over
and starts tapping out his own beat on the jukebox. This is the scene in
which one of the girls is about to ask him what he's rebelling against. His
answer, borrowed from an outlaw biker on a research jaunt to Hollister,
would become the classic statement of a new rock 'n' roll generation,
launched atop that very jukebox.

Watch the scene again and you'll notice that Brando is tapping out that
beat the way he would on his bongo drums. Brando is playing imaginary
bongos on the jukebox—jazz bongos—and that's something viewers
might overlook, just as they might overlook a key factor in this movie

that launched a rock 'n' roll revolution: *There's no rock 'n' roll music in the movie at all.*

The soundtrack to *The Wild One* is jazz, all jazz, sometimes with a dash of Latin rhythm composed and conducted by film and radio veteran Leith Stevens. The sound is reminiscent of the adventurous hard swing of Stan Kenton from the 1940s, because most of the West Coast jazz players Stevens brought in had passed through the Stan Kenton Orchestra. The jazz contingent was led by trumpeter Shorty Rogers, and included saxophone players Bud Shank, Jimmy Giuffre, and Bob Cooper; Carson Smith on bass; pianist Russ Freeman; and drummer Shelly Manne. Rogers would work with the Monkees in the late 1960s, but rock 'n' roll was not his bag. Nor was it Brando's.

That bongo riff tapped on the jukebox was from the heart. Jazz, and jazz drumming, were Brando's passions, more so than the acting that came so

The jazz soundtrack album from *The Wild One*. Author's collection

easy. Brando remembered the moment: he was fourteen. His mother had reconciled with his father, two summers after she'd left Marlon Sr. and taken the kids to their grandmother's house in California. "I can still feel the rhythm of the train that returned us to Illinois. While it rocked and swayed, I walked to a vestibule between two cars and felt the energy of the wheels rattling across the steel joints in the tracks. Spontaneously, I started banging on the doors and walls with my hands, grooving to the beat of the train as if it were a jazz quartet. After that, I was a changed boy: I wanted to be a drummer."

Young Bud Brando's idols were jazz drummers Gene Krupa and Buddy Rich. His parents bought him a set of Slingerland drums just like Krupa's, and he played along at home to records and the radio. When he was sixteen, he started a band called Keg Brando and His Kegliners. And after he arrived in New York City, he experienced the jazz clubs on 52nd Street and had his life changed again when he "discovered Afro-Cuban music" at the Palladium. "I had always been stimulated by rhythm, even by the ticking of a clock, and the rhythms they played were irresistible." He recalled that each band "usually had two or three conga drummers and I couldn't sit still because of their extraordinary, complicated syncopations." Brando gave up stick drumming, bought conga drums, and studied Afro-Cuban rhythm with the pioneering Black dancer and choreographer Katherine Dunham. Meanwhile, he always had bongos that he'd bring along to parties. He'd asked more than once to sit in with the players at jazz clubs in Harlem, and memorably, in the summer of 1946, was busted for bongo beating in Provincetown. Years later, when a reporter asked Brando what he would have done if "show business" wasn't an option, he replied, "Could've been a drummer, drummed for a while."

"*The Wild One* captures the spirit of rock 'n' roll," fashion historian and writer Andrew Luecke says.

When you look at trends and you look at pop culture, so often it's hard to explain why certain things all explode at once. It's almost as though there's an ineffable air in the zeitgeist, and so *The Wild One* is not a rock 'n' roll movie per se—there's no rock 'n' roll in it whatsoever—but it comes out right at the same time that rock 'n' roll is emerging, and those two cultural elements, rock 'n' roll and *The Wild One*, create this sort of perfect storm of rebellion.

Brando and the director and the writer, they're not rock 'n' rollers. Brando is twenty-eight and even though it's presented as a teen juvenile delinquent thing, they're grown men. They're men, and rock 'n' roll is a youth thing. But the look and the energy that's coming out of the biker culture and presented in *The Wild One* perfectly encapsulate the rock 'n' roll sound. And the teenagers see it and immediately they go, "Okay, rock 'n' roll is our sound, and the

Brando was a jazzman. From an early age, his passion was drumming. Photofest

leather jacket and the jeans, that's our look." And by the end of the fifties, that's pretty much codified in both the United States and in the UK.

If Brando was part of any group that was aligned with the rock 'n' roll generation, it would be the Beats: the literary, art, musical, and social movement whose rise coincided with his own. Led by figures including poet Allen Ginsberg, writer William S. Burroughs, and the fast-living character Neal Cassady, and popularized by the novels of Jack Kerouac, the "Beat Generation" rejected "square society," sought enlightenment through sex, drugs, and Zen Buddhism, and, drawn to marginalized sub-cultures, was heavily influenced by African American culture. The Beats used hipster vernacular, dug bebop jazz (Kerouac incorporated bebop into his "spontaneous prose"), and copied the African oral performance traditions with poetry readings.

Later, the Beats and their followers would be dubbed "Beatniks," first as a pejorative, then an easy label to mark the evolution of the American rebel, from hipster to beatnik to rocker to hippie to punk. (The most famous "beatnik" character arrived in 1959, on television, with Bob Denver as Maynard G. Krebs, sidekick in *The Many Loves of Dobie Gillis*. Brando had Maynard beaten on the bongos by more than a decade).

"In one sense, the 'Beat Generation' was not unlike a semantic vacuum cleaner, pulling all manner of rebellion together in one place," Alan Bisbort wrote in his book, *Beatniks: A Guide to an American Subculture*. "Even motorcycle rebels like Brando's character or leather-jacketed juvenile delinquent hotrodders like James Dean's character in *Rebel Without a Cause* were pulled into the Beat Generation orbit, partly because the label gave the media something around which to weave narratives of youthful rebellion."

"To be 'beat' is tantamount today to being 'punk,'" Bisbort explains in an interview. "And I always have thought of Brando as more in the beatnik camp than rock 'n' roll. He was more psychologically and intellectually affiliated in my mind. Plus, he was older than the rock 'n' roll generation. He and Kerouac were roughly the same age. Kerouac was born in 1922, Brando in '24, and they had gone probably through similar experiences. This is why I think Kerouac had some kind of fantasy that Brando would be on his wavelength. Kerouac really loathed pop culture, but he respected Brando."

Bisbort produces a typewritten letter that Kerouac sent to Brando in 1958, in which the author begs the actor to star in a movie version of his breakthrough novel (and Beat Bible), *On the Road*. Kerouac envisioned Brando in the role of Dean Moriarty, the embodiment of the reckless, rebellious, free spirit of the Beat Generation based on Neal Cassady. "I want you to play the part because Dean (as you know) is no dopey hotrodder but a real intelligent (in fact Jesuit) Irishman."

"Kerouac was kind of in awe of Brando, frankly," Bisbort says.

> I don't recall him ever saying anything about James Dean. I mean, he would scoff at the idea that these juvenile delinquents had anything to do with the Beatniks, but Brando was always spoken of with respect. There was no

sense of mockery, because Brando was also a smart guy. He was kind of an intellect. He would go to the jazz clubs. I never read anywhere or saw anywhere where the two of them crossed paths in a jazz club in New York. Boy, that would have been an incredible scene. And *The Wild One* was not rock 'n' roll in any way, shape or form. It was soundtrack music, full of orchestrated jazz, which was kind of weird, watching it. I was thinking "Rock Around the Clock" or something, and no. It's like the dance music that Kerouac loved. When you go back into Kerouac's childhood, the stuff that he gets really nostalgic about is Glenn Miller, those dance bands. If you read his books, where he's looking back on his teenhood, he's talking about getting the boys together and they go down to some dancehall and listen to a full-fledged dance band orchestra, with all the intricate arrangements and horn arrangements. It's strange to realize that the rock 'n' roll genera-tion really gravitated to Brando and Kerouac, and yet they were not of that generation at all.

By the time the youth was gravitating, Brando had moved on. He was wrapping his work on Elia Kazan's *On the Waterfront*, in which he played a character very different from Johnny Strabler, and was in a battle with 20th Century-Fox after he backed out of his role *The Egyptian*. In a syndicated profile in April 1954, Associated Press reporter James Bacon pointed out that Brando was not catering to the youthful demographic he was helping create. "He's a rage with the teenagers, but discloses they give him little trouble." Bacon quoted Brando: "When I see two or more of them congregated, I just walk a little faster than usual."

It's partly because of that disconnect, and Brando's connection to an earlier, adult generation, that many observers believe that the rock 'n' roll revolution wasn't sparked onscreen until the following year, with the premiere of Richard Brooks's *Blackboard Jungle* on March 18, 1955—a date that also marked the end of the first week of production on *Guys and Dolls*, the movie musical starring Brando and Sinatra. Based on *The Blackboard Jungle*, a popular novel by Evan Hunter, the film starred Glenn Ford as an English teacher trying to get through to students at a violent, gang-ridden, inner-city trade school. *Variety* described *Blackboard Jungle* as "an angry picture that flares out in moral and physical rage at mental sloppiness, be it juvenile, mature, or in the pattern of society's acceptance of things as they are because no one troubles to devise a better way. . . . These are no mischievous youths Ford deals with, but hoodlums, some of whom are already well along the road to crime. . . . The story uses the shocker technique of profanity, racial slur, attempted rape, and similar socially unacceptable motivations for emphasis. . . . All of this can be box office fuel."

Crowther in the *New York Times* agreed that the film version of the "sen-sational and controversial" novel is "a full-throated, all-out testimonial to the lurid headlines that appear from time to time . . . a blood-curdling, nightmarish picture of monstrous disorder in a public school." He adds, tellingly, that "Vic Morrow, as the most rebellious pupil, is a sinister replica of a Marlon Brando roughneck."

Like *The Wild One*, *Blackboard Jungle* opens with a disclaimer, this time with words scrolling up the screen while a snare drum beat a military tattoo. "We, in the United States, are fortunate to have a school system that is a tribute to our communities and to our faith in American youth—" Seven seconds in, it's clear the drum pattern is no martial cadence but a drum *solo*, a jazz drum solo, as the scroll continues like a *Star Wars* crawl. "Today we are concerned with juvenile delinquency—its causes—and its effects. We are especially concerned when this delinquency boils over into our schools. The scenes and incidents depicted here are fictional. However, we believe that public awareness is a first step toward a remedy for any problem. It is in this spirit and with this faith that BLACKBOARD JUNGLE was produced."

The words on the screen then fade to black and the drum solo cuts to the two-beat drum count-up to "Rock Around the Clock" and Bill Haley's "One, two, three o'clock! Four o'clock rock!" And, just as the image of Marlon Brando straddling that Triumph canceled out any disclaimers at the top of *The Wild One*, so is the rock 'n' roll music over the credits of *Blackboard Jungle* a celebratory invitation to anarchy. This is when the grownups in the movie houses noticed the teenagers jumping out of their seats and dancing in the aisles. In some theaters, gangs of teens ripped out those seats or slashed them with their switchblades. The song continues after the credits fade. Glenn Ford arrives at the school and looks through the fence at a group of young punks swing-dancing and jitterbugging together, boy on boy. A group of them are hanging on the fence, catcalling a woman passing by on the sidewalk—just as the Black Rebels did in *The Wild One* (although this film features young Black actors—Sidney Poitier is a costar—and this scene offers glimpses of multiracial homosocial dance couples). When the song ends, there is no more rock 'n' roll in *Blackboard Jungle*. The movie's score, composed by Charles Wolcott (known for orchestrating Disney films, including *Bambi*), was the standard fare for dealing with young delinquents: jazz. In fact, the opening credits list three songs in the picture: the aforementioned "Rock Around the Clock," and numbers by Bix Beiderbecke and His Gang—and Stan Kenton and His Orchestra.

Cinematically, *Blackboard Jungle* was more brutal than *The Wild One*. The young thugs were more frightening, the violence more visceral, and the attempted rape scene more terrifying. Yet each outrage had already been played out in *The Wild One*.

On July 9, 1955, "Rock Around the Clock" became the first rock 'n' roll recording to hit the top of *Billboard*'s pop chart, and remained at number 1 for eight weeks.

On September 30, James Dean was killed in the crash of his Porsche. His film, *Rebel Without a Cause*, premiered in October. That movie did not contain rock 'n' roll music, not even a number in the opening credits, but it gave the rock 'n' roll generation a martyr—one who even in death would be belittled by critics as a Brando imitator.

The premiere of *Guys and Dolls* took place on November 3 at the Capitol Theatre on Broadway, just north of Times Square.

On December 1, 1955, Rosa Parks was arrested in Montgomery, Alabama, for refusing to give up her seat on a city bus to a white man. The Montgomery Bus Boycott, the United States' first widescale demonstration against segregation, began four days later.

Brando, the man whose image helped launch the societal and cultural revolutions, always took the position that he was an innocent bystander. "The public's reaction to *The Wild One* was, I believe, a product of its time and circumstances," he told Robert Lindsey. "Right or wrong, we were at the beginning of a new era. . . . Young people were beginning to doubt and question their elders and to challenge their values, morals and the established institutions of authority. There was a wisp of steam just beneath the surface when we made that picture. Young people were looking for a reason—any reason—to rebel. I simply happened to be at the right place at the right time in the right part."

Eight

Meet the Beetles

You know, I missed you. Ever since the club split up, I missed you. We all missed ya! Did you miss him? Yeah! The Beetles missed ya! *All the Beetles missed ya!*

—Chino, portrayed by Lee Marvin in *The Wild One*

It came in a vision—a man appeared on a flaming pie and said unto them, "From this day on, you are Beatles with an A."

—John Lennon, *Mersey Beat*, 1961

The power of Marlon Brando's seductive performance in *The Wild One* and the fears of the delinquency and violence it could encourage, or even provoke, led local censors and bluenoses in regions far beyond the realm of octogenarian movie examiner Lloyd T. Binford to outlaw showings of the film. *The Wild One* was banned in the Canadian provinces of Alberta, British Columbia, and Quebec, and more consequentially, in one of Hollywood's most lucrative foreign territories. But despite the drastic decision by censors in Great Britain to suppress the film, *The Wild One*'s influence throughout the United Kingdom would prove to be substantial, and may have given name to its most influential and far-reaching cultural contribution of the twentieth century.

The British Board of Film Censors was very much like the MPAA's Production Code Association, with the same concerns and similar restrictions on images of violence, adultery, nudity, sexuality, and controversial topics. But while the PCA was under the authority of the movie producers' trade association, the BBFC worked very closely with the British government. The BBFC also had more flexibility in its final rulings once the filmmakers made revisions they demanded. In 1951, seventeen years before the MPAA instituted a ratings system, the group had issued its own classifications that would allow a film to be released, but with a restricted viewership. An "A" rating would allow children to view the film if they were accompanied by an adult. An "X" meant that no one under age fifteen would be admitted. Producers and distributors would go out of their way to avoid an "X," which would severely reduce the number of theaters willing to run the film.

The British censors received their copy of *The Wild One* in January 1954, around the same time that Lloyd T. Binford viewed his. Just as Binford decried the film as "the most lawless picture I ever saw," the BBFC called it "dangerous to the extreme."

Arthur Watkins, the board secretary, provided the film's distributor with a summary of some of the problematic components. "The film deals with organized hooliganism and deliberate outrage of all law and order by a group of young toughs who at weekends ride about the countryside on motorcycles under an acknowledged leader," he wrote.

> The story is said to be based on an actual incident in the United States which emphasizes the seriousness of all that happens, and the happenings include a long series of unprovoked insults and attacks on old and young alike in a small town, looting and destruction of property in a wild orgy, and finally the death of an innocent old man. The local police officer is helpless and ineffective and his daughter against her better nature "falls for" the leader of the gang, demonstrating the morbid attraction which such young toughs can have for immature girls. When police reinforcements finally appear, the youths are allowed to get away with a mild and quite inadequate caution and so made to appear rather clever fellows than dangerous young fools.

"The hooliganism in the film (goes) unresisted and in the end virtually unpunished," board member John Trevelyan argued, and British youth would take away from the film the message that "if there were enough hoodlums and they behaved in a menacing way, they could get away with it."

The BBFC's reasons for concern went beyond what was being offered in a script that had already been watered down to clean out the most controversial messaging. Just as authority figures in the United States were dealing with a supposed epidemic of postwar juvenile delinquency, so were leaders in Great Britain in a panic over "rowdy gangs of youth" brawling and breaking laws in their cities. And these were not just "any gangs." These groups, in dandified British fashion, were in many ways disturbingly real-life counterparts to Johnny Strabler's Black Rebels Motorcycle Club: teenage males, decked out in a uniform that identified them as separate from polite society, showing disrespect for their elders, causing trouble, and engaging in violent fights with their rivals. They were, for the most part, members of Britain's working class, happy hooligans and products of a disruptive jazz age who would soon be identified with rock 'n' roll. And for all the negative connotations that went along with their activities, they were the first group that would lead to the creation of a market directed at teenagers. They were the Teddy Boys.

Teddy Boys: the name was derived from their style of dress. At the end of World War II, tailors on Jermyn Street in London's West End came up with the idea of a style, based on turn-of-the-century Edwardian garb, that they could sell to officers mustered out of military service. The veterans would certainly stand out in long draped jackets, waistcoats, and tight, high-waisted "drainpipe" trousers. Unfortunately, the "Ted" style didn't catch on, and the overstock was eventually laid off onto inexpensive men's stores in South and East London. By the early 1950s, the flashy suits began to be scooped up by teenagers, many of them kids from the lower- and working-class council flats, the first generation that was not absorbing and copying the tastes of their fathers. The Teddy Boy look was similar to the oversized zoot suits popular in Black and Latino subcultures in the United States in the 1940s. The trousers, though, were tighter. The Teds covered their feet in suede shoes with fat crepe soles, known as "brothel creepers," and sported greased hair, combed back from a quiff at the front. They were also known to sport weapons, including flick knives, razors, bicycle chains, knuckledusters, and socks filled with coins.

Teddy Boy gangs were usually based in neighborhoods and would fight with competing neighborhood gangs on a regular basis. The British censors could see the obvious parallels to Brando's older, though equally immature, Black Rebels. And while the Teddy Boys didn't cause nearly as much trouble as the Fleet Street newspapers would have one believe, at least two recent incidents indicated that Marlon Brando's latest picture had been dropped into the UK at precisely the wrong time.

The country, with news media and politicians pushing the issue, was still dealing with fallout from a notorious cop killing more than a year earlier. On the night of November 2, 1952, two teenagers, sixteen-year-old Christopher Craig and Derek Bentley, nineteen, had broken into the warehouse of a confectionary company in Croydon when they were interrupted by police. Craig was carrying a gun, which he drew when confronted by the officers. A policeman asked him to hand over the weapon. Bentley supposedly called out, "Let him have it!" and Craig "let him have it"—he shot and killed the lawman. As a minor, Craig did not face the death penalty. As an accomplice, although he was not carrying a gun, the older Bentley did face execution. Despite the ambiguity of his call to "let him have it" and other circumstances of the case, and amid much publicity and controversy over his mental deficiencies, Derek Bentley was found guilty and hanged at Wandsworth prison on January 28, 1953.

The pundits and politicians were still debating youthful criminality and the miscarriage of justice in killing the impaired young man, when, on the evening of July 2, 1953, a new outrage played out on Clapham

Common, a two-hundred-acre park and green space in south London. A month after the coronation of a new queen, the park was teeming with couples and families. At the park's center, a couple of hundred teenagers gathered at a bandstand, where a musical group played hits of the day. Among the crowd of dancers were many Teddy Boys, who tussled among themselves, eyed rival gang members with disdain, and preened for their female followers. Later that evening, after the band packed up, four teenagers who were not Teddy Boys, nor part of any local gangs at all, sat chatting on two park benches. Seventeen-year-old John Beckley and his friends got into a confrontation with a Teddy Boy who was a member of the Plough Boys, a gang named for The Plough, a nearby pub they frequented. Punches were thrown. Other Plough Boys rushed over. Knives came out. Beckley and his friend Matthew Chandler scrambled out of the park and onto a double-decker bus. It seemed they'd made a getaway, but Plough Boys followed and dragged them back into the street, where a group of the gang members beat and stabbed the pair in full public view. Chandler, knifed in the groin, managed to run away. John Beckley hobbled about a hundred yards up the road, then stopped at the entrance to the Okeover Apartments. He leaned against the wall and slid down to the pavement, where, in a sitting position, he bled out and died.

The police rounded up six suspects and charged them with the stabbing murder of John Beckley. Each Plough Boy had his own story, minimizing his role in the attack, or denying being there in the first place. When the case went to trial in the Old Bailey in September, Fleet Street's coverage was rabid, and stirred up Teddy Boy panic throughout the country. No murder weapon was produced, and five of the defendants were acquitted of the charge, but all received prison sentences for common assault. Michael John Davies, a twenty-year-old laborer, had pleaded not guilty and was tried in October. He'd never denied being part of the mob, but insisted, "I didn't have a knife, I only used my fists." He was identified, however, by a woman who was riding a bus that passed by at the time of the fight. Davies was convicted and sentenced to death. (His sentence was commuted to life in prison, and he was granted a reprieve and released from Wandsworth in 1960.)

Near the end of *The Wild One*, Johnny Strabler is attempting to ride out of Wrightsville when one of the town vigilantes hurls a tire iron at the back wheel of his motorcycle, causing Johnny to fall off and the bike to slam into a crowd, killing an old man. To the BFCC, that premise of a death caused by a perpetrator who can't be identified was all too similar to the Plough Boys murder case. The resolution in *The Wild One* was seen to be even more dangerous. "A man's dead, on account of something you let get started," the sheriff says to Johnny. "But I'm gonna take a big fat chance and let you go." In the eyes of the BBFC, this was the point at which a crime went unpunished. Even Brando's disclaiming prologue, the one that Breen insisted be added to the film, worked against the film. "Once the trouble was on its way, I was just going with it," was seen as a reflection of the Teddy Boy philosophy, and the censors believed that Brando was so charismatic in the role that not only would young viewers see the events through his characters' eyes, but British moviemakers would want to produce more teen rebel movies. To ensure that no one missed the point, the BBFC stated that the character Johnny Strabler got away with "larceny, malicious damage to property, false imprisonment, assault and battery, insulting behaviour, reckless driving, and whatever federal offense it is to break into a government telephone exchange and prison and control them." Move over, Memphis, *The Wild One* was banned in Britain.

Not that the picture wasn't shown.

Urban legend has it that *The Wild One* was kept out of British cinemas and out of sight of British movie fans from 1954 until the ban was lifted in 1968. That was not the case. The BBFC's ban was not the last word. Local authorities were allowed to ask local magistrates to grant the picture a local X rating. The first action was taken in Cambridge, the university city. Leslie Halliwell, a Cambridge University graduate and manager of the Rex Cinema (later known for his *Halliwell's Film Companion*), booked the film for a three-week run in the spring of 1955. "It seemed worth trying," he wrote in *Picturegoer* magazine, "especially as Cambridge has very little Teddy Boy trouble and is thus less likely to suffer from their film's allegedly harmful effect on young people." Halliwell's bet paid off. The screenings became a cause célèbre, attended by movie stars, politicians, civic leaders, and groups of well-behaved Teddy Boys. The only trouble reported in the Cambridge city center was a lack of parking. *The Wild One* received local X ratings in other cities in Great Britain.

Derek Walker reported on the premiere for *Picturegoer*, writing that for the most part, people who viewed the film didn't think it was so wild, after all. One person leaving the cinema remarked that the violence in *On the Waterfront*, which had opened in London the previous September, was worse. One youth club leader said *The Wild One* was "nasty," but that it should be up to local authorities whether to screen it. "It's all right showing it in Cambridge," said Frank Hardy. "We have a low juvenile delinquency rate. But in some places it could be a harmful influence. I wouldn't show it in Liverpool."

The Wild One would be screened in Liverpool and other cities throughout the United Kingdom as more local committees decided to overrule the BBFC. But even if the film itself had not been shown, the publicity surrounding it made *The Wild One* almost ubiquitous in the UK. "Indeed, the fact that kids could not be trusted to see it only strengthened the film's mystique," Johnny Stuart wrote in his 1996 book, *Rockers! Kings of the Road*. "Brando/Johnny—through the legend, through the revered music stills and posters—provided the image that fired the imagination of 1950s youth."

Marlon Brando was already a major movie star, and his image, in a black leather jacket astride a British Triumph motorcycle, was even more popular than the poster for his previous film, *Julius Caesar*, in which he was pictured as a beefcake pin-up, bare-chested in a golden toga. It was a far sexier image than that of the battered, scarred boxer's face on posters for *On the Waterfront*. If the movie couldn't be screened in every theater, British teen and movie magazines made up for the drought and filled in the information about the plot. *Picturegoer* ran features; *Films and Filming* featured a special photo supplement in its March 1955 issue. It really wasn't necessary to actually see *The Wild One* to be familiar with its particulars.

"You didn't get a hundred movies a week or a hundred things on TV, so when something came out, it was a real celebration. Brando is this new star, so a Brando film is in a way a celebration of him," says UK journalist and author Douglas Thompson. "It's not like they'd gone to the movies and seen it. They'd know about it because it would be in the film mags, they would see the image of Brando, they'd read about the gang—they'd be fascinated by it. Because it was youth. It was youth rebelling, which they were all doing at exactly that time in the fifties.

"And in a way, by being banned, it's like, put a brown paper wrapper 'round a book, people will buy the bloody book. If you start banning the film you cannot see, the more you want to see it. That's certainly what happened with *The Wild One*."

When James Dean's *Rebel Without a Cause* was released in Great Britain in January 1956, moviegoers knew he was a junior, more sensitive version of Johnny Strabler. When Elvis Presley's "Heartbreak Hotel" entered the UK record charts in May, there was no doubt who Elvis emulated. Elvis said it in the teen mags: "Marlon Brando."

If there was any doubt that Brando's image in *The Wild One* was an influence on British youth long before 1968, when the ban on the picture was lifted, it only takes a look at the "Rockers" subculture. Also known as "Ton-Up Boys" (for their goal of driving "a ton"—a hundred miles an hour), "leather boys," and "café racers," the Rockers movement coincided with the rise of the Teddy Boys and came into its own as a troublesome influence in spring 1964, when they clashed in south coast resort towns with a rival group known as the Mods. The battles were memorialized in *Quadrophenia*, the rock opera album by the Who, released in 1973, and the subsequent movie version in 1979. The Mods were fashionable and stylish and got around in packs of motor scooters. The Rockers looked like the American rock 'n' roll and rockabilly stars who were making hay in the UK at the time. They wore black leather jackets, rolled-up jeans, and motorcycle boots. They rode motorcycles. Banned or not, *The Wild One* and Johnny Strabler were the models for the Rockers.

"The painted skull and crossbones supported by his gang on the back of their leathers became the most commonplace insignia of the Ton-Up Boys jacket," Johnny Stuart wrote. "His cycle cap, although not available in any English shop, was improvised by caps nicked off milkmen and train-drivers and then done up with chains, studs, and badge, and worn pulled menacingly low over the eyes. So amid the all-pervasive uniformity and quiet decency of the contemporary scene, it was Brando's uniform, stance and image which appeared on the streets of Great Britain."

John Lennon was a rebellious teenager from the Walton suburb of Liverpool when he entered the Liverpool College of Art College on Hope Street in October 1957. It was his talent for art and a recommendation from the headmaster at Quarry Bank High School for Boys that, despite his failing grades, led to his acceptance at the school, supposedly saving him from a life of drudgery. Not that too much drudgery was likely. Young Lennon's world had been rocked, literally, when he first heard "Heartbreak Hotel" the previous year, and he'd started his own band with his schoolmates. The Quarrymen, named for their school, played skiffle and rock 'n' roll, and Lennon saw more of a future in that rebel music than he did with the sweater-wearing crowd at the art school. The sarcastic, brilliant teen had been brought up in a nice semi-detached house with his Aunt Mimi and Uncle George, as his mother flitted in and out of his life (and bought him his first guitar). Lennon wasn't all that different from the other tweedy future art students—but he had a serious chip on his shoulder. He showed up on that first day of classes looking like some kind of working-class zero, dressed as a Teddy Boy in a blue-gray suit, slim Jim tie, blue suede shoes, hair piled high, just like Elvis, and doing his best Brando.

"I was never really a street kid or a tough guy," Lennon would admit in an interview a few nights before his death in 1980.

I used to dress like a Teddy Boy and identify with Marlon Brando and Elvis Presley, but I never really was in real street fights or real down-home gangs. I was just a suburban kid, imitating the rockers. But it was a big part of one's life to look tough. I spent the whole of my childhood with shoulders up around the top of me head and me glasses off because glasses were sissy, and walking in complete fear, but with the toughest-looking face you've ever seen. I'd get into trouble just because of the way I looked. I wanted to be this tough James Dean all the time. It took a lot of wrestling to stop doing that, even though I still fall into it when I get insecure and nervous. I still drop into that I'm-a-street-kid stance, but I have to keep remembering that I never really was one.

I look at early pictures of me-self, and I was torn between being Marlon Brando and being the sensitive poet—the Oscar Wilde part of me with the velvet, feminine side. I was always torn between the two, mainly opting for the macho side, because if you showed the other side, you were dead.

The Liverpool College of Art is where Lennon met his first wife, Cynthia Powell. More significantly, it's where he met Stuart Sutcliffe. Sutcliffe was a serious art student, already an accomplished painter, but he also had experience in music, and was even more of a Marlon Brando fan than Lennon.

Douglas Thompson wrote the 2001 book, *The Beatles Shadow: Stuart Sutcliffe's Lonely Hearts Club*, with Sutcliffe's younger sister, Pauline. "Stuart identified. He saw Brando as that rebel and understood all of that, trying to get out of the environment you're in. Pauline's point was that Stuart was trapped in a sense, because they were in a middle-class culture in Liverpool, which is a working class city, and Lennon is pulling him into music."

Paul McCartney, a year younger than Lennon and a student at the Liverpool Institute High School for Boys, joined the Quarrymen that October, and in February the group had been narrowed to Lennon, McCartney, and George Harrison. Lennon moved in with Sutcliffe in 1960. Together, they came up with a new name for the Quarrymen, and Lennon convinced Sutcliffe to join as bass player.

The group became The Silver Beatles, then the Beatles, and in the summer of 1960, was offered a gig on the Reeperbahn, the red-light district of Hamburg, Germany. With Liverpool drummer Pete Best along for the ride, they played for hours every night and into the morning and were adopted by an artsy German crowd that included photographers and artists Astrid Kirchherr, Jürgen Vollmer, and Klaus Voorman. Under the Germans' influence, the Beatles began wearing leather jackets and jeans, then head-to-toe leather suits onstage, and eventually ditched the greasy kid stuff and began sporting what would become their trademark "mop top" haircuts.

"At the time, Stuart's looking for an escape, a way out, and eventually he does. He goes to Hamburg, and he apes the Brando look, the James Dean kind of attitude—the method acting, if you like, the Brando way," Thompson says. "And of course he did that on stage when he was a Beatle—he turned his back to the audience and had the dark glasses and posed that way—being individualistic, being a guy apart. They weren't the first boys to wear leather jackets, but of course Stuart introduced them. And they were walking around like Teddy Boys at that point,

The *Wild One* was banned in the UK until 1968 but still had a tremendous effect on John Lennon—and may even have inspired the name of his band. Photofest

but especially Lennon. With that kind of combed-back quiff of hair, he could be straight out of one of the scenes in the Brando movie, without question."

Jürgen Vollmer took some of the most iconic photographs of the group, including one that would be resurrected for the cover for Lennon's 1975 "oldies" album, *Rock 'n' Roll*. The photo was taken in the spring of 1961 in a secluded courtyard called the Jäger-Passag. Lennon stands in a doorway, while the other Beatles walk past, out of focus. Any resemblance to Marlon Brando, anything that might bring to mind Brando's pose leaning against the jukebox in *The Wild One*, shrugging with a "Whaddaya got?" when asked what he was rebelling against, was purely intentional.

"I put John in the doorway because he looked the most *rocker* of them all—to me, he was like Marlon Brando in *The Wild One*," Vollmer said. "I made him stand still, then I got the other three to pass by. I put the camera on a tripod and set a long exposure so their bodies were out of focus, but I wanted their shoes to be sharp, so you could hear the hard steps."

Mark Lewisohn, perhaps the ultimate Beatles authority, wrote, "Here, then, is the definitive leather-jacket Lennon at twenty, leaning into the brick of a Hamburg doorway."

Stu Sutcliffe was gone from the group by the summer of 1961 (and dead, of a brain hemorrhage, the following April). Brian Epstein came in to manage the group in November, Pete Best was out, and Ringo Starr was in the following August, leather outfits made way for tailored suits, and a new era in cultural history was about to begin. And the story of how the group got their name, "The Beatles," was asked again and again.

"It came in a vision—a man appeared on a flaming pie and said unto them, 'From this day on, you are Beatles with an A.' 'Thank, you, Mister Man,' they said, thanking him," Lennon wrote in a jokey essay for the *Mersey Beat* newspaper in 1961.

"John thought of it, first of all, just for a name, just for a group, you know," McCartney said in December 1963. "We just didn't have any names. Oh, yeah, we did have a name, but we had about ten of them a week, you know, and we didn't like this idea, so we had to settle on one particular name. And John came up with 'the Beatles' one night, and he sort of explained how it was spelled with an e-a, and we said, 'Oh, yes, it's a joke!'"

The story was told over and over during the initial rush of fame and the heyday of the 1960s: Shortly after Stu Sutcliffe had been recruited by his pal into the Quarrymen, he came up with the name. It was a takeoff on Buddy Holly's group, the Crickets. He spelled it "Beatals," and Lennon tweaked it—or it was originally "Beetles" and Lennon liked the double meaning and wordplay. "I was looking for a name like the Crickets that meant two things, and from Crickets I got to Beatles," Lennon said in 1964. "I changed the 'B-e-a' because it didn't mean two things on its own—B, double-e, t-l-e-s didn't mean two things. So I changed the 'a,' added the 'e' to the 'a', and it meant two things, then. . . . It was 'beat' and 'beetles,' and when you said it, people thought of crawly things, and when you read it, it was beat music."

That was the origin story, more or less, until it took a turn in December 1975—a turn toward *The Wild One*. According to an impressively detailed 1996 chronology by Beatles historian Dave Persails, George Harrison, on the road on his concert tour with Ravi Shankar, revealed the surprising new information during an interview on the "Earth News" radio network. "John used to say in his American accent, 'Where are we goin' fellas?' and we'd say, 'To the top, Johnny!' And we used to do that as a laugh, but that was actually the Johnny, I suppose, from *The Wild Ones* [*sic*]. Because when Lee Marvin drives up with his motorcycle gang, and if my ears weren't tricking me, I could've sworn when Marlon Brando's talking to Lee Marvin, Lee Marvin's saying to him, 'Look Johnny, I think such-and-such, the Beetles think that you're such-and-such,' as if his motorcycle gang was called the Beetles."

(*"You know, I missed you. Ever since the club split up, I missed you. We all missed ya! Did you miss him? Yeah! The Beetles missed ya! All the Beetles missed ya!"*)

With Harrison's account, a second generation of Beatles fan lore began to unfold. Derek Taylor, the Beatles' former press agent and group insider, expanded upon Harrison's version in December 1983, with the publication of an autobiography, *Fifty Years Adrift* (with an introduction by Harrison). Taylor gave credit to Stuart Sutcliffe for naming the group, stating that "at that time, Stuart was into the Marlon Brando type of method acting.

"There has always been a big thing about who invented the name Beatles. John had said he invented it. But if you look at a movie called *The Wild One*, you'll see a scene about bicycle gangs where Johnny's (played by Brando) gang is in a coffee bar and another gang led by Chino (Lee Marvin) pulls into town for a bit of aggro. The film dialogue . . . shows how Stuart could have thought of the name Beatles."

Hunter Davies, the Beatles' official biographer, found Taylor's words noteworthy. In his 1968 authorized biography, *The Beatles*, Davies had written of the band's name that "Paul and George just remember John arriving with it one day. They'd always been fans of Buddy Holly and the Crickets. They liked his music, and the name of his group. It had a nice double meaning, one of them a purely English meaning which Americans couldn't have appreciated." But in the introduction to the book's second revised edition in 1985, Davies added a caveat: "I learned the other day through Derek Taylor (formerly their pressman) that it had come from that Marlon Brando film *The Wild One*. There's apparently a group of motorcyclists in the film, all in black leather, called the Beetles, though they are only referred to as such in passing. Stu Sutcliffe saw this film, heard the remark, and came back and suggested it to John as the new name for their group. John said yeah, but we'll spell it Beatles, as we're a beat group. Well, that's the latest theory. No doubt in the years to come, there will be many new suggestions, perhaps even some revelations."

It was ten years later, with the television airing of the autobiographical documentary miniseries, *The Beatles Anthology*, that many Beatles fans may have been confused by a nod to *The Wild One*'s influence. In the first of the eight-part series shown on ITV, there's a brief section in which Lennon alone is given credit for coming up with the band's name. His original quote from 1964 is Frankenbitten to say, "Um, I was looking for a name like the Crickets and then two things. And from Crickets I got the Beatles. When you said it, people saw crawly things and when you read it, it was beat music." And then the image of Lennon cuts to *The*

Wild One, the scene in which Marlon Brando shoves Lee Marvin off his motorcycle. Marvin gets up and ultimately says, "The Beetles missed ya! All the Beetles missed ya!"

Fade to commercial break.

Some explanation was needed! McCartney provided it two years later, when quoted by his official biographer Barry Miles in the book, *Many Years from Now*. McCartney said he remembered talking to Lennon about Buddy Holly and the Crickets, and the double meaning of the band's name, which led to "beetles": "We were turned on like nobody's business by the idea of a double meaning." But while working on the *Anthology* project in 1994, the ex-Beatle said, he did some research and new memories were stirred. "We were into the Marlon Brando film *The Wild One*, particularly John and Stuart, and in that they use the word 'beetles,' and we think that kind of clinched it. It was John and Stuart one night at their art school flat. I remember being told the next day the new idea for the name."

After rewatching the film and seeing Lee Marvin refer to his gang's groupies as "the Beetles," McCartney said, "I got this terrible thought, 'Fuck me, it's biker's molls.' I had to make notes for the *Anthology* and I was watching the video and I wrote in my notes, 'Does "beetles" mean girls or guys?' The director looked it up and found that in forties American slang, 'beetles' are girls. It's like 'chicks.' We were actually named after girls, which I think is fabulous. None of us noticed it."

Was that even accurate? McCartney, who was admittedly revisionist and score-settling when it came to Beatles history in Miles's book, said the story fit in with the fact that in their early years, the Beatles included many "girl group" songs in their repertoire, and recorded songs already made popular by the Shirelles, Cookies, Donays, and Marvelettes.

The Brando influence is seconded by Sutcliffe's younger sister, Pauline. "Stuart also dreamt up a new name for the group," she wrote in her book *Backbeat*, published in July 1994. "Buddy Holly had his Crickets, and, on a forthcoming month-long tour of Britain, Gene Vincent was going to be backed by the Beat Boys. How about 'The Beetles?' One of the motorbike gangs in *The Wild One* was called that too. A brainstorming session with John warped it eventually to The Beatles—you know, like in 'beat music.'"

Now if you ask a Beatles expert, it's most likely he or she would say it's all more revisionist history, that the name "The Beatles" was inspired either by Buddy Holly and the Crickets, or handed over by a man with a flaming pie.

Lewisohn wrote off the possibility of a connection to *The Wild One* in 2013, in a footnote to *Tune In*, the first part of his historical trilogy, *The Beatles: All These Years*. He claimed that Stuart Sutcliffe had but one chance to view *The Wild One* before 1960: "On November 24, 1956, the Merseyside Film Institute Society (a private club whose aim was to raise the standards and appreciation of films) held a one-off, members-only screening at the Philharmonic Hall. Stuart would have had to retain for more than three years a piece of dialogue inconsequential when he heard it (and yet not suggest it when they were looking for a name earlier), he would have had to gain access to the screening though at sixteen he was too young, and would have needed to be a MIFS member, and wasn't."

Lewisohn neglects the fact that amid the widespread publicity given *The Wild One* in the months and even years following the BBFC's ban, young people, especially those inclined to idolize Marlon Brando, sought out information about *The Wild One*, the forbidden film, and could find much information in newspapers and magazines that covered the movie in detail. Even a cursory summary of the plot might mention that the trouble in Wrightsville begins when Brando's Black Rebels Motorcycle Club is confronted by Lee Marvin and a gang that was called—or had "molls" called—the Beetles. Such a line of dialogue is hardly "inconsequential."

The influence of Brando on the Beatles' style and attitude is clear. But was the name derived from his film? In some circles, the fight boils down to whether Lennon or Sutcliffe deserves credit for naming the band. Revisionist or not, Pauline Sutcliffe wrote in *The Beatles' Shadow* that her brother "had seen *On the Waterfront* many times, and all the boys adored *Viva Zapata!*, but his favorite Brando film was *The Wild One*, which was first screened in Britain in cinema clubs."

"When you say 'cinema clubs,' it was a bit like book clubs today," Pauline's coauthor Thompson adds. "There would be groups of people who were film fans and they couldn't get to see a film, or a film would open, or it was always John Wayne and *Stagecoach*, so they wanted something different. And the European cinema was coming in, French cinema, the New Wave was happening as well, so that was part of the cinema clubs. The Brando film was coming through at that time and these guys are all artists, so I would think the university would have had the cinema club, which is where they would have seen the movie. They were teenagers at art college and looking at everything. It would have influenced them, whether they sat and watched every frame of the film or not. I mean, they're interested in the image. That would have been their way to it."

"The stills and press photos of *The Wild One* and Brando's role in the movie are almost as famous as the movie itself, or perhaps more famous," says Andrew Luecke.

I hesitate to use this word because it's overused, but in this case it's really accurate, you have that *iconic* photo of him sitting on the bike with the cap, with the outfit. It was almost an omnipresent piece of pop culture. I think that the visual stills of it are just as potent as the movie, and those spread wide and far, so I'm not surprised that it was able to influence the UK, even though the movie was banned. And the UK's reaction to American pop culture in the post-war fifties was just ravenous.

You have stories of rock 'n' roll bands and kids rioting in the UK. There was a big concern about juvenile delinquency, and rock 'n' roll, and what America is going to do to the youth of the UK, and Brando and *The Wild One* were a big part of that. And then you also have the issue of the clothing that he's wearing. Think about the conditions of post–World War II UK. You still have rationing. You still have war damage from the Blitz. It's really an environment of deprivation. And America is, at the same time, becoming a superpower, and its middle class is growing, with all of these consumer goods. So when you have that picture of Johnny from the Black Rebels Motorcycle Club on his bike circulating in UK magazines, it's not just an image of teen rebellion and subversion, it's also an image of opulence, a sort of rough-and-tumble opulence. I think all of that had a chokehold on the UK.

In May 1997, while promoting his album *Flaming Pie*, McCartney had to reiterate that the Beatles did not actually get their name from a man holding one. "It's a joke," McCartney said. "There are still a lot of things we have to fudge because of compromise. If we don't all agree on a story, somebody has to give in. And Yoko kind of insisted that John had to have full credit for the name. She believed he had a vision."

That need to compromise might be why Harrison's 1975 statement, the one that ignited the debate, was amended in *The Beatles Anthology* book, published in 2000. "It is debatable where the name came from," he's quoted as saying. "John used to say he invented it, but I remember Stuart being with him the night before. There was The Crickets . . . but Stuart was really into Marlon Brando and in the movie *The Wild One* there is a scene where Lee Marvin says. . . 'The Beatles have missed you.'. . . We'll give it fifty/fifty to Sutcliffe/Lennon."

"Pauline certainly had no doubts that Stuart came up with the name for the Beatles, very much originally, with the Brando connection," Thompson says after being read McCartney's words.

She was there. It was all going on in her front room. She was a teenager and she's got John and George and Paul and her brother in the front room. And Mrs. Sutcliffe is coming in, "Would you like another cup of tea, boys?" So she was witness to all. What happens, you see, is that after Stuart dies, they very much tried to bury—literally bury—Stuart from the memory of the Beatles. It's just easier to market, forget him because he was so enigmatic and popular. So this goes on for many years. But when they do *Sgt. Pepper*, Lennon insists that Stuart's on the cover, and you can see him there, but he's there because Lennon doesn't want to forget him. But when they do the *Anthology* later on, there's all this fighting with Pauline, because Stuart's on various records and copyrights and all that. And I think later on, when the marketing machine comes in, they want everything to conform, everybody's on the same page the whole time with the same story. But I don't think there's any question that Brando and *The Wild One* are not just influencing Stuart Sutcliffe and artists and young creatives like him. It's a whole country of young people affected.

An obvious omission in the arguments over the derivation of the Beatles name is the album, *Sgt. Pepper's Lonely Hearts Club Band*. The landmark Beatles album was released in the United Kingdom on May 26, 1967, with a front cover featuring the four Beatles in colorful costumes as members of the Lonely Hearts Club Band, standing in front of a crowd collage of cut-out pictures of more than sixty celebrities and iconic figures (including wax models of their younger selves, borrowed from Madame Tussauds museum). Stuart Sutcliffe is there, on the far left, fourth row, surrounded on three sides by illustrator Aubrey Beardsley, a hairdresser's wax dummy, and a "Petty Girl" pinup. Marlon Brando is also included in the collage. He is displayed prominently, directly behind the four wax figures of the Beatles in their Beatlemania-era suits and haircuts.

The photo of his face is from 1953, as Johnny Strabler in *The Wild One*.

"Brando's there and Stuart's up there, too," Douglas Thompson says. "And you've certainly got a straight line between the two of them. So the influences, however you play it, they knew all about him. Everybody they put on that cover, they debated, and Lennon insisted that Stuart be on it—and who's to say if he insisted that Brando be on it."

(There is a footnote to Brando's connection to Lennon: After Lennon's assassination, according to news reports, his killer was revealed to have a list of other potential targets, including Marlon Brando.)

Nine

You Need an Analyst

People are usually willing to blame somebody else before they'll blame themselves or even look at themselves. I was the same way, but I was blessed with enough sense to realize that if I wanted well-being, psychoanalytic help was just about the only, and last, way to get it.

—Marlon Brando

Even before Marlon Brando completed his work on *The Wild One*, he announced his "long term plan" to move on from Hollywood. As he told it, he intended to star in a film based on the Rodgers and Hart musical *Pal Joey* in the fall of 1954, followed by a trip around the world. "After that, I'll confine my work to the stage." As he made that definitive statement, however, Brando was well aware that he had one more motion picture obligation left to fulfill. When he refused to do so, the Hollywood system and its supporting institutions finally had a chance to get back at the Broadway brat who'd been so superior for so long. For Brando, the fight could be seen as a losing battle, but by waging it, he would be changing culture once again, popularizing and, through his accomplishments, legitimizing a theory and therapy that at the time was misunderstood and even ridiculed.

It all went back to his childhood. Brando spoke often about the emotional and psychological turmoil that dated to his early years—and with a distant, disapproving father who was unfaithful to his wife and a loving mother who was often wrapped in her own dramas and alcoholic stupors, there was no shortage of trauma in young Bud Brando's life. Within a year of his move to New York City where his sisters were living, the trauma followed him, as his mother separated from his father a second time and moved to the city, as well. Dodie set up house in a sprawling apartment on West End Avenue, where Brando and his sisters often stayed. This was a time when Brando's mother attended Alcoholics Anonymous faithfully, and seemed to be getting a handle on her problems. In 1945, while Brando was locked into his first tortuous Broadway engagement in *I Remember*

Mama, Dodie and Marlon Sr. reconciled, and she left New York City to move in with her husband in Chicago.

Her departure might have been expected to lift a burden from her son, but Brando recalled that in the aftermath, he experienced a "kind of a nervous breakdown that came on gradually, then was severe for several months." He stopped eating. His weight dropped from one hundred and seventy to one hundred and fifty-seven pounds. He couldn't stand to hear arguing, or even loud voices. He was nervous, unable to sleep. He wandered the city streets and spent hours in Christian Science reading rooms, "searching for anything that could help me understand what was wrong with me and make me feel better." Brando never missed a performance, but "I sometimes thought I was losing my mind. If I was offended in the slightest, I wanted to punch somebody."

Brando began spending time with Stella Adler and her family, who, he said, "may have saved my sanity." He and his teacher had a close, flirtatious, and very intimate relationship. Brando said he would sometimes stroll into Stella's bedroom while she was dressing, and cup her breasts in his hands. *In Songs My Mother Taught Me*, he denied that things went any further. He did go on to have a long affair with Stella's daughter Ellen, which must have made things complicated, to say the least.

Brando's demons caught up with him again during his second long-term theatrical commitment. This time, the pressures of sudden stardom were added to the monotony of repeat performances and issues with his parents and women. In the final months of 1948, closing in on a year of performances of *A Streetcar Named Desire*, he slipped into another deep depression and began experiencing severe anxiety attacks. He was stricken with stomach pains. He worried about having a heart attack. He feared he might "kill somebody."

Harold Clurman, who had originally championed Brando for the role of Stanley Kowalski, understood that the young actor needed help. "Brando's mother was a hopeless alcoholic," he wrote in his 1974 memoir, *All People Are Famous*. "He suffered untold misery because of her condition, and the soul searing pain of his childhood lodged itself in some deep recess of his being. He cannot readily speak of what lies buried there: he hardly knows himself what it is. . . . He cannot voice the deepest part of himself. It hurts too much. That, in part, is the cause of his 'mumbling.'"

Director Elia Kazan believed he knew a way to help. He'd borrowed psychiatric techniques from his brother Avraam, a Freudian psychoanalyst, in order to get his actors to connect their own experiences with that of their characters. These techniques, based on the work of Sigmund Freud and used by a growing number of psychiatrists in post-World

War II New York, delved into unconscious feelings and attempted to pry out memories of past events, often repressed, in order to find the cause of problems. Kazan's Actors Studio, a drama school established weeks before *Streetcar*'s premiere, relied on the same concepts in teaching "The Method." Students were urged to make use of their real lives and pasts to, as some said, turn "trauma into drama," or as Kazan put it, "to make psychology public."

"Psychology is one thing," Kazan said. "Psychological complexity can be explored. Movement is another. Directing can be thought of as rendering psychology into behavior, into action."

During his *Streetcar* crisis, Brando had already been convinced to give psychiatry a try. At his sister Jocelyn's insistence, he visited the doctor who treated her and her husband. He walked out in the middle of the first session—and refused to pay for the hour.

Kazan counseled him to try again, and recommended that Brando meet Dr. Bela Mittelmann, another Freudian who happened to be Kazan's own psychiatrist (at the demand of his wife, who'd threatened divorce if he didn't agree to the therapy). Brando made an appointment at Mittelmann's home office at 130 East Sixty-Seventh Street, stretched out on the divan, and began to talk. And talk. "Something was chewing on me and I didn't know what it was, but I had to hide my emotions and appear strong," he remembered. "It has been this way most of my life; I have always had to pretend that I was strong when I wasn't. Why these feelings surfaced when they did, I don't know, although I suppose they had something to do with my mother going away."

Mittelmann, a short, unimposing, and chubby forty-nine-year-old Hungarian Jew, had a particular interest in psychosomatic disorder—physical ailments caused by internal conflicts—so he would seem to be a good fit. Brando's issues also fit in comfortably with neo-Freudian psychiatry in the post–World War II era, in which anxiety, and not the old standby, sex, was seen as the underlying cause of psychological maladies. There was also a focus on family dynamics, especially the need for emotional security in early childhood, which Brando clearly did not have.

Brando remembered Mittelmann as "the coldest man I've ever known," perhaps because the doctor worked mostly, in the Freudian tradition, by listening. "I saw him for several years, seeking empathy, insight and guidance, but all I got was ice. He had absolutely no warmth. Even the furnishings in his office were frigid; I almost shivered every time I walked into it. Maybe he was following the rules of his particular school of psychiatry."

The rules were very flexible in Brando's case. Sometimes, his friends came along and sat in on the sessions. Mittelmann crossed the traditional doctor-patient boundaries. But it was believed that the unorthodox methods worked for a celebrity like Brando, who needed to talk, and keep talking until the answers were produced.

Brando would later say Dr. Mittelmann "had no insight into human behavior and never gave me any help. I was still on my own, trying to deal alone with emotions I didn't yet understand." Yet he remained Mittelmann's patient well into the 1950s. (When Mittelmann died in 1959, at sixty, Brando found a new psychoanalyst.) Once he began his Hollywood career, Brando always scheduled appointments with Mittelmann for when he was back to New York, sometimes more than one session a week. He'd get on the couch and Mittelmann would let him talk, working out for himself how to overcome what Brando called "my acceptance of what I had been taught as a child—that I was worthless."

The seeds for Brando's latest, and most career-threatening, crisis were sown in 1951, when Kazan was preparing to film *Viva Zapata!* for 20th Century-Fox and ran into strong, unexpected headwinds when it came to casting his leading man. While he and Darryl F. Zanuck, Fox's head of production, both agreed they'd prefer a Mexican actor in the title role, Kazan always wanted Brando, the talent he had nurtured since *Truckline Café*, who'd just turned in an incendiary performance in the film version of *A Streetcar Named Desire*, and with whom the director could speak in shorthand when it came to the truth he sought in a performance. Zanuck's choice was Tyrone Power. When he said he could not envision Brando in the role of a Mexican revolutionary, Kazan pushed back. He even convinced Brando to do another screen test. Zanuck rejected it, claiming he couldn't understand Brando's "mumbling," but eventually gave in. He even gave in to Brando's agent's salary demand, so long as the actor agreed to sign an option to star in another 20th Century-Fox picture, to be determined.

Two years earlier, Brando had vowed to Bob Thomas that he'd never sign a deal with a studio, which would have him waiting to be cast as "a cannibal in a Johnny Weissmuller picture." But he agreed to the contract—which he later claimed he'd never bothered to read. The *Zapata!* shoot went on and led to Brando's second Academy Award nomination for Best Actor.

Brando was filming *Julius Caesar* in September 1952 when the option deal first came back to taunt him. Zanuck had returned from Europe, where Kazan was shooting *Man on a Tightrope*, and announced to the trades that he'd purchased the rights to *The Egyptian*, Finnish writer Mika Waltari's best-selling novel set in the fourteenth century BC, about a physician in the court of the pharaoh Akhnaton. The press release continued: "*Egyptian* will be Zanuck's only personal production for 1953, with Marlon Brando set for the lead." Brando put that out of his head, and eventually moved on to *The Cyclists' Raid*.

Brando did, as he'd promised, hightail it back to New York in March 1953, as soon as he completed work on *The Wild One*. By the time he arrived in Manhattan, *Pal Joey* was forgotten. Brando had checked in with Dr. Mittelmann and was making plans to sail to France with Billy Redfield, an actor pal from his earliest days on Broadway. He was in Greenwich Village when he ran into another friend from the old gang. Back when he was struggling through *I Remember Mama*, the young actors would meet up at Maureen Stapleton's apartment on West Fifty-Second Street for music and stew. When Brando learned that many of those old friends were again out of work and money, he hurried uptown and instructed his agent to arrange a four-week summer stock tour through New England. Brando would join his friends onstage, and everyone would share in the proceeds. Brando considered staging a politicized version of *Hamlet*. Redfield really pushed that idea. He wanted Brando to use the tour as lead-up to a *Hamlet* on Broadway, revolutionizing stage acting once more, and proving once and for all that he belonged alongside the greatest stage actors of all time. In the end, they settled on George Bernard Shaw's comedy, *Arms and the Man*.

Brando gave the leading, romantic role of Captain Bluntschli to Redfield. He took a secondary role, the pompous Sergius, for himself. No actor of Brando's stature in memory had settled for that part, but he wasn't out to prove anything. He said it would give him a workout, a chance to play a role in which he might not otherwise be cast and allow him to have a little fun. The four weeks in New England were going to be fun. There was some talk of taking the show to Broadway, after which Brando might even follow Redfield's advice and fulfill his destiny as a great actor by portraying Hamlet. For now, it was time to hit the road. In what could be seen as a precursor to Bob Dylan's Rolling Thunder Revue in 1975, the small-auditorium concert tour through the northeast that was hatched when Dylan met up with old friends in Greenwich Village, Brando and friends headed up the northern seaboard.

Arms and the Man opened on July 6, 1953, in Matunuck, Rhode Island, and moved on to a week each in Falmouth on Cape Cod; Ivoryton, Connecticut; and Framingham, Massachusetts.

Marjorie Adams, film critic for the *Boston Globe* since the silent film era, was granted an interview with Brando in Falmouth (apparently the first time he'd returned to the Cape since 1947, when he'd hitchhiked to Provincetown to meet Tennessee Williams). Although the actor was known to be "rude, moody and eccentric" in Hollywood, Adams wrote, she found his manners to be "exemplary." He was so solicitous that she "began to think that Marlon Brando was a transformed character"—until she asked why he received such adverse publicity out west. Adams wrote that he spoke "coldly, with thick eyebrows scowling and no smile lighting up his handsome face."

"Those Hollywood people ask such dull, such stupid, such irritating questions. They talk like cretins," he said. "But I really wasn't rude to them. I was merely taciturn, which is all one might expect of such superficial silliness. They call me smug and recalcitrant. But I am not interested in the idiotic falsehoods and exaggerations that the fan magazines turn out. I do not wish to give such interviews."

Then he surprised her. "I'm not crazy about the theater, you know. It's only my job and the one thing I can do well. But what I like most of all is travel."

The four weeks traveling with his merry troupe of old friends wasn't the low-key triumph Billy Redfield had hoped. Brando played it loose onstage, a bit too loose for Redfield, other castmates, and most all of the critics, who of course had shown up to see the Hollywood star back on the boards. Adams reviewed the show at Falmouth and focused on the large number of women in the audience. She wrote that Brando didn't make his entrance until the middle of the second act, but that when he did, "wearing a skin-tight white and gold uniform, an upturned and elegant wax mustache and heavy gold epaulets, the audience lost interest for the moment in anyone else.

"For the most part, he leaned toward the farcical, including the exit in which he made what is known on the stage technically as a pratfall. I don't believe any other actor ever played Sergius in just this manner." The audience, especially the women, she noted, were delighted by Brando's broad characterization. Other critics and Shavian aficionados at the stops were offended, none more so than Elliott Norton from the *Boston Post*, who raged that "in recent years, no major star, no actor with anything like Brando's reputation, has ever given such a ridiculous performance."

Brando was aware of the criticism. He wrote his parents at the end of July, "*Arms and the Man* has been received as the most embarrassing fiasco since Agamemnon goosed Agrippa, or the most exciting. . . bit of creative buffoonery since Aunt Betty played Santa Claus." But he claimed to be having a good time. "The audience seems to enjoy itself, and that is the measure of importance most worth considering."

Brando's casual demeanor, combined with the critical drubbing, scuttled any plans to take the show to a larger stage, or for Brando to take on *Hamlet*. Redfield was particularly disappointed and displeased that his old friend hadn't bothered to learn his lines and clowned his way through the summer jaunt. "He was brilliant once or twice a week, usually when nervous or otherwise disturbed," Redfield recalled. "The remainder of the performances he threw away. When I occasionally complained, he would say gently, 'Man, don't you get it? This is *summer stock!*'" Redfield was cheered somewhat when the two of them followed up by sailing off to France, after all. Brando was in Paris that fall with his friend Christian

Marquand, turning down scripts over croissants, playing it cool, and trying to ignore the prospect of *The Egyptian*. The year in which Zanuck had promised to produce the picture was nearing a close.

Then came an offer for a new project that Elia Kazan was developing. The movie was called *Waterfront*, the story of a longshoreman and former prizefighter who becomes a hero by defying the corrupt, mobbed-up union boss running the docks in New Jersey. It was written by Budd Schulberg, son of a Hollywood producer and author of the caustic Hollywood novel, *What Makes Sammy Run?* Kazan has said that Brando was his first choice for the role of Terry Malloy, but in the months leading to the call, Kazan had considered Paul Newman, then regarded as an "imitation Brando," reasoning that that Newman might be hungrier for the role. After the major studios passed on the project, independent film producer Sam Spiegel stepped in and began negotiating with Frank Sinatra, who was winning praise (and eventually a Best Supporting Actor Oscar) for the recently-released *From Here to Eternity*. But Spiegel knew the marquee name that would bring in the big money. Even while he was stringing Sinatra along, he concentrated on roping in Brando.

Spiegel assumed that the actor would be anxious to reunite with "Gadg," his former mentor, the one director he knew he could trust, an artist who'd be such a relief after working with László Benedek, who was in over his head with *The Wild One*, weeping with frustration in front of cast and crew during the final week of shooting. But Kazan warned that there would be issues. He and Brando were no longer close. They no longer had a working relationship, or any relationship at all, really, because Kazan had "named names."

On April 10, 1952, Kazan had testified before the House Un-American Activities Committee in Washington, D.C., and gave up the names of eight members of the Group Theatre (including the playwright Clifford Odets) who, along with himself, had been members of the Communist Party in the 1930s. Brando had been in Paris when he learned about Kazan's testimony, and like many in Hollywood, was shocked by what he considered a betrayal. He knew the people who'd be hurt by Kazan's statement, and he knew that many innocent people had been blacklisted because of these "commie hunters." Worse still, Kazan had taken out an ad in the *New York Times*, defending his actions, and urging others to follow his lead.

A year-and-a-half later, Brando was conflicted. This was a great role. Kazan was indeed one of the few directors he respected—professionally, at least. But how could he work with a rat? Some friends and people he trusted, including Stella Adler, counseled him to do what was best for his career, but the one who probably had the most influence was his psychotherapist. Dr. Mittelmann reminded his patient that if he wanted to get a handle on his rage, he'd have to learn to not judge others. Holding a grudge would not be "constructive." Accepting the role could be considered part of his therapy.

With his father giving him an extra nudge to put business and money before personal issues, Brando took the role. "Gadg had to justify what he had done and gave the appearance of sincerely believing that there was a global conspiracy to take over the world, and that communism was a serious threat to America's freedoms," Brando said later. "To speak up before the committee truthfully and in defiance of his former friends who had not abandoned the cause was a hugely difficult decision, he said, but though he was ostracized by former friends, he had no regrets for what he'd done."

The *Waterfront* script, written by Schulberg, who'd also "named names" for HUAC, was an obvious defense and glorification of the "squealer" Terry Malloy, who testifies against the mobbed-up union boss, and after the beating he takes in retaliation, tells him defiantly, "I'm glad what I done to you, ya hear that?!" Oddly, Brando said that when he agreed to make the film, he didn't realize it "was really a metaphorical argument by Gadg and Budd Schulberg: they made the film to justify finking on their friends. Evidently, as Terry Malloy I represented the spirit of the brave, courageous man who defied evil."

Brando's agent told him that Kazan and Schulberg were working for a percentage of the film's profits, and that there was potential for him to cash in with a similar deal should the low-budget film be a success. But Brando demanded he be paid up front, one hundred and twenty-five thousand dollars. He also had it written into his contract that he'd leave the set each day no later than 4 p.m., so he could cross the river to Manhattan to attend his psychotherapy sessions with Dr. Mittelmann. Brando had scheduled four sessions a week.

According to Kazan's papers at Wesleyan University's Cinema Archives, a source for William J. Mann's book, *The Contender*, Kazan later reminded Brando that "you told me repeatedly while we were shooting the picture that you weren't enthusiastic about it and were only making the picture 'because your psychoanalyst was in New York' and that you wanted to make enough to pay his bills while still remaining in that city."

Despite his tension with the director, his ambivalence toward the project, and a couple of disappearing acts (which had come to be known as "doing a Brando"), Brando continued with his therapy and came through with the character of Terry Malloy. His work would lead to his first Best Actor Oscar (Hollywood didn't hold a grudge against the "rats"; the picture would win eight Academy Awards, including Best Picture) and praise as one of the most powerful performances in cinematic history. But throughout the shoot and this entire period, the actor was in great emotional and psychic turmoil, relying on pills to get to sleep, leaning heavily on Dr. Mittelmann in order to deal with women problems, family issues, and most of all, the commitment with 20th Century-Fox that been hanging over him since 1951. As soon as he wrapped his work on *Waterfront*, Brando would be forced to return to Hollywood and pay the piper, Darryl Zanuck, by starring in *The Egyptian*.

With production set to begin at the end of January 1954, and aware of his star's commitment, Kazan rushed to shoot all of Brando's scenes in New Jersey and New York and release him from *Waterfront* before the end of filming so he could arrive on schedule on the 20th Century-Fox lot. Brando did not want to go. Did he find a way out? *Variety* reported the answer on January 20: "Marlon Brando left for the coast Sunday to begin work in *The Egyptian* at 20th-Fox. Sked for shooting *Waterfront* in Gotham and Hoboken under producer Sam Spiegel had been arranged so that Brando could complete his assignment in time to take the 20th job. Brando is teamed with Karl Malden and Eva Marie Saint in *Waterfront*, which is continuing before the cameras this week."

The Egyptian was to be a "spectacle," a four-million-dollar, widescreen, CinemaScope, "beefcake and cheesecake," tunic and headdress, historical drama also starring Victor Mature, Jean Simmons, and Gene

Brando scheduled his *On the Waterfront* shooting schedule around sessions with his psychotherapist. His openness about his treatment helped popularize psychoanalysis in the 1950s. Columbia Pictures/Photofest © Columbia

Tierney. Brando didn't like the script and its corny dialogue, or his role as Sinuhe, a physician who witnesses and participates in hanky-panky in the Pharaoh's court, but he showed up for wardrobe fittings and sat in for the first script read with the cast and director Michael Curtiz. The Hungarian-born, Academy Award-winning director was known for being versatile and prolific, but also as an imperious and brutal blowhard (three extras were killed during the climactic flood scene of his *Noah's Ark* in 1928; twenty-five horses died during the filming of *The Charge of the Light Brigade* in 1936). If Brando was teetering on the edge of backing out, the scales were tipping when he discovered that his love interest was to be played by Bella Darvi, Darryl Zanuck's mistress, an arguably "talentless" twenty-five-year-old beauty whom the fifty-one-year-old mogul was hellbent on making a star. Born Bella Zegler, she was given the name "Darvi" by Zanuck—combining the first letters of his name with those of his wife, Virginia—while Bella was living in the Zanucks' guesthouse.

After that first readthrough on Friday, January 29, Brando walked away. More to the point, he ran away. He was expected to return to work on Monday, and cameras were ready to roll on Thursday, February 4. But by the time Zanuck, Curtiz, or even his own agent realized that Brando was MIA from the Fox lot, he was on a train, chugging back to New York City and Dr. Mittelmann.

Psychoanalysis, still a controversial and exotic science to most of heartland America, was about to become a household word, thanks to Marlon Brando.

"Brando was driven off the picture by Curtiz," said Philip Dunne, a screenwriter brought onto the production as an "unofficial producer." "We had a reading and Brando read his part absolutely beautifully. It was quite poetic. Then Mike said, 'How can I, with all my genius, make you play this man who was one moment hero, the next moment villain?' Brando just looked at him." Dunne took it upon himself to type up a memo, explaining the character to Zanuck, Curtiz, and Brando. By the time he sent it off, Brando was already in the wind.

Zanuck was beside himself. Leading men just don't walk away from a picture, not after signing a contract, showing up for wardrobe fittings, and sitting through the first rehearsal. And no one knew where Brando had gone.

Zanuck and 20th Century-Fox got word on February 2. The telegram did not come from Brando, or his agent. It came from Brando's psychiatrist, Dr. Bela Mittelmann. The doctor informed Zanuck and the Fox attorneys that his patient was in New York City, under his care, and would be unable to return to work for the next ten weeks.

Fox replied with an offer to pay the doctor's expenses to make the trip to California with Brando so the doctor could remain with him during the making of the film. The offer was rejected. The studio then proposed that another physician be permitted to examine Brando, and asked to see his case history. There was no reply.

On February 5, 20th Century-Fox announced that it was going to sue the actor in order to recover, according to Zanuck, "the amount our auditors determine the studio has lost through the delay he has caused to the production." According to *Variety*, "Zanuck declared that he had come to expect a certain amount of temperament from actors, but never before concurred in instituting a lawsuit against one of them."

With his refusal to play ball with Darryl Zanuck, Brando had crossed a couple of lines. Many an actor had bristled against the power of the old "studio system" that had an ironclad grip on every aspect of filmmaking and distribution in the 1930s and 1940s. Olivia de Havilland's successful lawsuit against Warner Bros. for using excuses to extend her seven-year contract led to California's "De Havilland Law." The ruling gave more power to performers, but Brando's case was different. He'd given his word and then reneged. "He undoubtedly is going through some sort of personal crisis, but he should have bowed out of this picture before production," an anonymous "Hollywood big wheel" told James Bacon. "He decided to buck a major studio with the wrong tactics. That's the most unpardonable of all Hollywood sins. . . . No actor, no matter how good he is, can be bigger than a studio."

"Bigger than a studio." That alone gave the excuse for payback from all the columnists and writers who were forced to bend to the will of the "Broadway brat" for so many years. By adding "psychiatry" and "psychoanalysis" to the equation, Brando opened himself to ridicule. Everyone could say what they'd believed all along: He was *nuts*.

Within forty-eight hours of the telegram from Dr. Mittelmann, Louella Parsons was spreading Zanuck's message through newspapers across the country: Should Brando not return to *The Egyptian*, he'd lose out on Stanley Kramer's next picture, *Not as a Stranger*—and Kramer was already talking to Montgomery Clift about the role. "Darryl believes that Marlon will show up," she wrote, alleging that Brando had "walked out of *Julius Caesar* and was gone for several days, and he disappeared nine times from the picture *Waterfront*. Curiously enough, Brando has a fright complex and he's been seeing a psychiatrist in Chicago. Could be that he's getting himself some courage and that he will come back as Darryl believes."

The newswire stories were equally concerning. The United Press quoted Brando's agent Jay Kanter as describing him as a "very sick and mentally confused boy." A studio spokesman claimed the telegram from Dr. Mittelmann used the same verbiage. "An informed source said the thirty-year-old bachelor would be kept in seclusion for two months and perhaps longer," according to the *Brooklyn Daily Eagle*. "Persons who worked with Brando before Christmas on the filming of the movie *Waterfront* in Hoboken, said he showed signs of a nervous breakdown at that time and made numerous visits to a New York psychiatrist.

"Brando was considered eccentric even by Broadway and Hollywood standards. He preferred slovenly clothes, a motorcycle, third-rate bars, a pet raccoon, and African drums to the customary garb, travel, haunts, pets and hobbies of theater personalities."

The headline said enough: *Brando Mentally Ill.*

On February 16, lawyers for 20th Century-Fox arrived at the Federal Courthouse in New York City and filed a $2 million damage suit against Brando. The suit stated that the actor had signed an exclusive services contract on April 12, 1951, and understood at the time that he would act in *The Egyptian*. In charging that Brando "contemplates rendering his services to someone else," the Fox suit also sought to stop him from doing any other work on film or onstage.

Zanuck got *The Egyptian* back on track at the end of the month. He replaced Brando with British actor Edmund Purdom, who weeks earlier had taken over for Mario Lanza after Lanza was fired from *The Student Prince*. The AP's Bob Thomas described Purdom as "sort of hard to describe . . . sort of a combination of James Mason and Errol Flynn with a touch of Brando . . . the hottest young actor in Hollywood today." (Purdom's Hollywood career never took off, but the sobriquet "The Replacement Actor" stuck.) Brando, meanwhile, hid out in New York City for three weeks. A US marshal finally found him near his apartment and served him with the court papers. Louella Parsons, still relaying messages from Darryl Zanuck, reported that although the delays caused by Brando's disappearing act had already cost 20th two million dollars (an exaggeration), the studio was willing to drop the lawsuit if Brando would pay half the cost and fulfill his contract for two more films, beginning with *Désirée*, based on a best-selling novel about Napoleon Bonaparte. Brando was in a jam. His career was literally on the line. No major player in Hollywood would hire an actor who cost a studio millions by cutting out on a signed deal. He could either star as Napoleon when cameras rolled in June, or lose all his savings in a federal lawsuit he was never going to win.

And then Brando received word that his mother had collapsed at the home of his Aunt Betty, on whose couch he'd slept when he first arrived in Los Angeles, and was taken to Huntington Memorial Hospital in Pasadena. Brando rushed there immediately, and when he arrived, the family stayed with Dodie in shifts. Marlon Sr. went with Fran; Bud with Jocelyn. The vigil went on for two weeks, with Dodie in and out of a coma. Brando and Jocelyn were with her, holding their mother's hands, when she died on the morning of March 31, 1954.

The following day, 20th Century-Fox announced that the suit had been settled. Brando agreed to star as Napoleon Bonaparte in *Désirée*. The brat had been taken down a peg, and all the reporters who once had to bow to his genius could now condescend to his "nuttiness."

Days after the settlement was announced, James Bacon opened a long syndicated feature story by asking, "What is Marlon Brando? The greatest living actor? A crazy mixed-up kid? World's highest-paid geek?" It was ostensibly a story focusing on the real Marlon Brando, who, according to Bacon was regarded by many as "the strangest of Hollywood's strange people." Bacon used *The Egyptian* situation as an example of Brando's "strangeness" by laying out 20th Century-Fox's side of the story through the words of a "studio spokesman." The unnamed spokesman claimed that Darryl Zanuck had offered Dr. Mittelmann "fifty thousand dollars if he would pick up his couch and come to Hollywood and psychoanalyze Brando between takes. When that was declined, Zanuck offered to install a direct cross-country phone line so that the doctor could consult with Brando at any time.

"Hey, sure we knew he was a screwball. But aren't all actors? We had no alternative but to sue him."

With the dispute settled, the spokesman said that the studio was certain Brando would show up in June for *Désirée*. He added, "What psychiatric patient who ever lived wouldn't jump at the chance to play Napoleon?"

And there was the message, boiled down to a few key words: The "screwball" with a "psychiatrist" should be eager to play "Napoleon." The "studio spokesman" and Bacon were connecting Brando to "the Napoleon Delusion," one's false belief that he or she is Napoleon, emperor of France. It is, according to the *British Journal of Psychiatry*, "a classic stereotype in psychiatry, which seems to have been assimilated in modern pop culture as well. In artworks, films, comic books and strips, the unusual but characteristic bicorn hat and hand-in-jacket pose are a strong visual that immediately suggests the madness of its wearer."

The delusion was first recorded, according to the British journal, among numerous patients in 1849, when Napoleon's remains were returned to France. It was referenced in literature, and made it into the movies in 1922, in the silent films *The Misleading Lady* and *Mixed Nuts*, the two-reeler in which Stan Laurel played a salesman selling books about Napoleon who is hit on the head with a brick and begins to believe he is the emperor of France. Would-be Napoleons are dragged off to insane asylums in the 1956 Bugs Bunny cartoon, *Napoleon Bunny-Part*, as well as in the 1966 hit novelty record, "They're Coming to Take Me Away, Ha-Haaa!" written and performed by Jerry Samuels as "Napoleon XIV."

By conflating the two, Bacon was intimating that Brando was not suffering from an artistic crisis, but delusions of grandeur known to occur in people with a wide range of psychiatric diseases, including schizophrenia and bipolar disorder. Napoleon was indeed the symbol of the lunatic in a straitjacket, muttering to himself in the padded room of a mental ward. And how far-fetched was the idea in 1954? Brando was, after all, very publicly "seeing a psychiatrist," and his status as a leading man and highly paid actor meant little to him.

"Do you know what a geek is?" Bacon wrote that Brando asked him. "A geek is the lowest form of show business, the guy in the carnival who bites the head off live chickens. They usually get paid off in cheap whisky. Press agents made me a geek who gets paid $150,000 a chicken head." He laughed. "I don't give a damn. Every time somebody writes about my torn T-shirt, it's money in the bank. When you reporters are up at midnight thinking about some new phrase that will still mean 'slob,' I'll be over on the Riviera lying on the beach with some beautiful doll dropping grapes in my mouth."

But Bacon also noted that "psychoanalysis is nothing new with Mr. Brando. An actress friend disclosed more than a year ago that she and Mr. Brando shared a psychiatrist in common." The actress theorized that Brando's "personal crisis stemmed from a desire to throw away his torn T-shirt which so identified him with the brutish Kowalski. He even went so far as to order three custom-made suits from an expensive tailor." While that layman's diagnosis had little bearing on Brando's psyche, it did highlight Brando's bravery in not shying away from talking about his therapy. The actress's admission was another example of how he'd been working to remove the onus from seeking help for mental issues. "Mittelmann" had been a factor in his decisions and conversation since the doctor was first recommended by Kazan. And just as Brando seemed to subliminally channel the sexually-fluid leading man out of the closet through his characterizations, so did his public acceptance of psychiatry help in the spread of its popularity beyond the urban centers and intellectual subcultures.

It was, in fact, a natural component of his acting. Brando was using psychotherapy to plumb the depths of his past. His childhood with his alcoholic parents, mistreatment that he and his sisters and mother experienced at the hands of his father—even his early years sleeping nude with his nanny—was intrinsically connected to the techniques of Method acting he was using to find his characters. It's no coincidence that after an uncomfortable encounter with his slavish follower, James Dean, Brando would suggest that he see a psychiatrist. He offered that advice to many people in the 1950s, as more people began to take to the couch.

Brando fulfilled his commitment in *Désirée*. When the movie was previewed in New York City in November 1954, *Variety* said Brando's acting "rates as a masterful exhibition of thesping." By then, *On the Waterfront* was four months into release, and the trade paper had raved that "Marlon Brando puts on a spectacular show, giving a fascinating, multi-faceted performance." By March 1955, when he won his first Academy Award, it appeared that Brando had settled into Hollywood, in fact to have "*gone* Hollywood." He was filming that musical, *Guys and Dolls*, starring as Sky Masterson. Frank Sinatra, who felt he deserved the part because he, unlike Brando, could sing, was in the supporting role of Nathan Detroit. Sinatra was still fuming, and in fact suing Sam Spiegel for reneging on his agreement to cast him in *Waterfront*.

Consulting with his psychotherapist and finding new ways into diverse roles, Brando lost thirty pounds from an admittedly expanding frame, put rubber lids on his eyes and a black wig on his head to play a Japanese interpreter in *The Teahouse of the August Moon*. He later returned to Japan for *Sayonara*, as a US Air Force pilot who falls in love with a Japanese dancer during the Korean War.

Psychoanalysis, meanwhile, grew in popularity. By the late 1950s and early 1960s, more than half of psychiatrists were trained in psychoanalysis or were psychoanalytically inclined. According to the medical trade publication *Psychiatric Times*, "by 1960, virtually every major American psychiatry position in academia was occupied by a psychoanalyst." Later in the decade, movie stars as diverse as Cary Grant and Dustin Hoffman gave credit to the therapy for helping them in their lives and careers. For Brando it was something else. Psychoanalysis showed him how to follow his original instincts and seek out a life beyond acting.

He was directing (for the first and last time) the film *One-Eyed Jacks* in 1960 when he told a reporter from *Life* magazine, that "Acting by and large is the expression of a neurotic impulse. Acting is a bum's life. . . . You get paid for doing nothing and it means nothing. . . . Acting is fundamentally a childish thing to pursue. Quitting acting, that is the mark of maturity."

He'd later add, "The principal benefit acting has afforded me is the money to pay for my psychoanalysis."

But perhaps the greatest measure of psychotherapy's acceptance came in 1964. Ten years after Brando went so public with his treatment, Allan Sherman, the comedian and song parodist who had a finger on the pulse of middle-class American suburbia, released the album, *Allan in Wonderland*. The record included his takeoff on "I've Got a Little List" from *The Mikado*. The song offers a simple answer to those who are plagued by the likes of obsessiveness or imaginary ills, appreciate dubious modern art, or answer to the name "Bonaparte."

The title? "You Need an Analyst."

Ten

Poor Man's Brandos

While Marlon Brando continued his rise through Hollywood, many performers were influenced by his work. Others were swept along in his incredible path. Then again, you've got to feel at least a little sorry for the actors who followed or came up alongside Brando and found themselves unavoidably in his shadow, influenced, sometimes more than they'd admit, by his style and technique. Some became stars; some would be enshrined as legends. A few even went on to develop qualities that were recognized as unique from Marlon Brando's. Almost.

Of course, it all goes back to December 3, 1947, opening night for *A Streetcar Named Desire* on Broadway. The critics were awestruck by the complexity and power of Tennessee Williams's great artistic achievement (so great that, as *New York Times* critic Brooks Atkinson wrote, "it almost seems not to have been written but to be happening") and the performance of Jessica Tandy, who, in the starring role of the tragic Blanche DuBois, "is hardly ever off the stage and when she is on stage she is almost constantly talking." But although fewer words were offered in admiration of the rest of the cast, it was Marlon Brando as Stanley Kowalski who electrified the theater with a style that was so natural, so real, that it almost seemed to be happening. The *New York Times*: "Very high quality"; *Daily News*: "Magnificent"; *The New Yorker*: "Brutally effective"; Audience: "Pure Sex." Taught by Stella Adler, working with director Elia Kazan, Brando had not only changed the game, but raised the stakes.

Weeks before *Streetcar*'s opening, Kazan and his colleagues had opened The Actors Studio, a workshop for the Stanislavski method of using experience, emotional memory, and imagination to create a character. The method eventually morphed into "The Method," and because of his close work with Kazan, Brando was hailed as the ultimate "Method Actor." Brando disassociated himself from the term—and from Method acting guru Lee Strasberg, a Group Theatre founder who was handed the reins to the Actors Studio in 1951. Brando gave all credit to his New School teacher and mentor Stella Adler, the only Group Theatre member to have studied under Stanislavski. Strasberg taught the original version of The Method, which encouraged actors to find their characters through experience. For "experience," Adler substituted imagination, and Brando found that difference to be crucial.

(Brando did not always disavow The Method. In advance of the scene in *The Wild One* in which Johnny Strabler is beaten by the town vigilantes, stunt coordinator Cary Loftin found him running in place. "Hey, I'm a Method Actor," Brando said. "I have to be out of breath." Loftin recalled that Brando "seemed to be embarrassed.")

Wherever it came from, whatever it was, this was something new, something revolutionary, something *real*. So how could this be approximated? Give Strasberg credit for that, at least. Brando would claim he only ever sat in at an Actors Studio workshop because it was a good place to pick up chicks, but thanks to him, there would be a parade of aspiring actors, showing up in jeans and stained T-shirts, taking it all in, acting out scenes for Strasberg, mumbling their lines, trying to "be," and sitting through hours of dissections and critique. These would-be Garfields and Clifts, the first class of the "dungaree-and-dirty-shirt school of acting" wanted to be Brando, whether they admitted it or not.

Two of these Brando-point-twos were most obvious. There was the more sensitive "baby Brando," but despite his protestations, perhaps the saddest, most undeniable case was that of the "pretty boy Brando." He was a young actor from Shaker Heights, Ohio—well, not all *that* young, he was only nine months younger than Brando—a US Navy veteran who'd performed in summer stock theater and spent a year at the Yale School of Drama. He was already twenty-seven and married with a child when he arrived in New York City via Staten Island and managed to pass an audition into the Actors Studio. Though he'd stumble forward to success through roles originally intended for his much-younger friend and contemporary, this actor would not be known as "a second-rate James Dean." No, from the start, Paul Newman was derided as "the poor man's Marlon Brando."

"It was," author Shawn Levy claimed in *Paul Newman: A Life*, "a damning and frankly, dunderheaded claim. The two looked almost nothing alike; Brando was wide-faced with a bigger nose, thicker lips and heavily-lidded eyes; his vaguely simian air looked sensual and subversive. . . . Newman's features were always more angular and delicate. . . . He was pretty, preppy, and decent." Levy admits the "the two did share a similar brow line . . . but for the most part it was an absurd comparison." In 1955, however, there was no denying, with Brando already moving on beyond his sex symbol status and settling into a new kind of Hollywood stardom, that Newman was playing the Brando role, in live television drama and on Broadway.

The iconic, most telling image at this time was Eve Arnold's photograph of Newman in a workshop class at the Actors Studio. There are more than two dozen people in the picture, sitting on folding chairs, all eyes directed toward a performance, or more likely, a lecture. The men and women are well-dressed. The men wear ties; most wear jackets. All but one man: Paul Newman, in the foreground. He's the one watching intently, but posing. He's the only one in the picture who's sitting casually. His folding chair is turned around; he's got one foot on the seat, revealing a rolled pant leg, white sock, loafer, and a hint of ankle. He uses the back of the chair as an armrest, holding a cigarette, and—oh yeah, he's wearing, not a jacket, not a dress shirt—but a T-shirt. A white T-shirt. Add the Mark Antony haircut and, well, it does seem that the *Saturday Review* nailed it when they came up with the "poor man's Marlon Brando" tag.

Newman didn't like being compared to Brando, but he couldn't seem to step defiantly into his own. His time at the Actors Studio helped him grow "from his collegiate acting habits into something fluent, realistic, and professional. . . . 'It was monkey see, monkey do,'" he remembered. This blue-eyed Brando found work in television, and, in February 1953, made his Broadway debut as the second male lead in William Inge's *Picnic* (he was understudy for star Ralph Meeker, who'd replaced Brando in Broadway's *Streetcar*). He also began an affair with another understudy, Joanne Woodward, who in the past had dated Brando.

Newman continued to work in television during the *Picnic* run and began fielding film offers. In the summer of 1953, Elia Kazan considered casting him as Terry Malloy in *Waterfront* if Brando didn't come through. "He's just as good looking as Brando, and his masculinity, which is strong, is also more actual," Kazan wrote to Budd Schulberg. "He's not as good an actor as Brando yet, and probably will never be. But he's a darn good actor with plenty of power, plenty of insides, plenty of sex."

Months later, when Kazan set about casting *East of Eden*, a Cain and Abel story based on a section of the John Steinbeck novel, he first looked to Brando and Montgomery Clift to play the twin brothers Caleb and Aron Trask. Officially, the actors were unavailable. Realistically, they were too old for the parts. Kazan, who always liked working with new talent, looked to the Actors Studio bench. In February, he tested Newman and pal James Dean for the parts. The film clip shows that the two young men had chemistry. Perhaps the wrong kind of chemistry, for their behavior before the camera was, at the least, flirtatious. Kazan went with Dean as Cal. Richard Davalos would play his twin. Newman moved on. He signed a contract with Warner Bros. in April, parked his family in Wisconsin, where he and his wife had met in regional theater, and continued on to Hollywood.

By the time cameras rolled on *Eden* in May 1954 at the Warner Bros. studios in Burbank, Newman was also on the lot, filming his movie debut. *The Silver Chalice* was a first-century Christian historical epic filmed in big, colorful, widescreen CinemaScope. Newman had the central role of Basil, a Greek sculptor sold into slavery and later commissioned to create a silver case for the cup used by Jesus at the Last Supper. Dean had been offered the role, but he and his agent passed after reading the script.

As the premiere date approached, Newman may have gone out of his way to dismiss comparisons to Marlon Brando, but thanks to the studio flaks and gossip hacks, anticipation of the second coming was only stirred up. Two weeks before the film's premiere in New York City, the *Daily News* ran a preview article that featured a quote about Newman from his costar Virginia Mayo: "You are in for a surprise when you see this young actor. I think he is the most exciting personality to hit the screen since Brando arrived. He is a fine actor and suggests the same physical strength that Brando does."

The Silver Chalice opened in New York on Christmas Day, 1954, a year to the day after *The Wild One's* premiere, and five months after *On the Waterfront*. The opening credit read "*Introducing Paul Newman.*" The film would not get him closer to the Hollywood grail.

Kate Cameron, who'd penned the *News* preview piece, reviewed *The Silver Chalice* on Boxing Day. Newman, she wrote, was "disappointing"; his performance, "static." The *New York Times'* A. H. Weiler was more to the point about the suggestion of Brando. "Paul Newman, a recruit from Broadway and video, who is making his film debut in the role of Basil, bears a striking resemblance to Marlon Brando, but his contribution is hardly outstanding. As a youth who has been cheated of his rich inheritance by a covetous uncle, sold into slavery and eventually chosen to create the Holy relic, he is given mainly to thoughtful posing and automatic speechmaking. And despite the fact that he is desired by the extremely fetching Helena and the wistful Deborra, his wife, he's rarely better than wooden in his reaction to these fairly spectacular damsels."

Another tastemaker, Marjory Adams in the *Boston Globe*, wrote that Newman "looks so much like Marlon Brando that you blink a couple of times when he first appears on the screen. However, he does not match Mr. Brando when it comes to acting ability."

Newman was a month away from turning thirty. Brando had already moved on to a new phase in his career, playing the Hollywood game and making movies for the money. No longer Stanley Kowalski, Mark Antony, Johnny Strabler, or even Terry Malloy, he was most recently Napoleon in *Désirée*, another CinemaScope historical drama, which had opened in November. Brando would shock the columnists in February, when he, described by the United Press as "the leading exponent of the sweatshirt school of acting," showed up as "a new Marlon Brando, dapper in a tuxedo," at the Cocoanut Grove nightclub in the Ambassador Hotel for the Golden Globe awards. He was there to accept a Best Dramatic Actor award for his work in *On the Waterfront*. In March, he'd attend the Academy Awards show to pick up his Oscar for Best Actor.

In wake of the disappointing response to *The Silver Chalice*, Newman's attempts to tear off the Brando label seemed half-hearted. He returned to Broadway in February in *The Desperate Hours*, as one of three escaped convicts who hold a family hostage in their home. The role had him going up against Brando's *Streetcar* costar Karl Malden. "Paul Newman plays the boss thug with a wildness that one is inclined to respect," Brook Atkinson wrote in his *New York Times* review. Paul Newman was a wild one. The Brando name didn't need to be spelled out. (Newman later complained that during the run, "two fans approached me within forty seconds. The first one thought I was Jimmy Dean, and the second character mistook me for Brando.")

Newman did a nice, unexpected turn on live television in September, after he stepped in at the last minute—replacing James Dean—to play a teenager (at thirty) in a musical version of Thornton Wilder's *Our Town*. Frank Sinatra was the star of the NBC broadcast—with Nelson Riddle as music director and bespoke music and lyrics by Jimmy Van Heusen and Sammy Cahn. Newman "registered extremely well," according to *Variety*, "at the other end of the acting sphere from his more-typed *Desperate Hours* 'heavy' characterization." Reviews like that might have helped him step farther from the Brando comparisons—if the highlight of Newman's performance was not his duet with Eva Marie Saint, now a Hollywood star thanks to her Academy Award-winning role in *On the Waterfront*. And Sinatra? Well, he'd recently wrapped filming the musical *Guys and Dolls*, with Brando in the starring role that Sinatra wanted and felt he deserved.

That same month, Newman signed for another NBC television play. *The Battler* was based on an Ernest Hemingway short story in which the writer's fictional, wandering alter ego, Nick Adams, meets up with a punch-drunk, washed-up former boxing champ. No worries about *Waterfront* comparisons here. Newman was to play Nick Adams. The boxer role would be handled by his pal, James Dean. All was moving forward until the last day of September when, two weeks before the live broadcast, Dean crashed his 1955 Porsche 550 Spyder on US Route 466 near Cholame, California, about nineteen miles east of Paso Robles. Dean, whose second film, *Rebel Without a Cause*, had not yet been released, and who had just that week completed work on *Giant*, was dead at twenty-four.

The show, it was insisted, had to go on, but how? Paul Newman was convinced to switch roles. He would play Ad Francis, the battler. Dewey

Martin stepped in as Nick Adams. It was a risky move, days before a live television broadcast, but it paid off. *Broadcasting* magazine said Newman's portrayal was "a gem." The *New York Times* called it "quite effective." Newman got off easy. He was free to move on to something unique. He chose another boxing movie.

It was another role in another project that had been left open by the death of James Dean. *Somebody Up There Likes Me*, directed by Robert Wise, was based on the autobiography of Rocky Graziano, the former middleweight boxing champion and current television personality and actor. With this choice, there were bound to be more Brando comparisons in store. Brando had not only won an Academy Award for his portrayal of the former pug Terry Malloy, but it was public knowledge that Graziano had been his muse. Years earlier, when he was appearing on Broadway in *Streetcar*, Brando had kept in shape by boxing and working out at Stillman's Gym on Eighth Avenue and Fifty-Fourth Street, where crowds would gather to watch Graziano train for his prizefights. The actor stuck up a friendship with the boxer, all the while studying Graziano, incorporating parts of him into his Stanley Kowalski. Graziano revealed in his book that he'd assumed that Brando was just another mug. "He looked like he might have been a fair fighter once, but he was in bad condition for the ring now and his punch looked slow. I felt sorry for the kid. He rode round town on a secondhand motorcycle, wearing patched-up blue jeans. Whenever we went downstairs for a cup of coffee or anything, I always paid for it."

A few years later, when Brando was cast as a boxer in a live television pilot called *Come Out Fighting!*, he based his character on his old pal, Rock. "I am watching the television, and they introduce this show about fighting and his name is on the screen, and then he comes on and it's me!" Graziano wrote. "The son of a bitch is talking like me and walking like me and punching like me! How you like that? I got conned into learning this bum his part by a motorcycle and a pair of blue jeans."

Somebody Up There Likes Me, starring Paul Newman in a part originally set for James Dean about a real-life figure who'd already been a model for Marlon Brando, opened at the Loew's State Theatre in Times Square on July 5, 1956. Somewhat ironically, this would be the film in which Paul Newman would step out of Marlon Brando's shadow.

Bosley Crowther agreed that Newman "plays the role of Graziano well," although he said the actor did so by "making the pug and Marlon Brando almost indistinguishable. He is funny, tough and pathetic in that slouching, rolling, smirking Brando style, but with a quite apparent simulation of the mannerisms of the former champ."

By now, it seemed that critics were ready to give Newman a break, understanding that he had incorporated some of Brando into his very

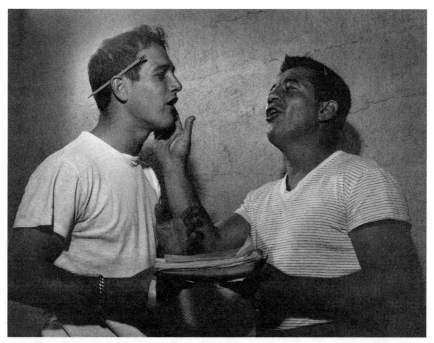

Paul Newman hated being compared to Brando, but he came into his own in *Somebody Up There Likes Me*, in the Brandoesque role of boxer Rocky Graziano, Brando's friend and model for Stanley Kowalski in *Streetcar*. PictureLux / The Hollywood Archive / Alamy Stock Photo

being while showing enough individuality to distance himself from the young rebel Brando—just as Brando had done. "Everything about his Graziano has a blistering rightness, a sense of the factual," Harold C. Cohen wrote in the *Pittsburgh Post-Gazette*. "A lot of people will see a striking similarity between Mr. Newman in *Somebody Up There Likes Me* and Mr. Marlon Brando in *On the Waterfront*. Mr. Newman insists he copied Mr. Graziano for the role; there have been inklings that Mr. Brando did, too. So let the matter drop. After all, Mr. Brando has no monopoly on this school of acting."

Newman's career continued and began to thrive, but the Brando comparisons stuck. In November 1958, he exploded when UPI's entertainment reporter Vernon Scott made a mention. "Why does everyone have to put labels on actors? It never fails. Sooner or later, every newcomer to Hollywood is told he is 'another somebody or other!' First they said I looked like Brando. Then it was agreed that we had the same 'quality,'" he raged, his voice giving air quotes to "quality." "All I want to know is *what quality*? I've yet to have anyone come up with the answer to that."

Scott wrote that "Paul simmered down somewhat," and eventually admitted that Brando did indeed have a "'quality'. . . a rebellious attitude which I don't believe I have. I've also been compared with Jimmy Dean, but Jimmy's quality was a lost little boy point of view.

"I've met Marlon several times. Neither of us thought we resembled one another. I probably could have capitalized on the comparisons by tearing around on a motorcycle and being as independent as Marlon is, but I don't want any part of that. I try to keep my off-screen life to myself. Not long ago, I told Brando I have signed more autographs with his name than he has."

Newman spelled out what he felt were the important qualities that separated him from Brando. "Some actors deal best with the roles that are most closely associated with themselves. I think Marlon is one of them. The closer the characterization to his own personality, the better. It's the opposite with me. I'm more effective playing parts which are farthest from my own self. I also enjoy doing them most.

"Any way you look at it, I don't think Brando and I look alike, act alike or do we have the same 'quality.' Frankly, I'd like to drop the entire subject once and for all."

Then he went off to his small, rented house in a Hollywood canyon, where he'd shared a very Brandoesque aphorism with James Bacon, Associated Press's Hollywood correspondent: "The only sane way for an actor to maintain his integrity in this town is to be a bum."

Decades later, Newman was still explaining his way out of the Brando label and why he was truly a contender and not a bum at all. "I tried very hard to put at least my version of Graziano on the screen. They accused me of imitating Marlon Brando," he told Iain Johnstone of the BBC in 1982. "Marlon and I had both the same basic character that we were dealing with. He had taken Rocky and put him up on the stage in *Streetcar* and I put him up on the screen in *Somebody Up There Likes Me*."

Paul Newman did not have a monopoly on Brando-aping, and he wasn't even the most blatant example at the time. Newman's friend and rival James Dean had a similar but quite different story. Newman was less than a year younger than Brando, a late bloomer to whom the Brando comparisons were an irritation. Dean, close to seven years Brando's junior, did not resemble Brando. If Brando was full-lipped and sensuous, Dean was delicate and shy. Where Brando could exude cockiness, Dean was awkward and withdrawn. He lacked the danger of *The Wild One*. He was submissive. But from the time he stepped into the Actors Studio, first under the eye of Lee Strasberg and then under the tutorship of Elia Kazan, he was imitating Marlon Brando. James Dean loved Marlon Brando, He loved his art and abilities. He loved his style. He wanted to be him. He wanted to be with him. His legacy was rescued by the fact that his Brandoisms were confined to some television work and three films.

And then he died.

Dean was a Midwesterner like Brando. Born in Indiana, he, like Brando, spent time in California as a boy. He was six when his parents moved to Santa Monica. Dean's mother died of cancer three years later, and his father shipped him, along with his mother's casket, back to Indiana, where he was raised by an aunt and uncle in the town of Fairmont. He attended Fairmont High School, played sports, acted in plays, and after graduation in 1949, returned to California.

He enrolled at Santa Monica College, where he studied pre-law, and spent a semester at UCLA, where he transferred his major to drama, played Malcolm in a student production of *Macbeth* in the fall of 1950, and soon quit school to pursue acting. His first television role was in a Pepsi Cola commercial. He did some bit parts, walk-ons in films and television, and moved to New York City in 1951.

Dean was accepted at the Actors Studio in 1952 under Lee Strasberg, and at that time was already obsessed with Brando. In his book, *The Method: How the Twentieth Century Learned to Act*, Isaac Butler writes that "to study Brando's mannerisms, Dean watched *The Men* again and again and read press reports about his idol's research process." Dean got more work on live television, and on December 3, 1953, made his Broadway debut at the Cort Theatre in *See the Jaguar*. The play closed on December 6, after five performances, but Dean was a standout in a supporting role as Willie Wilkins, a naïve boy from the mountains. Walter Kerr in the *Herald Tribune* praised his "extraordinary performance in an almost impossible role: that of a bewildered lad who has been completely shut off from a vicious world by an overzealous mother." *Jaguar* led to more substantial "teenage" roles, including another part on Broadway the following February. Dean received good reviews, smeared in brown makeup as an effeminate Arab houseboy in *The Immoralist*, but he wasn't comfortable playing a homosexual and tendered his resignation on opening night.

Dean's friends and colleagues thought he was crazy to quit a play hours before the positive notices showed up in the morning papers. They didn't know that Elia Kazan had seen the play in previews and was considering Dean for the role of Caleb Trask in *East of Eden*. The screen test with Paul Newman followed. In March, Kazan announced the casting of Dean, "bright new star of the New York stage," as the male lead. In a letter to Steinbeck, Kazan wrote that he'd "looked thru a lot of kids before settling on this Jimmy Dean . . . the best of a poor field.

"He hasn't Brando's stature, but he's a good deal younger and is very interesting, has balls and eccentricity and a 'real problem' somewhere in his guts, I don't know what or where." Dean also had, in Kazan's view, "a real mean streak and a real sweet streak."

As filming on *East of Eden* commenced near the end of May, Kazan didn't have the same collaborative relationship with the young actor that he once had with Brando. The director did see immediately that Dean had an affinity for his former leading man, and had soaked up some of the Brandoisms and techniques that Kazan helped instill. But there was something more. After moving to Hollywood, Dean was emulating Brando in real life, tearing up the streets on a motorcycle, walking into proper joints in T-shirt and jeans, mumbling, and being described as "rude, moody and eccentric," as Brando had once been. Dean was even playing conga drums! Kazan got hold of Brando, who was wrapping *Désirée* on the 20th Century-Fox lot. "You've got to meet this kid."

"Before introducing us, Gadg told me that his new star was constantly asking about me and seemed bent on patterning his acting technique and life after me—or at least on the person he thought I was after seeing *The Wild One*," Brando recalled in *Songs*. "He was not only mimicking my acting but also what he believed was my lifestyle. He said he was learning to play the conga drums and had taken up motorcycling, and he obviously wanted my approval of his work." That was problematic. Dean had confused Marlon Brando with Johnny Strabler. That character, after all, was one a young would-be rebel could easily identify with. Brando, however, was not Johnny Strabler any more than he was Stanley Kowalski or Napoleon. His role in *The Wild One* was just that—a role—and any similarities between Brando the motorcycle racing, T-shirt-wearing, mumbling rebel were, as far as he was concerned, purely coincidental. He was playing the Hollywood game, now, going along with the charade and taking studio roles in CinemaScope pictures because that's how he could make money. Easy money. James Dean, like Paul Newman, was inheriting a style that Brando had, simply, outgrown.

Brando could, of course, identify with the kid. Dean was a midwestern boy who'd spent time on a farm, and part of his childhood in California. Like Brando, he had daddy issues. Brando could sympathize with Dean's awkwardness, sensitivity, and sudden celebrity. Dean was twenty-three, the same age as Brando when *Streetcar* opened on Broadway. Brando says he felt sorry for him.

The day after they met and posed for some photos on the *Eden* set, Dean showed up, unannounced, on the set of *Désirée*. Still wearing his wardrobe from the previous day's shoot, he sat and studied Brando, watching slack-jawed as Brando worked through a scene as Napoleon. A few nights later, there was a party at Sammy Davis Jr.'s house. Brando was there, and so was James Dean, hanging back, watching his hero, working up the courage to step up and chat. Brando turned away, iced the kid. Dean slunk off, went into another room, and started banging on a set of bongo drums. To be blunt, he was creeping Brando out.

Brando wouldn't say Dean's name in public, referring to him as "the kid." When Dean would call, invite him out, or ask for advice, Brando says he encouraged the kid not to imitate him. When Dean would open up about his traumatic childhood and insecurities, Brando ultimately told him to see a shrink. "I urged him to seek assistance," Brando, who was in regular consultation with psychiatrist Dr. Mittelmann, said in *Songs*, "perhaps go into therapy."

Because of the actors' bisexuality there have been many stories alleging that Dean and Brando had an affair. Darwin Porter and Danforth Price, the controversial and immensely entertaining Hollywood biographers whose intimately detailed recreations of celebrity sexual couplings and conversations during coitus veer to the edge of fan fiction and often tumble in, made headlines in 2006 when, in their book, *James Dean: Tomorrow Never Comes*, they alleged that Brando and Dean had an extended S&M master-slave relationship. Brando denied any sexual encounters. He said he believed Dean "regarded me as a kind of older brother or mentor, and I suppose I responded to him as if I was." He also insisted that although he and Dean talked on the phone and ran into each other at parties, they "never became close." Brando was more annoyed than honored by the admiration. "I told him I thought he was foolish to try to copy me as an actor. 'Jimmy, you have to be who you are, not who I am. You mustn't try to copy me. Emulate the best aspects of yourself.'"

Dean would have been better off taking big brother's advice. Three weeks before *East of Eden* premiered in New York City on March 9 (six months and twenty-one days before Dean's untimely death in the crash of his Porsche), *Variety* got the jump on the critics, publishing its review of *East of Eden*. Dean's debt to Brando did not go unnoticed.

"Much pro and con probably will develop about James Dean, unknown to whom Kazan gives a full-scale introduction. It is no credit to Kazan that Dean seems required to play his lead character as though he was straight out of a Marlon Brando mold. Just how flexible his talent is will have to be judged on future screen roles, although he has a basic appeal that manages to get through to the viewer despite the heavy burden of carboning another's acting style in voice and mannerisms. It should be interesting to see what he can do as Dean."

Bosley Crowther at the *New York Times* took his shot the day after the premiere. "This young actor, who is here doing his first big screen stint, is a mass of histrionic gingerbread," the critic declared. "He scuffs his feet, he whirls, he pouts, he sputters, he leans against walls, he rolls his eyes, he swallows his words, he ambles slack-kneed—all like Marlon Brando used to do. Never have we seen a performer so clearly follow another's style. Mr. Kazan should be spanked for permitting him to do such a sophomoric thing."

In Los Angeles, at the *Times* a week later, Philip K. Scheuer couldn't miss the Brando in Dean's Cal Trask. "The redoubtable James Dean—about whom, even for Hollywood an extraordinary amount of nonsense has been written . . . combines the worst features of the Marlon Brando prototype, the shambling and the mumbling, with such an instinctive feeling for the loneliness of a boy who wants terribly to be loved that when a pitiful crumb of that love is finally tossed his way, our tears rejoice with him."

"Straight out of Marlon Brando mold. . . . Never have we seen a performer so clearly follow another's style. . . . The worst features of the Marlon Brando prototype. . . ." Displaying such public obeisance and outright mimicry on screen and in life, what could Dean have expected? And how could he respond? How else, but denying all?

"I do not idolize Marlon Brando!" United Press writer Aline Mosby wrote that James Dean "snorted" the words when the subject came up in a feature story in April. "If I imitate him subconsciously, I don't know about it. If I do it consciously, I'd be a fool to admit it."

Mosby countered that "some observers think Dean took over where Brando left off after he gave up T-shirts for tuxedos," in light of the fact that he was known for wearing "blue jeans and T-shirts," and even renting "a house in the Hollywood Hills so he could ride his motorcycle up a cliff in his backyard."

"Brando drove a motorcycle for effect," Dean volleyed. "I drive one because I know how."

A month later, Bob Thomas was observing Dean at the Griffith Observatory overlooking Los Angeles, where the actor was filming a scene for *Rebel Without a Cause.* "In his first important film, he emerged as a star of first magnitude," Thomas wrote. "No other debut of a virtual unknown in recent years has appeared so auspicious." But then there was "the comparison to Marlon Brando . . . pointed out by most reviewers." By now, the Warner Bros. publicity department had prepared their young star on how to respond to such allegations. "It doesn't bother me," Dean insisted. "When a new actor comes along, he's always compared to someone else. Brando was compared to Clift. Clift to someone else, Barrymore to Booth and so forth. I don't particularly like the dwelling on the comparison of Marlon and me. But there's nothing in particular I can do about it. I can only do the best kind of job I can, the realest acting. They can compare me to W. C. Fields if they want to."

Noting "strong indications there is no love lost between Brando and Dean," Thomas brought up the comparisons in Dean's personal life, "because he rides motorcycles and beats jungle drums."

"I've been riding motorcycles since I was fifteen," Dean retorted. "And," Thomas added, "he plays the conga drums, not the bongos à la Marlon." (Brando beat on both bongos and congas.)

Months later, just prior to *East of Eden*'s opening in the United Kingdom, Dean was still spouting his denials. "People were saying I was like Marlon Brando before I even met him. I am not disturbed by the comparison or even flattered. I have my own personal rebellion. I don't have to rely on Brando's."

Jympson Harman in the *Liverpool Echo* had a different take. He blamed the Brando comparisons on "the studio 'build-up.' They tell me he tears about on motorcycles, wearing old clothes, with girls in the pillion seat. He is 'aloof and downright rude.' He reads 'six books at once for preference'—from 'Aztec culture to expressionistic literature.' He plays all kinds of sports and wants to be a bullfighter. He loves music and has an alarm clock on his gramophone to wake him in the morning with music. We heard this kind of thing about Brando. I'm sorry, but I don't believe it about Dean."

Harman wrote that although Dean "comes from the same New York school of naturalistic acting that produced Marlon Brando" and "talks with the Brando muddled slur," the younger actor revealed in *Eden* "a degree of sensitivity lacking in the other. . . . In my opinion, Dean is going to be better than Brando."

In her newspaper dispatch in April, Aline Mosby had written that her interview with Dean took place "in a white sports car, a German Porsche . . . while we wheeled around corners at 50 mph." "I would like to be a star in my own sense," he told her. "I mean to be a very consummate actor, to have more difficult roles and fill them to my satisfaction." Bob Thomas reported that Dean had "one of the most favorable contracts ever granted a newcomer by a studio . . . nine pictures in the next six years at Warners, with 1956 off for a Broadway play."

Everyone figured he had time to outgrow the comparisons.

At this point, is it "rubbing it in" to recall that Marlon Brando was the original choice for the starring role in *Rebel Without a Cause*? Eight years earlier, Warner Bros. had bought the rights to a 1944 book by Dr. Robert Lindner entitled *Rebel Without a Cause: The Hypnoanalysis of a Criminal Psychopath*. The book recounted the psychiatrist's work with a prison inmate named Harold, who, it would be revealed, lashed out against society because he'd witnessed his parents having sex when he was a baby. Screenwriter Peter Viertel had assembled a treatment; producer Jerry Wald gave the project some heat; stage actor Sam Wanamaker wanted to play the doctor and urged the producers to get "the greatest young actor in America today" to play Harold. So, months before he opened on Broadway in *Streetcar*, and under pressure from his agent and a need to

James Dean, another Hollywood rebel, was in love with Marlon Brando—although Brando soon realized the young actor was actually in love with Johnny Strabler from ***The Wild One.*** Warner Bros./Photofest © Warner Bros.

pay the rent, twenty-three-year-old Brando filmed the five-minute screen test for what could have been his first Hollywood picture. The project was eventually dropped, and when it was picked up again in 1955, there were new writers and a new script, the prison angle was gone, and the adult Brando was replaced by the teenlike Dean. Only the title remained.

Rebel wrapped production on May 26, and Dean jumped right into his next project. *Giant*, directed by George Stevens, was a sprawling epic based on Edna Ferber's book about a family of Texas cattle ranchers. Dean was Jett Rink, another troubled outsider, a ranch hand who becomes an oil tycoon, in a story that spans the course of twenty-five years. There was still work to be done on the picture on September 30 when Dean took his last ride. (Nick Adams, a young actor who'd appeared in *Rebel* and in fact loved Dean as much as Dean loved Brando, dubbed his voice in several spots.)

Rebel Without a Cause, directed by Nicholas Ray, opened at the Astor Theatre in Manhattan on October 26, 1955. It was immediately compared to, and paired with, *Blackboard Jungle*, Richard Brooks's recent film about a teacher trying to make a difference at a violent school for boys. Crowther in the *Times* called *Rebel* "an excessively graphic exercise . . . a violent, brutal and disturbing picture of modern teenagers . . . neglected by their parents or given no understanding and moral support by fathers and mothers who are themselves unable to achieve balance and security in their homes. Like *Blackboard Jungle* before it, it is a picture to make the hair stand on end."

Only this time, the terror was closer to home for middle Americans. The teens in *Rebel*, played by Natalie Wood and Sal Mineo, both sixteen when filming started, and Dean, more than slightly older, at twenty-four, "are several social cuts above the vocational high school hoodlums in that previous film. They are children of well-to-do parents living in comfortable homes and attending a well-appointed high school in the vicinity of Los Angeles. But they are none the less mordant in their manners and handy with switch-blade knives. They are, in the final demonstration, lonely creatures in their own strange cultist world."

Dean was twenty-seven days dead, yet Crowther didn't hold back on holding him and his costars to account for being "so intent on imitating Marlon Brando in various degrees." Dean's imitation was even more obvious than it had been in *East of Eden*. The red Harrington windbreaker jacket, T-shirt and jeans worn by his character Jim Stark were as much a costume as the fussy leather jacket and jeans combo sported by another "J. S.," Johnny Strabler, in *The Wild One*. And while Brando had made his bones with his anguished cries of "Hey Stella!" onstage and screen, Dean came out with his own rebel yell in the picture's opening minutes. In custody at a police station after being picked up as a drunk, facing his parents and other figures of authority, Jim suddenly wails, *"You're tearing me apart!"* Brando's cry was an expression of pure animal sex. It caused chills. Dean's was a whine from a boy. When Ray follows with a reaction shot of his parents looking down at him, out of frame, one could imagine them looking at a baby, having a tantrum in a crib. When his mother snaps, "That's a fine way to behave!" Jim wails and hides his face in the jacket that he clutches like a blankie.

That was a major difference. At twenty-four, Brando was *The Man*. At twenty-four, to many, James Dean was a boy. He was the teen idol version of the dangerous rebel. "He had a personality and presence that made audiences curious about him, as well as looks and a vulnerability that women found especially appealing," Brando said. "They wanted to take care of him. He was sensitive." That sensitivity, that awkwardness and self-doubt was something that the newly rising youth generation could relate to, and were reasons why, even before *Rebel* had screened across the country, the James Dean death cult was in full swing.

Would Dean have outgrown the Brando influence had his Porsche 550 Spyder not smashed into Donald Turnupseed's 1950 Ford Tudor at the junction of Highways 466 and 41? He may have been on his way. After *Giant* premiered in New York City on October 10, 1956, *Variety* raved that he'd delivered a "sock performance." Crowther gave him credit as well. "It is the late James Dean who makes the malignant role of this early ranch hand who becomes an oil baron the most tangy and corrosive in the film. Mr. Dean plays this curious villain with a stylized spookiness—a sly sort of off-beat languor and slur of language—that concentrates spite. This is a haunting capstone to the brief career of Mr. Dean."

Dean would receive posthumous Best Actor Academy Awards nomination in 1956 for *East of Eden* (he lost to Ernest Borgnine in *Marty*) and the following year for his work in *Giant* (Yul Brynner took the Oscar for *The King and* I). Just as Brando did not receive a nomination for *The Wild One*, Dean was not recognized for his most culturally significant role.

"People identified with his pain and made him a cult hero," Brando said in *Songs*. "We can only guess what kind of actor he would have become in another twenty years. I think he could have become a great one. Instead, he died and was forever entombed in his myth."

Eleven

"Johnny, I Love You"

Bosley Crowther, film critic for the *New York Times*, sensed there was something about Johnny Strabler and his rival Chino that he couldn't quite pin down, but in his review of *The Wild One*, he came close. Of Brando's character, he wrote: "In this taut and eerie hoodlum is fleetingly but forcibly revealed the consequence of youthful frustrations recompensed by association with a cult. Mr. Brando . . . barely exposes his battered ego from behind a ferocious front." With Chino, Crowther saw,

> a second wolf-pack leader, whom Lee Marvin gruesomely portrays as a glandular "psycho" or dope-fiend or something fantastically mad, there was briefly injected into this picture a glimpse of utter monstrosity, loose and enjoying the privilege of hectoring others in a fair society. Unfortunately, the picture is not permitted to remain in these realms. . . . They begin by bringing the gang leader, Mr. Brando, into contact with a girl—a good, clean, upright small-town beauty—who apparently fills him with love. . . . It so happens that Mr. Marvin is permitted to disappear when the romance begins to blossom, and that is unfortunate, too.

Crowther was indeed close—about as close as any film critic or censor at the time would get to the relationship between the two cyclists who'd known each other in the past. Strabler's "ferocious front" was the "consequence of youthful frustrations." Chino "is permitted to disappear when the romance begins to blossom, and that is unfortunate."

The critics didn't see it—or at least didn't say it out loud—but over the years, viewers and reviewers alike have come to recognize that what could be called a "queer reading" of *The Wild One* is a straightforward reading, as well. The choices Brando made in the way he portrayed Johnny Strabler, a young man who knew he could not fit in with straight society—the way he dressed, the way he spoke, and the way he moved—only added to what was already spelled out in the script. It was indeed unfortunate that Lee Marvin's Chino was "permitted to disappear when the romance begins to blossom," because the real romance in the film was not between Johnny and Kathie Bleeker, that "good, clean, upright small-town beauty"—or, as Johnny called her, the "sad chick"—played by Mary Murphy. It's clear that Johnny's romance with Chino was far more passionate, the breakup more painful. In most cases, especially in the waning era of the Production Code, these signals are subtext, between the lines. In *The Wild One*, they are text.

They *are* the lines.

We get a taste of Johnny and Chino's backstory about twenty-eight minutes into the film, when Johnny, clutching the admittedly phallic second-place trophy his boys "gleeped" (stole) for him at the races in Carbondale, is ready to pull out of Wrightsville just as Chino and his gang come rolling in. Johnny and Chino once rode together. They had a history, and quite possibly that history was romantic. Their breakup was a bad one.

The scene is worth summarizing: Upbeat jazz music heralds the arrival of the Black Rebels' rivals. Chino is at the head of the pack. He wears a striped shirt and vest. His visorless hat, affixed with aviator goggles and combined with a scarf, gives the appearance of a pirate's headscarf. Chino could be a pirate clown, and possibly a drunken clown, as he uncorks a stogie from his mouth and shouts out to the timid citizens on the sidewalks: "Hello! Hey! What you doing tonight? Hey!" The group he leads is a ragtag bunch as well, very different in style from the Black Rebels in their uniform of black leather and blue denim. The men in Chino's gang wear skunk hats, Scottish tams, fake beards, buckskins, and all styles of surplus jackets and coats. And they come with a contingent of women. While the boys in the Black Rebels Motorcycle Club look not unsimilar to the gay leather club members already showing up in cities including San Francisco and Los Angeles—where Brando had done some research before filming—this group is "rough trade" in appearance, far more like the real-life outlaw bikers who had taken to the highways after World War II (Lee Marvin modeled his character after Wino Willie—in turn, Hells Angels president Sonny Barger would adopt Chino's look).

Chino rides past the long line of Rebel motorcycles parked on one side of the main drag, circles around and recognizes right away the one bike among many that belongs to Johnny. As he regards the second-place trophy poking up between the handlebars, there is, for a flash, a serious look on his face. "Hey," he calls out to the gang. "The Rebels are here! Hey, the Rebels! Come on! Yeah, looks like Johnny's here!"

Johnny is in Bleeker's Bar with his boys. They'd stayed in town longer than expected because one of them, Crazy, had injured his ankle while drag racing in the town square. Now Crazy has been repaired by the local doctor, and the boys want to celebrate with beers all 'round. But Johnny, having found out that Kathie's father is the town police chief, had taken his phallic trophy and strapped it to the front of his Triumph. "Let's get outta here," he says. The boys protest. "No, man," he says, "it's a drag, come on."

Johnny exits the bar, walks through the crowd of Rebels, and comes face-to-face with Chino, slouched over the handlebars of his Harley, surrounded by his cyclists. Their eyes meet. Johnny looks down at the trophy that his boys had gifted him, now tied to Chino's bike.

"Hiya, sweetheart," Chino says. "Hey, what are doing in this miserable gully, Johnny, my love?"

Johnny stares back, then looks down.

Chino says, "I love you, Johnny. I been looking for ya in every ditch from Fresno to here, hoping you was dead."

Johnny's boys figure that Chino's expression of love is only an act. "Chino's givin' him the needle," one of them tells Kathie, who's joined the gathering crowd.

Chino looks around. He laughs, knowingly. "Uh. Hahaha. You've been having yourself a time, huh, Johnny?"

Johnny takes a step toward him.

"You know, you do look pale," Chino observes. "You been takin' care of yourself? You been staying out too late at night?"

Johnny motions toward the trophy. "That's mine, Chino. Take it off."

Chino strokes the little man on the motorcycle on the head of the trophy. Johnny reaches for it. Chino swats his hand.

"Don't do that," Johnny says, coolly.

Chino does it again and Johnny pushes him off the bike, into the dirt. Chino lands on his back, his head clanking against a cycle's fork. He recovers quickly, and smiles.

"Now that's better, Johnny." He gets to his feet. "You know, I missed you. Ever since the club split up, I missed you. We all missed ya! Did you miss him? Yeah! The beetles missed ya!" He gestures to the female contingent. "All the beetles missed ya! C'mon, Johnny. Let's you and me go inside and have a beer—and I'll beat the living Christmas out of you." Chino softens, approaches Johnny at his cycle, where Johnny is reclaiming his trophy, and reaches out. "Johnny, for old times—"

Johnny shoves him, hard. "Aw, don't take that away from Chino." As Johnny methodically unties the trophy from Chino's bike, Chino resorts to a type of baby talk. "It's so beautiful. Chino needs it. Makes Chino feel like a big strong man. Yeah, Chino wants to be a big racetrack hero with all these girls. Pow, huh?" When he doesn't get a reaction, Chino gets serious. "Look, I didn't win it, Johnny. I just gleeped it. But I gleeped it off a guy that didn't win it, either."

Kathie looks disappointed when she hears that. Johnny had offered her the trophy at their first meeting.

"Look, Johnny, you want one?" Chino whines. "How about you go gleep one someplace yourself, huh?" He grabs Johnny from behind in a bear hug and grabs the trophy. Johnny spins, throws Chino off and nails him on the chin with a right. Chino falls back and knocks over a couple of bikes. His boys pull him up; he's got the trophy in his hand. By now he's noticed he has a rival. Kathie is on the sidewalk, watching anxiously. "Now wait a minute, wait a minute. Wait a minute!" Chino announces. "All right, this is the main event. Now, ladies and gentlemen, this lovely young lady over here shall hold this beautiful object, signifying absolutely nothing." Now, he's giving Kathie the needle. "Now, watch closely! See how the timid maiden of the hill clutches the gold to her breast. And see how she fights back a tear, while her hero bleeds to death in the street." With that, Chino turns and sucker-punches Johnny, knocking him back to the street.

"C'mon! Get up, ya big hero!" As Johnny rises, Chino kicks him down and leaps on his back. In a headlock, his right arm pinned behind his back, Johnny uses his free arm to reach between his own legs and pull Chino's leg out from under him. He pulls Chino up—and with a couple of pops to the chin, sends him sprawling.

The crowd—cyclists and townsfolk alike—cheers, while one of the locals pushes through to old Jimmy, the dishwasher at Bleeker's Café and Bar. "What happened? What are they fighting about?"

"Don't know." Jimmy replies. "Don't know themselves, probably."

What are Johnny and Chino fighting about? The two men are locked in an embrace, rolling around on the ground. They wind up on their feet, in front of Miss Emma's Millinery shop, while Charlie Thomas, a "local bully," threatens to take action if the ineffectual police chief won't. "If you can't boot these jerks out, there's plenty of us who can—even if we have to bust a few heads." Another head is about to be busted. Johnny slugs Chino with a left that sends him crashing through the millinery shop window and its display, landing between two mannequins whose symbolism could hardly be more obvious: a groom and a bride.

When Johnny pulls Chino back onto the sidewalk, the mannequin groom has lost its head. The bride is no longer there at all. Five more punches and, despite the urging of his gang, Chino's had enough. He's flat out, on the street. He struggles to stand before falling back. He smiles. "Johnny," he says, "I love you."

And there it is. Amid the clowning by Chino, the references to the "beetles"—his gang's female followers—and the plot machinations setting up the conflict between the vigilantes and the trouble-making cyclists, a love scene has played out—a love scene between two males, one old-school macho, the other a sensuous new kind of adolescent—in the only way it could be played out on screen in 1953. And it's Chino,

"Johnny, I love ya!" With Lee Marvin in *The Wild One*. Johnny's relationship with Chino was passionate, and then some. Columbia Pictures/Photofest © Columbia

the "butch" half, who makes it clear: "Hiya, sweetheart. . . . I love you, Johnny. I been looking for ya in every ditch from Fresno to here. . . . I missed you. Ever since the club split up, I missed you." And finally, after Chino comes between a bride and groom and literally knocks the bride out of the picture: "Johnny, I love you."

"Johnny, I love you." *The Deer Hunter*, Michael Cimino's picture released twenty-five years after *The Wild One*, leads to a scene in which Robert De Niro returns to Saigon in search of his lost love played by Christopher Walken. While attempting, desperately and in vain, to rescue his man from a life as a heroin-addicted professional Russian Roulette player, De Niro's Michael reveals his passion for his former housemate Nick, exclaiming "I love you" while playing the game, holding a revolver to his head. What did he have to lose? Chino's expression of love for Johnny was far more daring, and dangerous, and had to be covered up by humor, or violence.

"This dialogue is pointedly gay," says film historian and author David Del Valle.

It's very thinly-veiled homosexual banter which Brando would have heartily approved of. It's all there. It's all in the script. And it didn't register because of the way it was directed and handled. By using Lee Marvin, whose voice and persona, if he's in a kind of playful mood, as he is in this, you don't interpret anything sexual. They're not being overtly sexual but they're giving a tip of the hat to what they're like in private. "Johnny, I love ya," that would just go over the heads of a 1953 audience. The whole idea of the gang being outside the law, they're also outside the normal community of behavior. So what you see there is male-male bonding, which would only be interpreted like that in 1953. But it's very easy now that we're looking at it to see what it really is.

In his book *Phallic Frenzy: Ken Russell and His Films*, Joseph Lanza writes of the groundbreaking scene in the 1969 film *Women in Love*, in which Alan Bates and Oliver Reed—as "Rupert and Gerald"—wrestle in front of a crackling fireplace, in the nude, "a prelude to Rupert's verbal flirtation to Gerald on 'two kinds of love,' neither of them platonic."

"There was certainly never anything like it on the screen before: two males, entirely naked, locked in combat yet suddenly looking as if they're dying to taste each other." Perhaps no mainstream director had yet gone as far in portraying repressed sexual longing as did Russell in his adaption of the D. H. Lawrence novel, yet surely the reflections of the embracing, heterosexual matrimony-smashing Chino and Johnny Strabler can be seen reflected in the firelight amid the sweaty grappling between the macho, heavy-drinking Oliver Reed and the sensitive Alan Bates (Reed in real life was a heavy drinker—as was Marvin; Bates, like Brando, had many homosexual relationships). Bates and Reed would express their passion by wrestling nude in front of a fireplace. In *The Wild One*, Johnny and Chino fight, as closeted men amid a hetero male subculture might, expressing their repressed homosexual desires by brawling, wrestling, and embracing while clothed.

"The fight scene in *The Wild One* is choreographed exactly for this purpose. Wrestling is a Greek exercise," Del Valle says. "*The Wild One* is an influencer, and I know Ken Russell saw it. I know Ken has talked about *The Wild One*. It's not a favorite, but like everyone else he recognizes the iconic status of Brando's costume and posturing."

Del Valle saw another unmistakable a parallel to the Johnny-Chino relationship in *The Wild One* when, in 1985, he was invited to an early screening of *Top Gun* on the Paramount Studios lot. "The film was relentless in hammering home the homoerotic longing among the attractive male cast," he said. "One scene after another paired Maverick and Ice, played by Tom Cruise and Val Kilmer, nose-to-nose, shirtless and wet. The attraction between Maverick and Ice was far more intense than that between Cruise and Kelly McGillis as the flight instructor. And her role might have made more sense had it been played by a man, since I don't know how many women were teaching that craft in a Naval Fighter Weapons School at the time."

The reunion of Maverick and Ice was the emotional high point of the 2022 sequel, *Top Gun: Maverick*.

Johnny Strabler's struggles with his sexuality are also expressed in his interactions with the women he encounters. The character Britches, a "beetle" in a bullet bra, approaches him after his fight with Chino, and asks if he remembers the time they spent together a year earlier—"before the club split up." Johnny says that he doesn't and walks away. Later that evening, after the trouble has begun, Britches sees Johnny ride up and runs to him. "I wanna know how you been, Johnny. I'm singing tonight. I'm really singing, I'm on the Christmas tree." She's been drinking. She holds a beer bottle and again reminds Johnny of their one-night stand. "Johnny, remember the night? The first time I went out scrambling with the Rebels. Remember? That was the first time I ever saw you. I haven't seen you since. We really got ourselves hung on the Christmas tree, didn't we?"

Johnny looks at her impassively. Either he doesn't remember the night they were on the Christmas tree, or he wants to forget. "But we had a lotta yaks, anyway. Didn't we, Johnny?" Britches begs him to acknowledge the evening. "Can't you say something?" He does. "Whaddaya want me to do? Send you some flowers?" Johnny walks away, leaving Britches in tears.

Johnny's issues are made most clear after he rescues Kathie from potential rape—or at least continued shenanigans—by his own Black Rebels. As the nighttime revelry descends into chaos, a half-dozen cyclists have chased and encircled her, engines roaring while they tease and terrify her until Johnny rides in, orders Kathie to climb on behind him, and drives off with her. She holds him tight as they glide on a romantic moonlight ride into the countryside before stopping in a park. Kathie takes her hands from Johnny's waist, and as she stands, they share a meaningful look that Johnny breaks from. She walks away with a look on her face that says she's ready for romance, and as she sits on a log that could serve as a bed, Johnny takes a deep breath and walks toward her, doing what he knows is expected. "Get up," he orders, then grabs her and, animalistically, almost in a parody of Stanley Kowalski, takes her face in his hand and kisses her forcibly. Then he steps back to see her reaction. She looks stunned, and doesn't respond, so he goes in again, this time burying his face in her neck, like a vampire. "I'm sorry," she says. "I, I can't fight back. I'm too tired. That would be better, wouldn't it? Then you could hit me." Is she referring to his fight with Chino? Does she realize that is where his true passion lies?

Johnny gets it. He takes offense. "You think you're too good for me. Nobody's too good for me. Anybody thinks they're too good for me, I make sure I knock 'em over sometime. . . . Right now, I can slap you around to show you how good you are, and tomorrow I'm someplace else, and I don't even know you or nothing."

She teases him, gives him an opening, as Chino did. "Do you want to?" Cornered, Johnny replies, "I wouldn't waste my time with a square like you. What do I want to knock myself out for? I'm gonna take you back and dump you." He grabs her arm. "Come on, where're you going?" As he turns toward his cycle, Kathie tries once more for tenderness, gently touching the sleeve of his leather jacket. "Johnny—" He slaps her away. "Quit that."

And the subtext kicks. "It's crazy, isn't it?" she says. "You're afraid of me."

Johnny places his hands on his hips and asks her if she's "cracked." She lets him know she's his for the taking. But Johnny is afraid to take her.

"I wanted to touch you," Kathie says. "I wanted to try, anyway. . . . I wanted to make it the way I always thought it would be sometime. With somebody. The way I always thought it might be. You're still fighting, aren't you? You're always fighting."

Kathie drops to the dirt, against the front wheel of Johnny's Triumph. She strokes the fender and runs her hand suggestively up and down the thick fork. "I've never ridden on a motorcycle before. It's fast. Scared me, but I forgot everything. Felt good. Is that what you do?" She's not talking about riding motorcycles. But if she's created a mood, he breaks it instantly with a tantrum unbefitting a romantic hero.

"I'm going to leave! That's what you want me to, do isn't?"

She's disappointed again, so she levels with him. Kathie had hoped Johnny might be the man to rescue her from Wrightsville. "I used to think about it a lot after my mother died—that somebody would come here and stop at Uncle Frank's place, and buy a cup of coffee or something, and he'd like me right away. And take me with him. Johnny, you were going to give me that statue. Will you give it to me now?"

"Why?"

"I don't know. I just wondered if you still wanted to give it to me, that's all." She shakes her head. She knows. "It's crazy. I wish I was going someplace. I wish you were going someplace. We could go together." She realizes he's not going to that place where men and women can be together. Ultimately, Kathie grabs and hugs him. "Johnny! Johnny!" she sobs. If Johnny was going to "give it to her," now would be the time. But he pushes her away. He looks very confused. She runs off, in tears.

Johnny gets on his bike and rides after her, but when he catches up, she slaps him and runs again, this time stopping to watch Chino and his boys loot the market. Chino wears the top hat that fell with the head of the top-pled mannequin groom. One of his boys wears the bride's headpiece and veil, another, walking unsteadily, arm in arm with another biker, wears over his duds, the wedding dress. Johnny pulls up and motions to Chino. "Hey Chino, how'd you get outta the can?" Chino falls across the front of Johnny's bike. "Johnny, I love you. Hey, look, let's you and me have a beer and I'll beat the living Christmas out of you!" Chino laughs. Cut to Kathie, watching from a distance, hearing all, hearing Chino say, "I love you."

"No, man," Johnny replies. "C'mon. Get everybody together. We're gonna get outta here!"

Kathie watches as the bikers roll off, leaving only one, the man dressed as a bride, in the parking lot. The others are going someplace . . . they could go together.

The queer interpretation? Blame it on Brando, whom author Matthew Rettenmund refers to as "the king of effeminacy inside hypermasculin-ity," with what film critic Armond White calls "bisexual magnetism." In portraying Johnny Strabler, Brando brought his own sexual inclinations and abilities to the role, creating a character very unlike any he had yet brought to the screen. "Brando was Johnny the biker in *The Wild One*, a very camp figure," David Thompson wrote in Brando's obituary in *The Guardian*, "a gay icon."

"His posture, his stance—and the little Nelly number with the hand on the hip when Kathie tells Johnny he's afraid of her, it's all there," Del Valle says after watching the scene again. "This is a man who knows he has power. What Brando is doing is taking the female power that's recog-nized and has been celebrated in movies and flipped it around."

"He is our most sensitive actor and uses more of the feminine side of himself than anyone," said actor Gene Hackman. "Yet, he has tremendous masculinity."

The special qualities he brought to each role notwithstanding, Brando played aggressively heterosexual men in each of his first four film roles—the young paraplegic war veteran in *The Men*; the brute Kowalski; Emil-iano Zapata; the statesman Mark Antony. Strabler, with his lilting voice and adolescent belligerence, was far softer than the role of the ex-boxer in *On the Waterfront*, which would snare Brando's first Academy Award. Had Johnny Strabler been portrayed by other prominent members of the Black Rebels Motorcycle Club—Jerry Paris, who played Dextro, later to be recognized for his television role as Jerry Helper, Rob and Laura Petrie's neighbor on *The Dick Van Dyke Show*, or Pigeon, played by Alvie Moore, the future Hank Kimball on *Green Acres*—there would most likely be a very different interpretation and reaction.

"I think there's a couple things going on there," Andrew Luecke, the fashion historian, says.

Partly, it really just is Brando and his own sexuality, with instances of bisexuality, or sort of an undefined sexuality. As I understand it, he dated and slept with both men and women at a time that certainly wasn't acceptable, so I think that sort of shines through in his persona in *The Wild One*. But I also think it's very interesting that biker gangs themselves and then the Black Rebel Motorcycle Club in the movie, are very homosocial groups. Outlaw bikers even have this tradition of kissing one another, even though they're ostensibly straight. They say, "Oh, we're trying to freak out the squares." There's no male kissing in *The Wild One*, but I remember the dancing scene, and I think that those elements of the biker culture are in the air there. But I really do think that it's Brando. There's no one like him, with his ultra-specific personality and presence and smoldering look, and I think the fact that he had relationships with men in his own life shows through in the role. He's just so cool, he's so good-looking in that role and in other roles that I don't know if anyone else could have pulled off those homoerotic or homosocial elements—certainly not in the early fifties.

It has been acknowledged by Brando himself that he was very comfortable having sexual relations with men as well as women, and sometimes with men and women together. In *Brando: The Biography*, Peter Manso listed no less than sixteen index entries under "Brando, Marlon, Jr. ('Bud'): bisexuality of," with witness testimony dating back to his school days at the Shattuck Military Academy, where he had an open relationship with a fellow cadet, who "was several years younger than Marlon, finely featured to the point of almost being pretty."

Truman Capote interviewed Brando in Kyoto, Japan, during the filming of *Sayonara*, for what would be an uncomfortably revealing piece in *The New Yorker*. During their conversation, Capote mentioned a mutual friend who claimed he'd had sex with the actor. "I asked Marlon and he admitted it," Capote told his biographer Gerald Clarke. "He said he went to bed with lots of other men, too, but that he didn't consider himself a homosexual. He said they were all so attracted to him: 'I just thought I was doing them a favor.'" Brando told a French magazine in 1976, "Like a large number of men, I, too, have had homosexual experiences and I am not ashamed." There were more questions and Brandoesque mumbles about Brando's sexuality when he appeared, for no explained reason, in drag in the 1976 western, *The Missouri Breaks*. "I've never paid attention to what people said about me," he said. "Deep down I feel ambiguous, and I'm not saying that to spite the seven out of ten women who consider me, wrongly perhaps, a sex symbol. According to me, sex is something that lacks precision. Let's say sex is sexless."

At that time, he added, "Homosexuality is so much in fashion, it no longer makes news." His revelation did make news—as did his *Last Tango in Paris* costar Maria Schneider's comment a few years earlier that one thing

"His posture, his stance—and the little Nelly number with the hand on the hip." Any **excuse to not go all the way.** Columbia Pictures/Photofest © Columbia

she and Brando had in common was their bisexuality. ("He said, 'Let's go for a walk,'" Schneider told Judy Klemesrud of the *New York Times* of her first meeting with Brando. "Then he said, 'Maria, you're going to have to put your finger up my rear, so let's get to know each other.'")

There were his relationships with the writer James Baldwin, the French actor and director Christian Marquand (for whom Brando named his son in 1958, and in whose film, *Candy*, Brando appeared ten years later), and most controversially, his oldest friend, Wally Cox. Brando and Cox were both born in 1924 and had known each other since they were nine years old. "Wally Cox wasn't really my friend. He was my brother, closer to me than any human being in my life except my sisters," Brando said, and while Cox was known to have preferred women, there's speculation that Cox stepped into some of the anything-goes orgies Brando favored in his days on Broadway. It was at Brando's suggestion that Cox became comfortable with his interest in sadomasochism. "Get it out in the open. People like all sorts of things," Brando said he told his pal. He gave Cox the confidence, according to Brando biographer William J. Mann, to facilitate his interests by setting up a trapeze (in front of a mirror) in his apartment. "He'd dress up in boots and have girls whip him. They would make him grovel, and it made him sexually happy," Brando told Robert Lindsey in the original interviews for *Songs My Mother Taught Me*.

When it comes to Brando's comfort with his sexual fluidity and its prominence in *The Wild One*, it may be only coincidence that months before he returned to Hollywood from New York to begin filming in February 1953, he was featured in another picture that remained underground for more than fifty years—until the Internet made it available to anyone who could Google it.

It is a photograph of Brando with his lips wrapped around an erect penis. The member was said to belong to Wally Cox, although its ownership has been subject to great debate. The picture had been talked about in show business circles for decades. Kenneth Anger, the imaginative author of *Hollywood Babylon*, told an interviewer that he possessed a copy and for years was unsuccessful in his attempts to convince a publisher to print it.

In his Brando biography, Charles Higham called the picture "a vicious forged photograph" with faces "cleverly superimposed on other people's bodies in a studio lab." But when the picture first appeared online in 2004, and was published in 2006 in Darwin Porter's book, *Brando Unzipped*, the only face shown is Brando's, the person he is attached to is not identified, and by most all accounts, the photo is genuine. Porter wrote that the picture was taken at a celebrity party in Harlem thrown by Phil Black, a female impersonator well known for sponsoring the Harlem "fancy dress" drag queen balls that attracted the literati and Hollywood stars, and inspired the voguing balls that began in the 1970s (and inspired Madonna's number 1 single, "Vogue"—a song that namechecked Marlon Brando—but more on that ahead). Black supposedly dared Brando to take the photo. Porter quoted actor Tom Ewell as saying that "Wally went along with it." Whoever went along was certainly "up" for it. Porter writes that within weeks, the photograph was in wide circulation on both coasts. Roddy McDowell told Porter that he "found the picture being sold openly at kiosks along the Seine" in Paris. Further proof of its legitimacy was a snapshot that showed a framed print of the photo in the living room of French artists Pierre et Gilles.

According to Porter, Brando's first wife, Anna Kashfi, intended to show the photo in court, as evidence of his "perversity," in the bitter divorce and child custody fight that began in 1959. "Later, Marlon admitted to friends that he did indeed pose for the photograph, but dismissed it, saying, 'It was only done as a joke at a party. It's not to be taken seriously.'"

Brando's nonchalance at what was at the time, and would be today, a very scandalous photo of an A-list leading man, was the foundation beneath the quiet sexual revolution that he pioneered, himself. Twenty years later, Brando instructs Maria Schneider to penetrate him anally in *Last Tango in Paris*, an activity that supported Swedish director Ingmar Bergman's contention that *Last Tango* was "not really about a middle-aged man and a young girl, but about homosexuals." Armond White agreed that the "foolishly guilt-free sexcapades" between the characters Paul and Jeanne "undeniably resembled the libertine exploits that gay men enjoyed pre-AIDS." The quick, anonymous "hook-ups" also foreshadowed twenty-first-century dating apps like Tinder, Grindr, and AdultFriendFinder.

With the exception of a scene in which he "moons" a room full of tango dancers, Brando offers no explicit nudity in *Last Tango*. The one "full-frontal" nude scene he had been scheduled to perform led, he said, to "one of the more embarrassing experiences of my professional life. . . . It was such a cold day that my penis shrank to the size of a peanut."

"I realized I couldn't play the scene this way, so I paced back and forth around the apartment stark naked, hoping for magic. . . . I concentrated on my private parts, trying to will my penis and testicles to grow; I even spoke to them. But my mind failed me. . . . I simply couldn't play the scene that way, so it was cut."

The issue of Brando's sexuality resurfaced unexpectedly in February 2018, in an interview with music producer Quincy Jones that was posted on *New York* magazine's pop culture website, *Vulture*. "Brando used to go cha-cha dancing with us," Jones, then eighty-four, said of his longtime friend. "He could dance his ass off. He was the most charming motherfucker you ever met. He'd fuck anything. Anything! He'd fuck a mailbox. James Baldwin. Richard Pryor. Marvin Gaye."

"He slept with them?" interviewer David Marchese asked. "How do you know that?"

Jones, Marchese reported, frowned. "Come on, man. He did not give a fuck!"

For some reason, revelations about the mailbox, Baldwin, and Gaye slipped under the pop culture radar, but mention of sex with the legendary comedian Richard Pryor spread across the Internet and made news around the world (as well as providing material for months of comedic reenactments by comedian Gilbert Gottfried on his popular podcast). Pryor's widow, Jennifer, basically confirmed the story. "It was the seventies," she said. "Drugs were still good, especially quaaludes. If you did enough cocaine, you'd fuck a radiator and send it flowers in the morning." Speaking on behalf of Brando's survivors, his son Miko expressed disappointment "that anyone would make such a wrongful comment about either Marlon Brando or Richard Pryor."

In examining the queer subtext of *The Wild One*, another issue should not be overlooked: at the time *The Wild One* was being prepared, homosexuality was cited by experts, politicians, and lawmen alike as a factor in the rise of juvenile delinquency. In *The Myth of the Queer Criminal*, Jefferey P. Dennis points out that "during World War II, criminologists in the United States and France became disturbed and perplexed by the practice of juveniles who weren't being seduced by simpering inverts or flirting with elderly degenerates as a prelude to robbing them, but engaging in sexual acts with each other." Child psychiatrists at the time blamed the activity on the effects of wartime, which caused the youngsters to "grow up too fast." At an age when they might usually be in the "pal and gang" stage of homoerotic latency, they acted out on the sexual instinct. The experts agreed that the anomaly would fade when the war ended.

> Their hopes were dashed during the 1950s when they were faced with blatantly homoerotic youth subcultures. High school and college graduation rates soared as technological advances in economic prosperity pushed the age of entry into adulthood from fourteen or fifteen to the mid-twenties, pushing the putative "pal and gang" stage well past the age of sexual potency. Teen-oriented mass media regularly flaunted androgynous pretty boy singers. . . . Movies such as *The Wild One*. . . portrayed juvenile boys "running wild," engaging in acts of vandalism, intimidation, robbery, and theft in obviously homoerotic pairs.

Whether Brando, with his interest in psychiatry, was aware of this element of gang mentality and wanted it explored in the plot, there are, as mentioned previously, allusions to the camp and queer aspects of the Black Rebels Motorcycle Club. In addition to Johnny's final scene with Chino, where the biker in the wedding dress is left standing alone, there was more questionable activity earlier. After the sun went down and the cyclists ran riot in Wrightsville, the club members went from pogo stick bounces and beer bottle slaloms to serious looting and homoerotic pairings the experts had warned of. Drinking and whooping outside Mildred's Beauty Shop, with not enough local women to go around, Black Rebel Mouse (Gil Stratton) dons a flowing white mop head as a wig, camps it up and dances a tango with Pigeon. Then the men from both clubs join in and swing dance, holding and twirling each other, without a woman in sight. Scenes like that led Brian Eggert in *Deep Focus Review* to describe *The Wild One* as "a film of unintentionally conflicting ideas and ironic uncertainties, resulting in a work that lends itself to a camp sensibility and an inadvertent challenge to traditional masculine roles." The scene of men in wigs and black leather dancing, combined with "Brando's performance and the camera's ogling of Johnny's tight blue jeans," he writes, "has a sexual uncertainty that leads to queer interpretations." The "queer interpretations" may have been another factor in why, along with the stated fear that the film would incite teen riots, *The Wild One* ban was not lifted in Great Britain until 1968—a year after Parliament decriminalized homosexual acts.

In February 2020, days before the 87th Academy Awards ceremony at the Dolby Theatre on Hollywood Boulevard, Armond White, the film critic, announced his answer to the Oscars, which "usually rubber stamp mainstream movies with big budgets and hype but ignores breakthroughs in movie history and gay culture." White came up with a list that honored performances "that deserve the big prize but never got it . . . iconic characterizations (that) recognize gay experience and, through imagination, compassion and talent, validate gay people's humanity." He called his awards "The Brandos."

The name, he wrote in *Out* magazine, saluted Brando's performance in *Reflections in a Golden Eye*, "an act of artistic genius and cultural courage" in which "the great actor revealed depths of desire and critiqued the misery of repression." This characterization, White wrote was "revolutionary," creating "an unforgettable signpost for cultural awakening two years before Stonewall." *Reflections*, in which Brando played a repressed homosexual US Army major, opened in October 1967. It would be followed by his equally courageous role in *Last Tango in Paris* five years later. The same could be said of his characterization in The *Wild One* in 1953.

Twelve

Hell for Leather

"There is no other piece of pop culture that appears more across different subcultures than *The Wild One*. It is quite simply the most influential sub-cultural movie of all time." Andrew Luecke, the fashion historian, writer, and former style editor, studied the film's influence. "It pops up with bikers, English bikers known as the Ton-Up Boys and the Rockers, and you see the leather Perfecto-style jacket pop up in American greasers. By the end of the fifties, that's pretty much codified in both the United States and in the UK—and even in Switzerland."

Luecke cites photographer Karlheinz Weinberger, born in Zurich in 1921, and known for his homoerotic photographs of working-class men, rebellious youth and, in the 1950s, the *Halberstarken*. Translated as "half-strong," the term refers to the greasers, rockers, and juvenile delinquents in Switzerland, Austria, and Germany. Their look and attitude were directly inspired by Johnny Strabler. "Weinberger worked in a Siemens warehouse, but his passion was photography and he's got this whole body of work stemming from the fifties all the way up until his death in 2006. And he's shooting these Swiss biker kids (who've) got their own take on the leather jacket and jeans. It comes out at the same time, and it's obvious to the young people that they go together."

Weinberger's homoerotic photographs were distributed in the late 1940s in the underground gay journal, *Der Kreis*, under the pseudonym, "Jim." Fifteen hundred miles north, in Helsinki, Finland, an artist named Touko Valio Laaksonen had his own—and very influential—take on homosexual masculinity, and worked under a similarly short and sweet nom de guerre.

The Wild One was released in Sweden in May 1954; in Denmark in February 1955 (in both countries as *Vild ungdom*—"wild youth"); and in 1956 in Norway (*Vill ungdom*). The picture did not open in theaters in Finland (under the titles *Förvildad*—"undomesticated" and *Hurjapäät*—"crazy heads") until December 23, 1966, but the image of Brando as Johnny

Strabler, astride his Triumph motorcycle, decked out in full biker gear, had spread throughout Scandinavia within months of the film's initial rollout. Few reactions to the vision of the leather- and denim-clad antihero would lead to a greater worldwide cultural effect than that of Touko Laaksonen, the shy advertising employee and amateur artist in Helsinki. Touko was born in 1920 in Kaarina, a rural, cold, and cloudy town in the southwest corner of the country. His parents were schoolteachers. He was brought up with an appreciation for art and music, and soon realized he had an even greater appreciation for men. The image from childhood that was seared into his memory was that of a neighboring farmboy, said to be a strapping youngster named Urho (which in the official telling of his story translates conveniently to "Hero"). At nineteen, Touko left home to study advertising in Helsinki, and there, with the memory of Urho surging through his mind and loins, began to draw figures of men: handsome men, beautiful men, men with other men, eroticized pictures of men drawn from his own fantasies and urges that he would not dare show to others, let alone put on public display. Homosexuality was illegal, not to be decriminalized in Finland until 1971 (and even then, its "promotion" was a crime). "Even though I had to hide my own desires—or maybe because of it—I started drawing fantasies of free and happy gay men," he said.

When Touko was drafted into the Finnish Army in 1940, he destroyed those seminal (in more ways than one) "dirty drawings," and as the country entered World War II, achieved the rank of second lieutenant as an anti-aircraft officer. Finland fought alongside the Germans, and it was during this time that Touko had his first sexual experiences—relations with civilians and other soldiers, including Nazis. The intimate collaborations with German officers made as deep an artistic impression as did the masturbatory memories of Urho. Touko said that this was the time he developed a fetishistic interest in the uniforms and leather boots of Hitler's officers. Despite the inherent political nature of his work and the glorification of Nazis his art contained, he would deny any ideological influence or intentions. "I am thinking only about the picture itself," he told his biographer F. Valentine Hooven III. "The whole Nazi philosophy, the racism and all that, is hateful to me, but of course I drew them anyway—they had the sexiest uniforms! . . . Naturally—the designer of the Nazis' uniforms was gay!"

After the war, Touko studied music and blended into the Helsinki bohemian scene, playing piano in bars and at parties, while doing freelance drawing, advertising, and display work. He eventually was hired by the international advertising firm, McCann Erickson, while keeping his explicit homoerotic artwork on the down-low. His drawings were soft and romantic, and often colorful, featuring handsome, middle-class men with gentle features.

Then Marlon Brando roared in.

"Laaksonen would continue to create what he called his 'dirty drawings' through the 1950s, but they took on a new look after Brando's Johnny Strabler appeared," according to Elyssa Goodman, who did a study of Touko Laaksonen's work in time for the centennial of his birth. "What were once vibrant color gouache or pencil illustrations of men in brown leather jackets and cloth caps or army greens became strictly graphite. Black leather jackets, black boots and black jeans on rippling, lustfully swollen he-men."

With Brando as a muse, and the leather and denim of Johnny Strabler as an inspiration, Touko's fantasy ejaculated into a fantasy world of hypermasculine, hypersexed musclemen whose overdeveloped chests and arms broke through their tight T-shirts, while from the open flies of their tight leather pants protruded genitals of a size theretofore only seen on the cart horses back in Kaarina. These were handsome men, wielding batons, wearing aviator sunglasses, many sporting mustaches, engaged in various sexual acts in both private and public scenarios, gleefully, lustily, without shame. While the younger Touko intimated an alternative homosexual universe in his early work, he had now created a clear, crushing alternative to the stereotype of the mincing, effeminate gay man. By replacing the "sissy" with a new, strong, very "manly" image, he was not only claiming, but creating an ideal that would become a stereotype and subculture of its own.

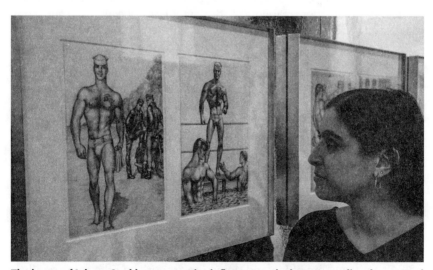

The image of Johnny Strabler was a major influence on the hypermasculine, hypersexed work of the artist Touko Laaksonen, better known as Tom of Finland. Photofest

It was also clear that Johnny Strabler's working-class outfit—denim jeans, leather jacket, cap, T-shirt, and leather boots—had inspired Touko to shift his focus from the middle class, middle-management subjects of his earlier work to working-class heroes, in occupations, roles, and body types that straight men would love to resemble.

"Male sex appeal prior to that Brando moment had been limited to men in suits for the most part," Goodman writes. "Laaksonen found sexiness in the style and rebellious status of Brando's *Wild One* garb, and it inspired him to perpetuate that clothing's erotic potential. . . . Beginning with the Brando look, there became a subversiveness attached to working-class identification that Laaksonen's work also adopted."

By co-opting these stereotypically heroic "straight" roles—not only macho bikers and soldiers, but cowboys and cops, lumberjacks and linemen, sailors, and stevedores—Touko was able to turn his work into pure art, calling dibs on the images on behalf of gay men while simultaneously parodying the heterosexual stereotypes—very much as Brando had done in *The Wild One*.

In 1956, one of Touko's friends convinced him to send some examples of his work to an American publication called *Physique Pictorial*. Editor and publisher Bob Mizer was a photographer and filmmaker who in the 1940s had established a "beefcake" empire with his Athletic Model Guild. Based in his studio in downtown Los Angeles, the AMG was positioned as a modeling agency for male bodybuilders, allowing Mizer to photograph and film thousands of strapping men, many of them nude, loan out models to other photographers, and assemble a collection of thousands of films and millions of photographs. His work also made him a frequent target of the law. Mizer had been arrested and did time in jail, but found new ways to carry on his mission at a time when the Los Angeles Police Department targeted gay men and the US Postal Service considered any publication or art depicting homosexuality to be obscene. *Physique Pictorial* was his way of operating undercover in plain sight. Marketed not as homosexual erotica, but a quarterly magazine dedicated to mainstream bodybuilding culture, classical figure art posing, and outdoor activities, the magazine could be sent through the mail and sold on newsstands.

When Bob Mizer received Touko's drawings, he knew there was something special in his hands. He featured the sketch of two strapping, shirtless lumberjacks, riding logs down a river, on the cover of *Physique Pictorial*'s spring 1957 issue. Still lying low, Touko Laaksonen signed his work "Tom." Soon, to make his origins a bit clearer, Mizer began to credit the artist as Tom of Finland. A subculture, born of *The Wild One*, began to rise.

"So you have Tom of Finland doing the artwork and the amazing illustrations, and from mid-century, on for the next fifty years, homosexual cultures are very into traditionally masculine iconography," Luecke says.

You not only have the bikers, you also have the biker cops, who interestingly wear the same leather jacket. You have the sailors and the military. So it's that attraction to traditional tough masculinity—not only an attraction, but a desire to take an aesthetic on for yourself. At the same time, on the West Coast, San Francisco in particular, but also in New York City, you have this gay leather culture emerging. So you're seeing this archetype of traditional masculinity. It's attractive to gay men, but I think it's also attractive to gay men because it presents an armor against the world. It can give you immense power, a look you create, a look like Marlon Brando's. Copying that look, the leather jacket, gives you a presence, but there's also the look and feel of the leather jacket and the boots and the denim. The leather is such a sensual material. It wears in. It has a little bit of shine. You have all of the zippers and metal furnishings. You put a Schott Perfecto motorcycle jacket on and it's a heavy, burly garment. And it's got the belt. You almost feel like a gunslinger with your spurs and your holster jangling as you walk through the streets. So it's got this immense power. And I think that's what attracted people to it.

Tom of Finland's influence began to spread into mainstream culture in the 1970s, around the time that Touko Laaksonen made his first visits to the United States. French music producer Jacques Morali introduced the Tom of Finland image into the seventies disco scene, and then into "straight" mainstream pop culture when he cast his disco music group, The Village People, through an ad calling for "gay singers and dancers, very good-looking and with mustaches."

Each of the five singing and dancing members of the group was given a persona and costume mirroring one of Tom's "superman" characters, including the construction worker, cop, soldier, cowboy, and "leatherman." The double entendre nature of the band's name—the "Village" referring to Greenwich Village, a homosexual enclave, and the presentation of and lyrics to songs like "Macho Man" and "In the Navy," made the gay context obvious—except perhaps to the *Washington Post* music critic who wrote in June 1979 that "all the Village People have distinct identities rooted in the American machismo mythology," while "unfortunately, some people wondered about the lurking homosexual undertones of the lyrics" to the "musical tribute . . . 'Y.M.C.A.'"

In interviews at the time, Morali and his group were cagy, denying the obvious and arguing that each character could be seen as representing classic "straight" masculine American heroes—all of course, but "The Leatherman." Buff, shirtless, with a thick horseshoe mustache, and wearing a peaked leather cap, studded leather jacket, leather pants, and chains, Glenn Hughes could have stepped out of a graphite Tom of Finland drawing or a gay leather bar (which in fact, he did, being a habitué of The Mineshaft, the gay BDSM leather bar and sex club in Manhattan's meatpacking district).

Glenn Hughes, the "leatherman" from the disco group the Village People, exemplified the influence of Johnny Strabler's image on gay subcultures. Paul Quezada-Neiman / Alamy Stock Photo

"I present what is probably the most recognized sexual, and largely gay sexual, pose of any of us," Hughes admitted to London's *New Musical Express* in February 1979. And although he was inexact in his knowledge of cinematic history, Hughes gave credit to the source. "The leather image . . . is very much wrapped up in the sexual overtones of rebellion, rock 'n' roll, what have you—the hard-ass biker right from Marlon Brando in *On the Waterfront* through to today, where you have someone like the Fonz."

Hughes died of lung cancer in 2001. His obituary in the *New York Times* referred to his Village People character as "the Biker."

The combined influence of Tom of Finland and Johnny Strabler blended into the fields of fashion and pop music most prominently through the designs and connections of Jean Paul Gaultier. The French designer saw Laaksonen's work for the first time in the 1970s as well, and used the clothing and uniforms of his characters as inspiration for many of the looks he developed. "I was attracted to the fact that they were covered. It shows the fetishism of fabric, of leather, and there were different types," he said. "In reality, I think he loved clothes." The prototype for many of Gaultier's designs and work with leather jackets was *The Wild One*. When he was honored at the Ischia Global Film and Music Fest in Italy in 2017, Gaultier cited Brando as a major influence. Five years later, Gaultier oversaw the *Cine y Moda* (Cinema and Fashion) exhibitions in Madrid and Barcelona, which focused on the influence of movies on fashion. He included a display dedicated to *The Wild One* (released in Spain as *Salvaje*), featuring a life-size version of the iconic photograph of Brando as Johnny Strabler, behind a mannequin wearing a cockerel-adorned biker jacket Gaultier had designed *"to pay homage to the rebelliousness and masculinity of Marlon Brando in Salvaje."*

Gaultier introduced the Tom-Johnny influence to the pop music arena when he created the costumes for Madonna's 1990 Blonde Ambition world tour—the tour that included the "cone bra," which became as iconic as any pop culture fashion item. The show featured a performance of the singer's latest single, "Vogue," which includes a spoken rap section in which Madonna namechecks sixteen Hollywood legends, including Brando. (Brando's estate sued Madonna in 2012 for projecting his image, allegedly without permission, that year on her MDNA tour. The suit was settled.)

"When it comes to Madonna, she was certainly well aware of Marlon Brando and found his allure appealing enough to warrant writing him into 'Vogue,'" says Matthew Rettenmund, author of several editions of *Encyclopedia Madonnica*. "No small accolade, considering she left out such luminaries as Joan Crawford and Mae West.

"At this time, 1990, she also appeared to either consciously or subconsciously tip her hat to Brando via an androgynous shoot she did with Patrick Demarchelier that wound up serving as the cover of her 'Justify My Love' single. Looking like *The Wild One*–era Brando, she pouts from behind newly-collagened lips, and it's tempting to deduce her decision to echo Brando was intentional, since the song was undeniably a gender-fuck—a woman asserting herself sexually so frankly at that time in pop music was unusual. And of course, Brando was the king of effeminacy inside hypermasculinity.

"The only other Brando reference that leaps to mind when it comes to Madonna is more gossipy," Rettenmund adds. "Norris Burroughs (Madonna's boyfriend in 1978, after her arrival in New York City) wrote that during their passionate time together, she would command him, 'Get that Brando body of yours over here.' And he did."

"Madonna's new-wave look is very much a downtown look and probably comes out of that mixture of subcultures she's seeing down there at the Mudd Club, with punk and rock 'n' roll," Andrew Luecke says.

> The other thing that's interesting is that there in that subcultural mix of eighties New York, that *"Brando to fetish culture to punk rock"* also seeps into hip-hop. A lot of the early-eighties hip-hop groups are also in leathers and in mariners' bikers' caps and in studs. And then in the late 2010s and early 2020s, we have artists like Playboi Carti, who's doing the rock and leather and studs thing once again, and I think he's drawing that more from punk than he is from Grandmaster Flash and those early hip hop acts. But it's interesting that it's a part of that conversation as well, because for so long, hip hop and rock 'n' roll have been seen as totally separate worlds and paths, when of course, they're not at all. They come out of the same traditions of R&B and things like that, so there is that part of the conversation, as well. And yeah, *The Wild One* is the single most influential. I think one of the things that's really interesting is Rob Halford, the singer of Judas Priest, who was a closeted gay man in the mid-seventies when Judas Priest started and through the eighties up to the nineties. There's a closeted gay man who was interested in the leather subculture, and he brought the leather subculture to heavy metal, with all the studs and the Perfecto-style jackets and the belts and the chaps and stuff. It became this very masculine-seeming thing, but of course he was influenced by the gay leather culture that he was a part of. And of course, the gay leather culture takes that leather stuff, partly because it seems so traditionally masculine. So it's sort of this dance of subversion.

Andy Warhol and photographer Robert Mapplethorpe attended Laaksonen's first American exhibition, at Stompers, an alternative gallery in Greenwich Village, in 1979. Mapplethorpe, openly gay and deep into the BDSM leather subculture, befriended Laaksonen, photographed him, and arranged more prominent exhibits. (Tom of Finland's work has since been displayed in respected galleries around the world, and made part of many museums' permanent collections, including the Museum of Modern Art in New York City, Museum of Contemporary Art in Los Angeles, and Kiasma, the contemporary art museum in Helsinki.)

Mapplethorpe became famous in the 1970s and 1980s for his stunning black-and-white celebrity portraits, nudes, and still-lifes, and was infamous for his graphic depictions of male nudity, documentation of denizens of Manhattan's BDSM gay leather culture (he was for a time the "official photographer" at the Mineshaft), and, most memorably, his "Self Portrait with a Whip," a photograph heavily influenced by Tom of Finland, in which he posed, back to the camera, with a bullwhip jammed into his asshole.

Mapplethorpe photographed himself in many guises, from a devil to a transvestite. Like Laakonsen, he challenged a prevailing gay stereotype, which in his later years was the pitiful image of the dying victim of AIDS. In 1988, when he was suffering from the disease, Mapplethorpe photographed himself, looking defiantly into the camera, gripping a cane topped by a small human skull. (Mapplethorpe died from AIDS complications in 1989; Laaksonen, hobbled by emphysema, died after a stroke in 1991).

Self Portrait (1988) was one of Mapplethorpe's final statements, but the self-portrait Mapplethorpe chose as the cover of his 1985 book, *Certain People: A Book of Portraits*, shows his debt to Brando and *The Wild One*. Mapplethorpe sports a fifties-style coif and wears a black leather jacket, with a cigarette dangling from his lips, like Johnny Strabler at the counter of Bleeker's Café.

Thirteen

Andy Warhol's Pants

Long before he was regarded as the most influential visual artist of the twentieth century, Andy Warhol worshipped Marlon Brando. Brando was a movie star, a handsome, tough-yet-tender actor whose sexual activity with men as well as women was already rumored and confirmed by some among the gay crowd of 1950s Manhattan. Warhol was a pale, pockmarked, balding, insecure, yet very successful commercial illustrator and artist, but he loved sex, and he loved Marlon Brando. One of his good friends, production designer Charles Lisanby, recalled the time Warhol showed him just how close he kept his screen idol to his . . . heart. "I do remember Andy coming to the display department once, and he said, 'I was just at *Harper's Bazaar,* and he gave me a picture of Marlon Brando. Would you like to see it?' And I said, 'Sure, Andy. Yeah.' And he went into his pants and he had it in there. . . . And he showed the photo to me. Then he put it back in. And he was walking around New York with Marlon Brando in (his pants)."

Brando, the leather boy biker in *The Wild One* and the brutish Stanley Kowalski in *A Streetcar Named Desire,* could be seen as the man Warhol always wished he could be, or at last the man he wished he could have. Warhol had been infatuated with cinema and movie idols since he was a child in Pittsburgh, Pennsylvania, collecting movie fan magazines and sending away for photos of the stars, and Hollywood was a focus of the pop art that Warhol pioneered. So, it is not surprising that Brando, a man whose rebellious attitudes on screen and in life mirrored his own, would be a major influence on some of Warhol's most celebrated—and valuable—work.

Warhol worked in many mediums, including illustration, painting, silk-screening, photography, sculpture, film, and video. His work embraced and satirized consumerism, mass media, and celebrity, and his use of related items, products, totems, scraps, and images from popular culture—sometimes produced on a mass scale—created a statement that went far beyond the label of "pop art."

By 1962, Warhol was already considered a great talent and a force to be reckoned with on the New York art scene, but the major fine arts dealers considered his pop art paintings to be too outré to be featured in major gallery exhibitions, let alone a solo show. When he received an offer for his first one-man show, it was from an art dealer based in Los Angeles, for an exhibition at the Ferus Gallery on North La Cienega Boulevard. Los Angeles wasn't even on the map as far as the East Coast art establishment was concerned. Irving Blum and his partners at the Ferus Gallery had attempted to make an impression by featuring the West Coast's most cutting-edge artists. Now, they were reaching farther.

Blum recalled visiting Warhol in his townhouse on Lexington Avenue near Eighty-Ninth Street in Manhattan. "What really made an impression was that the floor—I may exaggerate a little—was not a foot deep, but certainly covered wall-to-wall with every sort of pulp movie, magazine fan magazine, and trade sheet having to do with popular stars from the movies or rock 'n' roll. Warhol wallowed in it."

Warhol's show at the Ferus Gallery opened on July 9, 1962, and the highlight was not Hollywood, but the supermarket shelves. *Andy Warhol: Campbell's Soup Cans* was the first exhibition of his *Campbell's Soup Cans*, thirty-two separate twenty-by-sixteen-inch canvases, each displaying a painting of one of the thirty-two varieties of Campbell's canned soup. This masterwork was the introduction of pop art to the West Coast.

By the time the Ferus show had opened, Warhol was back in New York, concentrating on a vision of Hollywood that stemmed from his lifetime of obsession with movie stars, wrapped in the queer culture and the Hollywood scandals revealed, detailed, and embellished by avant-garde filmmaker Kenneth Anger in his book *Hollywood Babylone*, published in France in 1959 (published in the United States in 1965 as *Hollywood Babylon* and quickly banned).

Some of Warhol's first silkscreen experiments in 1962 made use of a publicity photo of Elizabeth Taylor, enlarged, turned to a stencil, transferred to a canvas, painted over, and reproduced like another commercial "product"—his own comment on the Hollywood machine. His other subjects included Warren Beatty, Troy Donahue, Elvis Presley, and Marilyn Monroe. Warhol was working on a series of Monroe paintings depicting a detail from a bust-length publicity still from the 1953 film *Niagara*, when Monroe died on August 4.

The death gave the work even more importance when the dozen paintings of Marilyn Monroe, later known as the *Flavor Marilyns*, were the highlight of his first solo show in New York City. The exhibit opened on November 6, 1962, at the Stable Gallery on East Seventy-Fourth Street in Manhattan. Each acrylic and silkscreen image was painted on a twenty-by-sixteen-inch canvas with a different colored background. (The paintings were offered for sale at two hundred and fifty dollars apiece.) Warhol's first show also included paintings and silkscreens depicting Elvis, Donahue, Coca-Cola bottles, dollars bills, and a Pepsi-Cola matchbook. "Shock value was built into pop art and Andy Warhol, one of its stellar performers, capitalizes on just that," Stuart Preston wrote in the *New York Times*. "Popular images such as coca-cola bottles; Marilyn Monroe's radiant smile; and Elvis Presley's sensual sulkiness are repeated in rows as if the canvases had been sprayed by image-making machine guns. This is 'art' in that Warhol knows more than a thing or two about color and layout, but its sociological value—that of making icons for sophisticates—is considerably higher."

Heading into 1963, Warhol's art had taken a darker, more serious turn as he began work on what would become known as the *Death and Disaster* series: images of car crashes, electric chairs, suicides, race riots, and other topics that reflected an American obsession with violence and tragedies. Simultaneously, he was attacking Hollywood mythology and celebrity culture straight on, with a more prominent queer sensibility, influenced not only by the fan mags and *Hollywood Babylone*, but *Flaming Creatures*, the recent underground film by Jack Smith. A sexually graphic display of performers in drag, transvestites, and orgies, *Flaming Creatures* was an underground sensation, local scandal, and cause célèbre, leading to obscenity charges, audience consternation, and Warhol's purchase of a Bolex sixteen-millimeter film camera and turn to filmmaking. For his first movie project, Warhol filmed his lover, stockbroker-turned-poet John Giorno, as he slept, then looped and slowed the film and added footage until he had a six-and-a-half-hour picture, *Sleeping* (Warhol later added ninety minutes to approximate the accepted eight-hour sleep time).

In January 1963, Warhol moved his studio from his townhouse to the third floor of an abandoned fire house a few blocks away on East Eighty-Seventh Street. He and assistant Gerard Malanga began working on several silkscreens for a second Ferus show. All were based on a single, oversized image of Marlon Brando as Johnny Strabler. Created from a promotional still from *The Wild One*, the image was silkscreened on a linen background that had been painted silver—as on the silver screen. "It was only natural that, in 1963, Warhol should have turned to the image of Brando leaning on his motorbike to create a silver-backed altarpiece to cool," according to a description of *Silver Marlon* from Christie's auction house, decades later. "Brando's character in the film even has a Warholian aspect in some of his terse dialogue. . . . Johnny's all-out, motiveless, empty war on the status quo was arguably echoed in the gauntlet that Warhol himself would take up with Pop almost a decade later."

"What are you rebelling against. . . Andy?" "Whaddaya got?"

Warhol also worked on reconceiving another photograph of Elvis Presley. This was a publicity still from *Flaming Star*, the western directed by Don Siegel in 1960. Elvis was in the role that had been written for Brando; one of the futile attempts to revive Elvis's Brando-influenced dramatic career after his return from military service. The photograph did not depict Elvis as a rock 'n' roll star or dreamy teen idol, but as a cowboy, the archetypal American hero, legs in a wide stance, right hand gripping and pointing a six-shooter. Warhol turned the photo into a life-size image on another silver background, on canvas, over six feet tall. In the mass production phase of his art, he made forty-eight copies and sent all of them, along with a collection of Elizabeth Taylor portraits, to Irving Blum at the Ferus Gallery.

"Andy sent a roll of printed Presley images, an enormous roll, and sent a box of assorted-size stretched bars," Blum recalled.

> I said, "You mean, you want me to cut them? Virtually as I think they should be cut and placed around the wall?" And he said, "Yes, cut them any way that you think you should. . . . The only thing I really want is that they should be hung edge to edge, densely—around the gallery." And that's exactly what I did. Sometimes the images were superimposed one over the next. Sometimes they sat side by side. They were of varying sizes. All the same height—roughly six and a half feet, as I recall. Really, life size. And I got as many stretched up as required to fill densely—the gallery, as per Andy's instructions. And I sent what was left on the roll back to Andy and opened the exhibit.

Warhol's second show at the Ferus Gallery was all Elvis and all he represented. The ten portraits of Elizabeth Taylor were relegated to a back room for viewing by appointment only, but with her inclusion, just as Jack Kerouac had once enshrined Presley, Dean, and Brando as America's "New Trinity of Love," Warhol announced his own trio of queer icons. All three were tragic figures, stars of movie mags and idolized by gay fans. Marilyn had died the previous summer; Liz always seemed on the edge of death and was famously reported dead erroneously in 1961 when she was stricken with pneumonia during the disastrous production of *Cleopatra*. She was saved only by having her neck slit open in a tracheotomy. Elvis Presley was, in some ways, the walking dead in cool pop culture, and Warhol saw the tragedy in what had become of his career and potential as a true rebel. There also was a far more openly queer subtext in a reading of this series of paintings. Elvis was presented as a "flaming star"—"flaming," as in the slang for a stereotypically effeminate homosexual. Elvis, once the rock 'n' roll rebel, was one of Jack Smith's "flaming creatures." With his crotch at the center of the image, legs spread and pointing that gun, the stereotypical phallic symbol, the King was reduced—or elevated—to a camp parody of the western hero.

Silver Marlon, the leather-clad motorcycle movie rebel, was not part of this latest attack on the mainstream. Brando did not figure into that picture—or at least that's what was believed at the time. Years later, Gerard Malanga pulled from a shelf in Warhol's library a book on French film theory that the artist had looked to as a guide while working on his first Marilyn Monroe project. One can imagine Malanga's shock when he opened the book and saw inside its front cover a display of ten identical photographs of Marlon Brando, with a gun, in the same position as Warhol's Elvises. Once again, Marlon Brando was the model for Elvis Presley, and the inspiration for Andy Warhol.

Brando's place in the Warhol pantheon would be enshrined a few years later, under very different circumstances, in a series of eight canvases titled *Marlon*. In 1966, Warhol, the avant-garde director of an eight-hour stationary view of the Empire State Building and seventy minutes of *Taylor Mead's Ass*, had ventured into the mainstream with *The Chelsea Girls*, a movie that was shot mainly at the Chelsea Hotel in New York City and

Brando was a major influence on and subject of Andy Warhol's revolutionary pop art. Early in his career, Warhol kept a picture of Brando "in his pants." Photofest

made use of black-and-white and color film stock and split screen—two separate images and soundtracks running side by side—for the three-and-a-half-hour duration. The picture had its first "non-underground engagement" in December at Cinema Rendezvous on West Fifty-Seventh Street. Dan Sullivan wrote in the *New York Times* that at its best, the film "is a travelogue of hell . . . at its worst it is a bunch of home movies in which Mr. Warhol's friends, asked to do something for the camera, can think of nothing much to do."

Warhol was admittedly influenced once again by the work of Kenneth Anger. *Scorpio Rising* was Anger's twenty-eight-minute experimental film about a gang of Nazi bikers preparing for a race that ends in death. Scored to a collection of sixties pop songs, with no dialogue save for some screams and animal roars, the film is a meditation on biker culture, leather fetishism, homosexuality, sadomasochism, the occult, Christianity, Naziism—and the heroes of this homoerotic cult, James Dean and Marlon Brando. While Dean is seen in photographs tacked to a bedroom wall, along with a skull-and-crossbones flag resembling the logo of the Black Rebels Motorcycle Club, Brando is seen in clips from *The Wild One*, on a blue-tinted television screen. Amid a party scene that evolves into a sadomasochistic homosexual orgy (that includes one biker pounding on a shades-of-Brando conga drum), the image of Brando as Johnny Strabler is intercut with that of Jesus Christ (in clips from the 1927 silent film, *King of Kings*), and, ultimately, Adolf Hitler, as Little Peggy March sings "I Will Follow Him." Anger takes whatever queer subtext was attributed to *The Wild One* and makes it religion.

"The main influence in *Scorpio Rising*, which is shown in great loving detail, is the leather jacket that Kenneth created for the movie, which was inspired by Brando," says the historian David Del Valle, a longtime friend of Anger. "But after watching these scenes in *The Wild One*, I see what else Anger is doing. The character of Johnny is an iconic representation of masculinity at its most sexual—homosexual. And the fetish of leather is also the promise of sexual conquest and sexual domination, which is part and parcel with a certain kind of sexual fetish within the gay community."

Del Valle says that Anger talked about Brando "all the time. Kenneth's apartment was like a shrine to Rudolph Valentino, but in another part of the room was the leather jacket from *Scorpio Rising* on a mannequin. I think he tried to bid in an auction on the cap that Brando wore (in *The Wild One*), but it went to somebody else. He liked 'bad boys.' It's attitude. It's being uninhibited. Brando represented all that in a very silent way. Kenneth Anger is the number one reason *The Wild One* became the fetish object it did. Kenneth Anger, Tom of Finland, and Andy Warhol, all three as artists saw what this film was stirring up."

(Anger spoke of the real-life bikers who were homoeroticized, fetishized, and demonized in *Scorpio Rising*, in an unpublished 1997 interview with pop historian Legs McNeil: "They weren't that outlaw. They weren't Hells Angels. They weren't involved in any criminal activity to speak of. They were Italian-Americans who worked all night in the Fulton Fish Market, but they were obsessed with motorcycles, and they put all their money into the motorcycles. And they were straight guys. They weren't gay, but their mistresses were the motorcycles, not their girlfriends. The girlfriends knew that they took second place. So they're going to have a Halloween party. I said, 'I'd like to do some filming.' I don't know what it would've been like if I hadn't been there with my camera, but I never said, 'Take your pants down.' I never said, 'Take your dick out.' That was their idea. So I got most of it on film and the funny thing is, during this time their girlfriends were all present behind the camera.")

Warhol used the same *Silver Marlon* image for the new *Marlon* series, but replaced the silver background with a raw, untreated canvas. This, according to the auction house, had "devastating effect. Warhol's decision to use the canvas in its natural state adds to the subversive nature of the painting, enhancing the feeling of masculinity and edginess and adding another layer to the depiction of the counter-culture that is already contained within the image itself." The image of Brando was relegated to the right side of the canvas, leaving a large section untouched, placing even more emphasis on the black lines of the image.

Now, Brando as Johnny Strabler in the *Marlon* series had been reimagined, reprocessed, and remade, not only by Kenneth Anger but Andy Warhol. Any fantasies that Warhol may have had about the actor were now being produced for public consumption. The iconic image of the cool motorcycle rebel, from his leather to his chains to his "whaddya got" attitude, no longer represented a tough, straight marauder, but was part of the Warholian gallery of Hollywood queens. All subtext had risen to the queer surface. In the summer of 1967, Warhol even directed a film that was his own take on motorcycle culture. In *Bike Boy*, he cast Joe Spencer, an actual biker gang member described in the *New York Times* as "a muscular youth with an angelic face and an early Brando dese-dem-dose vocabulary," as a motorcyclist who showers for the camera and is mocked by Warhol's clique of outré characters he dubbed "superstars." Once again, any pretense of straight macho heroism among the "vanishing breed" of outlaw bikers was skewered when tossed into the Warhol world.

Only three of the eight Marlon canvases repeated the image of Brando and his bike. One of the most effective and striking versions was *Double Marlon*, which featured two of the images stacked on the right third section of a very large canvas—84 × 95¾ inches—leaving two-thirds of the canvas untouched. This again makes the images even more powerful, as if they are frames on a strip of film. The vertical strip also resembles, an art curator wrote, "a screen awaiting projection (and) even recalls the dual projection techniques that Warhol had used in *The Chelsea Girls*."

Four Marlons, along with Warhol's *Triple Elvis (Ferus Type)*—three overlapping images of Elvis Presley—went up for bidding at Christie's Rockefeller Center Auction House on November 12, 2014. Elvis sold for $82 million. The lesser-known Brando sold for $69.6 million. On the eve of the auction, Brett Gorvy, Christie's worldwide chairman of postwar and contemporary art, told a reporter for the *New York Times* that of the two, Brando and Presley, "Marlon speaks to a younger audience, because there is a very raw sexuality to the image. He's the person every young actor wants to be."

In February 2023, Warhol's portrait of Brando was a centerpiece of Saudi Arabia's first exhibition of Warhol's works. FAME: Andy Warhol in AlUla was part of the second annual AlUla Arts Festival, a government-funded initiative to bolster the country's reputation as an arts destination (or, according to Human Rights Watch, "a deliberate strategy to deflect from the country's image as a pervasive human rights violator").

The show's curator, Patrick Moore, director of the Andy Warhol Museum in Pittsburgh, said in a statement that FAME was intended to reach new audiences and to introduce Saudi youth to Warhol through a "fascinating"—and relatable—aspect of his work. "Andy Warhol's journey, which started as a child staring at the movie screen and collecting publicity stills, is becoming more common through the rise of social media."

Fourteen

The Original Punk

.

Brando was cool without oppressing the audience with too much sharpness. He was powerful without having to be invulnerable. . . . He provided new, vicarious life for a public starting to feel intimidated by the always-competent film heroes of the thirties and forties. Vulnerability in a leather jacket.

—Joe Koch, "Marlon Brando: The Original Punk"

The surface, stylistic aspects of punk rock, a genre that in shorthand is often identified by spiky hair, black leather jackets, a "fuck you" attitude, and a basic, thrashing sound, can, from the sartorial decisions, persona presentations, and musical abilities of groups like the Ramones and Green Day and artists including Travis Barker and Machine Gun Kelly, be traced easily on the teen culture timeline to Marlon Brando as Johnny Strabler in *The Wild One*. Brando, in fact, did have a major influence on the actual genesis of punk—"punk" as a movement, ethos, and lifestyle—but was discovered as an inspiration in a manner and for reasons that had little to do with music.

Travel back to 1975. The latest Brando movie to have opened across America was *Last Tango in Paris* in February 1973, ten months after Brando's "comeback" as Don Corleone in *The Godfather*. In a ramshackle office in a former trucking company at the corner of Thirtieth Street and Tenth Avenue in a rough section on the West Side of Manhattan, within scent of the Hudson River and view of New Jersey, three friends from Cheshire, Connecticut, a suburban town about fifteen miles north of New Haven, have joined forces in pursuit of, in their words, "world domination." Eddie McNeil, aka "Legs" (not because of his dancing ability or likeness to flamboyant Prohibition-era gangster Legs Diamond, but because he was born with anisomelia) has just turned nineteen. Had he made up a few credits, he could have graduated from Cheshire High School the previous September. Now he has his sights on a career as a filmmaker. Ged Dunn, who did receive a diploma from Cheshire High in 1972 (and

165

died in 2015), is something of a "trust fund baby," and has the means to bankroll Eddie's dream, as well as the projects envisioned by the third, and in this story, most important figure of the trio. John Holmstrom is twenty-two. A brilliant illustrator and cartoonist, Holmstrom graduated from Cheshire High in 1971 and arrived in New York City to study at the School of Visual Arts, where he was a student of Harvey Kurtzman, a founder of *Mad* magazine. He later worked for the influential comic book artist Will Eisner. Now Holmstrom wants to start a magazine of his own, one that captures and encapsulates a rock 'n' roll "scene" that has not yet been dubbed with a formal title, does not yet exist in New York City, but whose course and development hundreds of miles away Holmstrom has charted.

"People say, 'Oh, punk started in here New York City.' I took every-thing from *Creem* magazine, which was published out of Detroit," Holm-strom says, recalling the legendary, irreverent rock 'n' roll monthly.

> And *Creem* would talk about punk rock. In fact, [*Creem* writer] Lester Bangs was kind of ticked off that he wasn't acknowledged as the guy who started punk rock. It was big in the Midwest. The Midwest is where rock 'n' roll really grew out of. Whatever band you can think of, all those mainstream bands made it big by touring the Midwest. Which is unusual, because doo-wop came out of here, and the jazz scene was very big in New York, and every kind of pop culture trend seemed to start in New York City—except for rock 'n' roll music, which was pretty much by the seventies being created in the Midwest. Iggy and the Stooges were big in the Midwest. They had a following and that's what really started punk rock. There was a magazine called *Gulchur* out of Indiana. Around there, there was a definite music scene. A band called the Gizmos put out records that sounded a lot like the Stooges' *Raw Power*. My big inspiration, though, was Alice Cooper. That was the first punk band that really got me excited about the music and he was on the cover of *Creem* in 1974, as "punk of the year." You could look it up.

The most prominent "punk-adjacent" rock 'n' roll artists identified with New York City at the time were Lou Reed, who'd emerged in the late 1960s with the Velvet Underground and their parasitic association with Andy Warhol, and the New York Dolls, a trashy, hard-rocking borderline transvestite glam band who'd peaked with the release of their debut album in 1973.

"The New York Dolls were dead by 1975," Holmstrom says.

> I always point to the April '75 show at the Little Hippodrome. It was the last time the Dolls performed in New York and their opening band the last week-end was Television. It was Richard Hell's last gig with Television, and to me that's when the torch was passed. The Dolls looked kind of ridiculous. They were wearing those red patent leather outfits Malcom McLaren designed for

them. But I liked the show. I wanted to name the magazine after the [Dolls guitarist Sylvain] Sylvain song, "Teenage News," which described what a cool magazine would have. But the Velvet Underground and the Dolls were more like inspiration because they were bands from New York that actually got a record deal. That was kind of a rare thing.

And then real inspiration—no, make that *salvation*—came in the form of an album released that spring on Epic Records. *The Dictators Go Girl Crazy* was a dumb rock 'n' roll album created by a group of smart New Yorkers, full of thudding tunes and pop and garbage can culture references that would resonate to the cheeseburger-munching teenager in anyone, and especially delivered a punch to the trio at the corner of Thirtieth Street and Tenth Avenue.

"I bought that first Dictators record and brought it to Ged's place and played it for them," Holmstrom recalls. "We all went nuts for it. It's a fun album."

"The Dictators wore black leather jackets and hung out at White Castle. Finally, someone was singing about our lives!" McNeil says. "Not that we went to White Castle, but we went to McDonald's. I can't remember all the lyrics, but they were fantastic: 'It's the dues you've got to pay, for eating burgers every day. Take my vitamin C, nothing's good for me. Don't do what we're told, and we're scared of growing old!' Instead of everybody singing about 'Don't stop thinking about tomorrow'—fuck that! Someone was finally reporting on what our lives were actually like and that was the Dictators, and we really embraced them."

The Dictators, incidentally, also ate at McDonald's, as noted in a line from *Weekend*, a song from the same album that incidentally contained a word that would become very important in the future: "Bobby is a local *punk*, cuttin' school and getting drunk, eating at McDonald's for lunch." According to founder Andy Shernoff, "'The Dictators' sounded tough. We wanted a tough name. But we weren't into being tough guys. I think we were more into having fun."

The Dictators Go Girl Crazy, according to Holmstrom, "really kickstarted the magazine."

"Holmstrom wanted the magazine to be a combination of everything we were into," McNeil says. "Television reruns, drinking beer, getting laid, cheeseburgers, comics, grade-B movies, and this weird rock 'n' roll that nobody but us seemed to like: the Velvets, the Stooges, the New York Dolls, and now the Dictators. And when we were starting, John said, 'Let's go to this place called CBGB's and see this band called the Ramones.' I said, 'Okay, sure.'" CBGB & OMFUG (Country, Bluegrass, Blues & Other Music for Uplifting Gourmandizers) was a former biker bar on the Bowery.

The Ramones came out in black leather jackets. They really did look like the SS. They were really scary, and they played the wrong song, and they threw down their guitars in disgust and walked off the stage. And it was real! It wasn't fake, and that's what we loved. I loved it! It was fantastic to see these guys fighting—"Fuck you!" "No!" *BAM!*—throw down their guitars and walk offstage. And they came back two minutes later and went into *Blitzkrieg Bop*, and they had us. And then we interviewed them. We said, "What are you into?" And they said, "1910 Fruitgum Company." Which I love, that '60s pop stuff.

Holmstrom was ready to launch *Teenage News*, but Ged Dunn nixed the name. "Well, Ged was coming up with the money and if he didn't like the title, I was out of luck," he says. "I came up with the name *Punk*," McNeil adds.

It seemed like we needed to create something, because at that time there were only two types to be. You could either be a pot-smoking hippie or a jock, and there seemed to be a need for room in the culture for more variations of the way people wanted to dress and behave. And it seemed like "punk" was a good fit for that because "punk" included everybody. We weren't rebels in high school. We were just outcasts. We were just outsiders. We were just outside of everything. Cheshire was kind of a rich town, it's Connecticut, and we were never going to be accepted into Connecticut society. That's why we embraced people like Lenny Bruce, because they were so great and so outside and successful at being an outsider. And we thought we could be successful being outsiders, too.

"I saw the Ramones and I said, 'Okay, this is punk rock and I want to write about the Ramones and the Dictators,'" says Holmstrom, "but there were not many others. There were no other punk bands really in New York, so it wasn't really a punk rock scene in 1976. It was kind of a wannabe scene with a couple of punk rock bands. Richard Hell always had the attitude, and I felt that I didn't understand it enough to articulate it at the time, but as Don Letts said in his movie, *Punk*, 'Punk is an attitude.' It was and is not necessarily music. I think music comes from the attitude."

Work got underway on *Punk*, Holmstrom's vision, his view of what mattered when it came to what was, actually, teenage news. As editor, artist, and illustrator, he made a decision that made the 'zine even more unique: rather than use professional typeface, the entire issue (and issues to follow) would be hand-lettered. Ged Dunn was now a publisher, putting up the money to print thousands of copies on newsprint. (The first issues would be folded in tabloid form, like the early issues of *Rolling Stone*.) Legs McNeil was the "Resident Punk."

"Legs insisted, 'You can't just start a magazine. It has to be a social movement,' and that's why he called himself the Resident Punk," says

Holmstrom. "Because he saw it as the anti-hippie movement—which was part of Alice Cooper. Part of rock 'n' roll at the time was turning away from glam and moving towards what became punk. Alice Cooper turned against it when they toured with *School's Out* and they'd perform *West Side Story* onstage. They'd be greasers this time instead of glam rockers. By '74, '75, glam rock was definitely over. Even the New York Dolls turned against it. Lou Reed's a good example. He was the original gay icon who was married—to a woman—but then he dated Rachel the transsexual, which was shocking at the time. But in '75, he shaved Iron Crosses into his scalp. When I saw him at the Academy of Music, he was dressed in leather with the dog collar—Iggy's dog collar."

Lou Reed was featured on the cover of *Punk*, volume 1, number 1, which was dated January 1976. The Ramones were in the centerfold, with an article, "Rock 'n' Roll, the Real Thing," written by Mary Harron, who'd go on to a career as director of films, including *I Shot Andy Warhol* and *American Psycho*. (In the article, Harron referred only to "punk-type," and only in relation to the Ramones' style and attitude onstage.) The issue featured two of Holmstrom's cartoon character creations, Sluggo and Joe.

Page One was reserved for the defining editorial, one that would define the spirit of punk—the magazine and social movement. "There was a cultural shift that I was aware of," Holmstrom says. "I don't think Ged or Eddie were aware of it. They were not rock 'n' roll fans, so I was making every creative decision on the magazine. And one of the things I wanted off the bat was a story about Marlon Brando."

The article was titled *Marlon Brando: The Original Punk*. And the inspiration did not come from films—at least not directly. "I was aware of Marlon Brando when I read the *MAD* magazine paperbacks and their take-off on *The Wild One* called *Wild 1/2*," says Holmstrom. "He was 'Marlon Branflakes.' It had a big effect on me. All those Harvey Kurtzman comic strips blew me away as a kid. And in high school I actually went to see *The Wild One*. 'I gotta see the movie that the comic strip is based on!' I think it was on a double bill with *Waterfront*, and I was just blown away. I was really affected by his performances. I went to see every Brando movie I could. I saw *The Men* and *Streetcar*, and those four movies were so amazing. You never saw an actor like that before—or since. He was just the greatest."

The Brando essay was written by Joe Koch, a friend of Holmstrom and another comic book aficionado. Accompanied by a photo from *The Wild One* set, showing Brando as Johnny Strabler, surrounded by members of the Black Rebels Motorcycle Club—and a few of the "beetles" from Chino's gang—the twelve-hundred-word piece opens with a description of a screening of *Last Tango in Paris* in a movie theater on Forty-Second Street in seedy Times Square, where audience members would shout

Brando's influence continued for decades, as he was hailed as "The Original Punk" in the first issue of *Punk* magazine. Courtesy of John Holmstrom

encouragement to the on-screen heroes and bottles would roll down the aisles and often fly through the air toward the screen.

"When the entire gallery got to its feet as he pinned Maria Schneider to the wall in the first five minutes of *Last Tango,* you knew something was happening," Koch wrote.

> It was the return of the prodigal son. The one who made undershirts fashionable in *Streetcar Named Desire,* and made black leather jackets the symbol of violence in the fifties counterculture. People liked him in *The Godfather.* He had power and class and he got a rise out of the audience for "the offer he can't refuse," but it's not the same. He was a distant authority figure, stroking snotty-looking cats with an aristocratic flair. But in *Last Tango,* it was the rebel again, with the same nervous cool. What the audience got to its feet for, and subsequently got depressed over, was Bertolucci's funeral oration for Marlon Brando, the punk.

Koch's thesis and conclusion would fit in almost any cinematic journal, and its insights were even more surprising, written out in the cartoon hand-lettering.

What comes alive in *Last Tango in Paris* is Brando's own iconography and his conclusions about the punk character he created. Even at the time, he was not sure about *The Wild One*. It seemed dangerously self-indulgent; if it enlightened America by certifying a character type she had been trying to ignore, then it also romanticized a life without direction. . . . Brando himself sometimes said that he only acted because he didn't know how to do anything else. So twenty years after *The Wild One*, with cycle and road movies in full swing, nostalgia on the rise, and Bruce Springsteen eulogies to today's street people just around the corner, Brando put himself in a film that showed what it all came out to.

Nothing.

"I haven't read the article for a while. I can pull it out if you want," Holmstrom tells the author. "Here's a good sentence":

Brando set up the public. The trilogy of *A Streetcar Named Desire, The Wild One,* and *On the Waterfront* provided media recognition for an inarticulate, rebellious character type, 'til then ignored by the popular media. America had watched a young man stroll into a diner with a motorcycle gang behind him, tear the place to shreds . . . and still felt like they were dealing with a human being. . . . *On the Waterfront* didn't have a single cool one-liner for Brando. It pulled its entire audience together on the mumbles and the promise of violence in Brando's nervous fidgeting. The audience had found a better fantasy: Brando was cool without oppressing the audience with too much sharpness. He was powerful without having to be invulnerable. . . . Vulnerability in a leather jacket. Brando prowled, not as a predator, but as a formidable victim.

Holmstrom takes a moment after he stops reading. "'Vulnerability in a leather jacket.' Well, that was the brilliance of Brando. I don't know if there's another actor who could have brought that to the table. 'He's not a predator but a formidable victim.' These are all ideas that Joe was expressing. I did not use a heavy hand editing people, but I was so lucky in that Joe wrote that great piece to start the magazine."

"Brando was a punk in a black leather jacket who showed vulnerability," says McNeil.

I think that was very, very important, and that's probably what we didn't really understand at the time, but it's written in that first article in *Punk*. I think he set the template for punk in *The Wild One*. It was the leather jacket which set the standard of what we would all be, but it wasn't until *On the Waterfront* that he actually gave it some depth. And I think what subconsciously we didn't get was that he was a loser. He was a failed boxer, and there's that great scene, "I could have been somebody"—everybody relates to that. "You could have helped me out. You could have done something." So I think what punks embraced about Brando was not only his look, but that he was failed and that he kept going and maybe he could succeed at something else. That was the hope and the promise of Brando.

"The magazine took off right away," Holmstrom recalls.

And when people were talking about this thing out of New York called "punk," they got confused between the magazine and the music. People didn't differentiate between the two until the punk scene started in England. For one year, 1976, we were punk rock. None of the bands wanted to be punk. Not even the Ramones. They didn't want to be the next "acid rock," they didn't want to be "folk rock," they didn't want to be "glam rock," because all of those musical movements came to a bad end—until they were revived years later, like glam rock in the MTV years. Before grunge kicked them out again.

"Some people would go, 'Question Mark and the Mysterians is punk,' and there were a few articles about our first album that used the term 'punk,'" Shernoff confirms.

But [punk] didn't become a common term in reference to music until *Punk* magazine came out. And that kind of spread the word. It wasn't until *Punk* magazine that it entered the common vernacular. And I acknowledge Brando, absolutely. I consider rock 'n' roll starting in 1955, when "Rock Around the Clock" came out. That song for me is Ground Zero for rock 'n' roll. But I acknowledge that he became an icon. I'd seen *The Wild One*. It didn't make that much of an impression on me, but obviously the rebel— "Hey, what are you rebelling against?" "What do you got?" Wearing a leather jacket, his whole attitude—it was a punk attitude.

Meanwhile, another interpretation of "punk" has its own connection to Brando's widespread influence. This one spanned his cinematic career, from the black leather jacket and jeans of *The Wild One*, to the military bearing of his sexually repressed Army Major Penderton in *Reflections in a Golden Eye*, to his character's activities, both as a giver and receiver of sexual assault, in *Last Tango*. Holmstrom could see from his office the aforementioned gay leather subculture growing simultaneously with punk. "When we had the Punk Dump on Thirtieth Street and Tenth Avenue, we were just about ten blocks north of the S&M leather bars. And the gays changed from glam to punk. They were dressing in leather jackets and it's evident that they were not posing as effeminate sissies anymore. They were dangerous leather boys."

Holmstrom insists that at the time, he did not know the alternative meaning of the word *punk*, as defined by Merriam-Webster: *"a young man used as a sexual partner by another man, especially in a prison."*

"I was totally unaware of all that, and that's pointed out in the second issue when we ran the definition of the word *punk*. We were getting informed by some of the people in the rock 'n' roll scene, like Peter Crowley at Max's Kansas City, what *punk* meant. It had a lot of different meanings. I mean, the word originally appeared in a Shakespeare play to describe a prostitute." ("My lord, she may be a punk, for many of them are neither maid, widow nor wife," said Lucio in *Measure for Measure*. "Marrying a punk, my lord, is pressing to death, whipping, and hanging.")

"People wrote us letters that said, 'Punk is someone who gets it in prison, takes it in the ass,' and that kind of bothered us," McNeil recalls. "I was thinking of 'punk' because I was born with one leg longer than the other, so I would always slouch. I always had incorrect posture, so everyone always called me a punk. 'What are you? Some kind of punk?' So when John said, 'Let's call the magazine *Teenage News*,' I said, 'Why don't we call it *Punk*?'"

The link to a specific gay subculture and the influence of Brando on the nascent punk movement could be seen, according to the historian and expert Andrew Luecke, in the studied image of Holmstrom's and McNeil's most immediate inspiration, the Ramones. The four young men from Forest Hills, Queens, took on a shared surname (based on "Paul Ramon," a pseudonym used by Paul McCartney early in his career) and won renown for short, sharp songs that took on the same subject matter as the Dictators, with an even more cartoonish bent. On the surface, their uniform of Schott Perfecto leather jackets, T-shirts, jeans, and sneakers was directly inspired by the Dictators, pictured on the inner sleeve of their first album seated at a White Castle restaurant counter, wearing matching leather jackets. "When the Ramones started, they were a glam band," Andy Shernoff says.

> Joey Ramone would come see the Dictators at the Coventry (a nightclub in Sunnyside, Queens), and he was wearing platform shoes and satin pants and he looked like the guy who got picked on—because he *was* the guy that got picked on. I don't know if Johnny ever saw us in the old days. Joey did. Dee Dee did. We wore leather jackets because we liked the image. MC5 wore leather jackets. Blue Oyster Cult, who were our friends, wore leather jackets. Other bands did it. Gene Vincent did it. We didn't make it a uniform. We wore leather jackets. We wore sneakers. We wore jeans, and once in a while we'd wear something else. The Ramones made it a uniform.

"At first, they were very influenced by glam rock, the pants and suspenders and the shoes with the little heels on them," says Monte A. Melnick, the Ramones' longtime road manager and author of *On the Road with the Ramones (Bonus Edition)*. "The glam rock days were phasing out into what eventually they called 'punk,' so they decided not to buy all the clothes. That stuff is expensive. They couldn't afford the glam clothes, so they were wearing just jeans and whatever they were wearing on the street. And they had those leather jackets."

"I think they realized when they're playing this simple music that they had to come up with a new look and I think they embraced this look that everybody could relate to," McNeil adds. "A black leather jacket, a T-shirt, and sneakers were what we were wearing then. I mean, I wasn't. John and I were still wearing blue denim jackets because we couldn't afford them, but after I saw the Ramones, I went out and bought a black leather jacket the next day."

Luecke says that the leather jacket, T-shirt, jeans, and sneakers may have been a uniform of the people, but it also gave an implicit nod to the gay hustler subculture. "Part of the Ramones were obviously smarter than they pretended to be. They've been coy about their exact intent, but in a sense, they're playing both sides. The leather jackets are what a young teen 'punk' would wear, and a young teen punk is likely to be a male hustler, since they're the ones who need money for drugs. And a good hustler would also know that a tough looking leather jacket would appeal to certain gay men because it connotes delinquency and bad boy appeal."

Johnny Strabler's Perfecto jacket was the uniform of punk rock icons the Ramones. "The leather jackets are what a young teen 'punk' would wear, and a young teen punk is likely to be a male hustler," says fashion historian Andrew Luecke. Photofest

Most obviously pointing to the teen punk, male hustler image was Dee Dee Ramone. Born Douglas Glenn Colvin in 1951, he was bass player and primary songwriter for the group and was known to wear a tight T-shirt that exposed his midriff. Dee Dee wrote the song "53rd and 3rd," about his experience as a male prostitute, "trying to turn a trick" on a corner known for its "chicken hawk" trade. "I know he (hustled) a little bit and he wrote that song," Melnick says. "He probably picked the jacket up along those lines—Brando and the gay scene. But Johnny and Tommy were wearing it, and they were influenced by Brando, not by the gay scene but the hardcore punk look."

"Dee Dee Ramone famously did turn tricks to support his habit, and so that's where the crop-tops and the tight jeans and the leathers come in," Luecke says. "That connection of *The Wild One*, the leather and the boots running through straight biker culture, running through gay leather culture, running through straight fetish culture, that all comes back full circle with the Ramones."

"In punk, there was that subtext of the gay scene," McNeil says in hindsight.

> Yeah. So the word *punk*, which was used in prison for "somebody's punk" or as a euphemism for getting fucked in the ass, made the whole scene bigger and accepted. There were a lot of gays at CBGB's. It was also the first time in the punk scene that gays and straights came together and worked together and were friends together. Whenever Patti Smith or the Talking Heads played, there'd be all the art scene kids. And Patti attracted a lot of lesbians because a lot of people thought she was gay. This bisexuality thing also applies to women. I bet a lot of people thought Tina Weymouth was gay because she was so intensely private. I think the whole idea of punk was to make it accessible to everybody. When you know [Ramones artistic director] Arturo Vega, who was gay, and [Ramones manager] Danny Fields, who was gay—we were working with these people all the time, and they were great fucking people! And once your best friends turn out to be gay, you can't be homophobic anymore. It was kind of forcing us to accept something that was opposed to us fundamentally, and I think that's what Brando did. Maybe not as obviously as you're pointing out, but he made it accessible and made them real people, so when you have the guy saying and doing these things and you see him and you relate to him and he also happens to be bisexual, what are you going to do then? You have to rethink your homophobia and dismiss it.

Punk survived through fifteen issues, and with the exception of special editions and spin-offs, lasted until 1979. An incident in February of that year, involving a notorious figure from the London punk scene and an American groupie in a room at the Chelsea Hotel on West Twenty-Third Street, probably sealed the fate of *Punk*—and punk.

"When Sid Vicious came along and stabbed his girlfriend, people said, 'See, they just shoot dope and kill their girlfriends' and punk became a noncommercial entity," McNeil says. "When Sire Records (the label for the Ramones and Talking Heads, among others) hooked up with Warner Brothers as their distributor, they took out these huge ads with Bugs Bunny in a black leather jacket saying, 'Don't call it Punk. Call it New Wave.' And that killed the magazine. No one wanted to advertise with us anymore."

Holmstrom looks back at those years with a sense of accomplishment, and pride. In 2023, he produced a special issue of *Punk* for an album by the original Midwest punk, Iggy Pop. "It's kind of crazy," he says.

> I graduated from Cheshire High School in 1971 and within four years, I put out a magazine that changed the world. We could have gone the James Dean route, really, because he was a bigger influence, I think, on juvenile delinquents than anyone. Growing up in Cheshire, our house was on a straightaway and so as a little kid I'd be kept up late at night by these kids who'd be drag racing down the street, and that was all James Dean, *Rebel Without a Cause*. But I'm remembering our high school. As soon as kids turned eighteen, they all bought Harley-Davidsons. And it was kind of horrendous because they weren't wearing helmets, and a lot of kids got really hurt. But that's a form of rebellion. That's why I chose Marlon Brando as the original punk. What other movie summarizes that attitude? "What are you rebelling against, Johnny?" "What do you got?" That's punk.

Fifteen

Wild Angels

Preacher: Tell me, just what is it that you want to do?
Heavenly Blues: We want to be free. We want to be free to do what we want to do! We want to be free to ride. And we want to be free to ride our machines without being hassled by The Man! And we want to get loaded! And we want to have a good time!

—The Wild Angels (1966)

"One of the things that's interesting in America and across the Western world is that you see these subversive cultures pop up, like your post–World War II bikers, and big movie studios become interested, and they sort of co-opt it, present it back to the subculture. It's sort of this conversation and dance," says Andrew Luecke, the fashion historian. "*The Wild One* pops up with the American biker scene, which obviously created the look that Brando presented to the world, but Brando made it bigger and more popular, and I think the way he presented it in *The Wild One* influenced the biker culture itself."

Images of the outlaw biker had already been entrenched in the public's imagination before *The Wild One* began appearing in movie theaters across the country in 1954. But the characters of Johnny Strabler and Chino refined the image, and became models, in style and attitude, for their real-life counterparts, much as movie gangsters influenced street wiseguys and hoodlums. The "conversation and dance" would continue over the next decade, until the outlaw bikers gave Hollywood a new and wilder version to exploit.

In the immediate aftermath of *The Wild One*, the major studios focused on the controversy over juvenile delinquency and gang violence with pictures like *Blackboard Jungle* and *Rebel Without a Cause*. If there was a focus on teens on wheels, the wheels were attached to automobiles. The 1950s was the decade of car culture. Work on Eisenhower's Interstate Highway System was underway, NASCAR and the National Hot Rod Association were formed, and in movieland, dangerous kids were speeding around in hot rods, stolen cars, or dying in chickie runs. It took some time for the bikers in Perfecto-style jackets to get their close-ups on the silver screen, and when they did, the screens were in drive-ins and grindhouse movie houses. A pair of producers, James H. Nicholson and Samuel Z. Arkoff, maneuvered to the pole position with their American International Pictures (AIP), which made low-budget flicks aimed at teenagers (assuming that their parents stayed home to watch television). In 1957, AIP released *Dragstrip Girl*, starring Fay Spain as a young woman who liked to race hot rods with hot guys. The movie was paired with *Rock All Night*, produced and directed by independent cinema pioneer Roger Corman, and featuring appearances by the Platters and a group called the Blockbusters, playing real rock 'n' roll. *Dragstrip Girl* worked out so well for the exploitation team that AIP shot and released a virtual remake the very same year—trading the hot rods for motorcycles. *Motorcycle Gang* (aka *Motorcycle Girls*), with the tagline *Wild and Wicked*—emphasis on the "wild"—featured young women who rode with bad boys in black leather jackets and jeans (and a character named "Speed," played by Carl "Alfalfa" Switzer from the *Our Gang* comedies). AIP introduced an actual biker gang, complete with those Perfecto leather jackets, in 1958, when it combined hot rods and motorcycles in *Dragstrip Riot*.

By the early 1960s, while Marlon Brando was becoming more deeply involved in political and social activism, and young, Hollywood-friendly John F. Kennedy had the nation looking toward the moon, *The Wild One* was one of the foundations of the new pop culture. When American International Pictures began to mine the teen vein with beach party movies starring Annette Funicello and Frankie Avalon, outlaw biker gangs were in the mix along with surfboards and hot rods—if only for comic relief. Harvey Lembeck appeared in a half dozen of the beach flicks, in Johnny Strabler drag, as Eric Von Zipper, leader of The Rats, described by one critic as "the Hells Angels as executed by the Three Stooges."

Memories of *The Wild One* were also kept alive in television sitcoms. Two days before Kennedy's assassination, CBS aired episode nine of the second season of *The Beverly Hillbillies*. In "The Clampetts Go Hollywood," Jed, Granny, Elly May, and Jethro decide to get into show business. Jethro, the naive, dimwit Clampett cousin played by Max Baer Jr., is seen in a movie theater, transfixed as he watches *The Wild One* on a big screen (actual clips of the film are shown). When we next see Jethro, he's Jethro Strabler, riding a motorcycle in the driveway of his mansion, wearing a leather hat, shades, and a leather jacket emblazoned with his name on the back. If viewers missed the joke, he makes it clear when a car pulls up. "Uh, hey, Stella," he says to the woman in the passenger seat. "What do you say, baby? Uh, you wanna drag me in that heap?" (Even in 1963, a Brando impression was signaled by uttering "Stella.") "Hot Rod Herman," the thirty-sixth episode of the first season of *The Munsters*, aired on

CBS on May 27, 1965. The highlight was a Johnny Strabler impersonation by Fred Gwynne as six-foot, ten-inch Herman Munster posing in a leather hat, jacket, and big, studded belt. (In the words of Grandpa Munster: "My son, the hundred-and-fifty-year-old teenage punk.")

That was Hollywood. Outside the studio walls, in the streets, while the "adult" mainstream made lame *Wild One* jokes, the beatnik and free speech movements had led to a rejection of "traditional values" by young people. The fight for civil rights was reaching a fever pitch. With the arrival of the Beatles, followed by a British Invasion, rock 'n' roll—soon to mature into "rock"—was dominating the music industry. Marijuana and other drugs were on the scene, someone acknowledged a widening "generation gap," and the escalating conflict in Vietnam and conscription of young American men was feeding an antiwar movement that was embraced not only by college students, but veterans who'd been drafted into combat in Vietnam. Many of these former soldiers had returned a little more haunted, a little crazier, and often with more than a little a taste for—or addiction to—heroin.

Amid these cultural shifts, the outlaw biker culture that emerged after World War II and was influenced by *The Wild One* was undergoing a rejuvenation and injection of recruits who were more extreme and violent than the weekend warriors who'd downed a few beers and did fishtails on San Benito Street in Hollister in 1947. By the mid-1960s, outlaw motorcycle gangs were rolling across the highways and backroads of California from San Diego to the Sierra Nevada, and no gang was more mythologized by the media and law enforcement than the Hells Angels. Organized in 1948 in Fontana in San Bernardino County, the club expanded as various chapters were formed over the next decade. Sonny Barger, a US Army veteran, started up the Oakland Hells Angels in 1957. Barger traveled the state, unified other chapters, codified the rules, and by 1958 was regarded as the Hells Angels president. By the early 1960s, he was the face of the outlaw organization and kept the conversation and dance alive as he helped the Hells Angels go "Hollywood."

Barger made it clear that he was influenced in a major way by *The Wild One*—but not by Johnny Strabler. "When I saw *The Wild One*, Lee Marvin instantly became my hero," Barger wrote in his autobiography. "Lee's character, Chino, was my man. Marlon Brando as Johnny was the bully. His boys rode Triumphs and BSAs and wore uniforms. Lee's attitude was, 'If you fuck with me, I'll hit you back.' Lee and his boys were riding fucked-up Harleys and Indians. I certainly saw more of Chino in me than Johnny. I still do."

It makes sense that a real rebel outlaw like Barger would be attracted to the Chino character—to the point that he reportedly purchased at auction the striped jersey worn by Lee Marvin in the film. Chino's gang, careening into Wrightsville in all their ragged rebel glory, looked a lot more like the real-life outlaw bikers at the time, and most of the bikers hired as extras in *The Wild One* were placed with them. Offscreen, Marvin was jealous of Brando, and played his opposite off camera as well. In contrast to Brando's quiet concentration, he was loud, boisterous, and often drunk, playing to the extras, and laughing when they referred to the Black Rebels as "the pussycat version of outlaw bikers."

The Hells Angels skidded into the headlines and went from curiosities to perceived threat to the nation in 1964, after hundreds of them descended on a town on the Monterey peninsula on a holiday weekend. It was in some ways reminiscent of Fourth of July weekend, 1947, in Hollister, but this was Labor Day weekend, and the town of Monterey, forty miles southwest. On Sunday, September 6, two underage teenage girls were allegedly gang-raped by bikers at their encampment on a nearby beach. The full force of the law came down upon the outlaws. A posse of state and local police, aided by volunteers, escorted three hundred of them to the county line. Four Hells Angels were arrested (the charges were soon dismissed for lack of evidence), and the attorney general of California ordered a report on this new threat to civilized society.

The attorney general's six-month investigation led to the Lynch Report, which tallied up many crimes committed by the gang members in recent years, including assaults, narcotics trafficking, forgeries, robberies, and thefts. Around the time the report was published in March 1965, so was an article in *The Nation* by journalist Hunter S. Thompson. Thompson had been riding and spending time with the Hells Angels and rebutted the conclusions and sensational news coverage that painted the outlaw bikers as some sort of mythic supervillains:

> The Attorney General's report was colorful, interesting, heavily biased and consistently alarming—just the sort of thing, in fact, to make a clanging good article for a national news magazine. Which it did; in both barrels. *Newsweek* led with a left hook titled "The Wild Ones," *Time* crossed right, inevitably titled "The Wilder Ones.". . . The vast majority of motorcycle outlaws are uneducated, unskilled men between 20 and 30, and most have no credentials except a police record. . . . They are out of the ball game and they know it— and that is their meaning; for unlike most losers in today's society, the Hells Angels not only know but spitefully proclaim exactly where they stand.

One of the first filmmakers to reflect the zeitgeist—and exploit the publicity—was Russ Meyer, an independent director, writer, and producer known for his "nudies" and "sexploitation" films featuring ample-breasted women and smutty jokes. His 1965 film, *Motor Psycho*, dramatized a rape and murder spree by a trio of bikers led by a sadistic and deranged Vietnam veteran who experiences combat flashbacks.

Motor Psycho was one of the first films to depict the post-traumatic stress disorder that would afflict so many who returned from the war.

"Bikersploitation" expert, author, and pop culture historian Edwin Lee Canfield points to *Outlaw Motorcycles* as another film, also produced in 1965, that "kick-started the biker flick," a genre that "can be traced back to the portrayal of the hell-raising outlaw motorcycle gang the Black Rebels, led by a devil-may-care Marlon Brando in *The Wild One*." The 16 mm short was written and directed by actor and director Titus Moede (aka Titus Moody), and recorded the exploits of Southern California motorcycle gangs and outlaw clubs like the Tikis, Monks, Coffin Cheaters, and of course, the Hells Angels. "It was made documentary style," Canfield says. "Moede got in tight with the motorcycle clubs and basically filmed their parties and get-togethers. It was the first real look at motorcycle clubs and gangs, although it's not as down-and-dirty as they probably really were. It talked about how, in their use of Nazi symbols like the swastika and iron crosses, they were more like stamp collectors, collecting historical objects. Instead of using them as part of their philosophy, it was for shock value, to scare the 'straights.'"

Actor Keenan Wynn, who had originally been chosen to play Chino in *The Wild One* (after weeks of preproduction, MGM refused to loan him out to Columbia Pictures), makes an appearance in *Outlaw Motorcycles*. Wynn and Lee Marvin were good friends and were among Hollywood's notable hard-drinking motorcycle enthusiasts.

Hunter S. Thompson's article on the Hells Angels led, in February 1966, to the publication of his first book. Kirkus Reviews praised *Hell's Angels: The Strange and Terrible Saga of the Outlaw Motorcycle Gangs* for debunking the exaggerations of the "New York Press establishment": "The phenomenal aspect of this press was that the Angels started believing the image. They trekked to the movies to see themselves portrayed on film by Marlon Brando and Lee Marvin in *The Wild One*. They got dirtier, tougher, meaner and for a while even had a public relations man to promote their madness into some sizable cash."

A month later, Roger Corman of American International Pictures began filming a low-budget exploitation flick called *The Wild Angels*. According to Canfield, Corman had been inspired by a *Life* magazine photograph of a Hells Angels funeral (just as a photo in *Life* led to *Cyclists' Raid*). He'd brought AIP the idea of a film about the gang, promising that the "biker flick" would be the "new western."

Peter Fonda was in the starring role as Heavenly Blues, leader of a motorcycle gang called the Angels. Nancy Sinatra, cast as "Mike," Heavenly's "old lady," would guarantee some box office returns. Her single, "These Boots Are Made for Walkin'," had recently hit number one on the *Billboard* pop chart. Bruce Dern played a character named Loser, who

THE MOST TERRIFYING FILM OF OUR TIME!

UPA®

Distributed by
UNITED PRODUCTIONS OF AMERIC.
600 Madison Avenue, New York, N.Y
Phone: 212-752-1464

Against everything
but each other–these
are today's real rebels,
with a chip on their
shoulder, a monkey
on their back and
a hate for the
world in their guts!

PETER FONDA · NANCY SINATRA

STARRING IN

THE WILD
ANGELS

CO-STARRING BRUCE DERN and DIANE LADD

WITH

MEMBERS OF HELL'S ANGELS
OF VENICE, CALIFORNIA

The Wild One was the model for the "biker flicks" of the 1960s, beginning with *The Wild Angels*, directed by Roger Corman and starring Peter Fonda, Nancy Sinatra, Bruce Dern, Diane Lane, and Michael J. Pollard. AIP/Photofest © American Int'l Pictures

loses his life and sets the stage for an Angels funeral that includes a coffin draped with a Nazi flag, a riot and orgy in a church, and finally, a funeral procession like the one in *Life* magazine. In this film and others to follow, Canfield mentions that Fonda's characterization reflected "Brando's coolness" in *The Wild One.*

"*Cyclists' Raid,* the short story *The Wild One* is based on, depicts the militaristic style of the gang, the way they pull into town single-file and split off, with the leader of the gang signaling them without being obvious. It's probably because they're veterans of the war, having this military leadership and at the same time being total rebels who want to be free and live free. Brando's leather jacket has stars on the epaulets, indicating he's the general. He's leading the group, but he's not a part of it. He's not like the rest of the guys. He wasn't out of control like the rest of the gang. He was pretty mellow, pretty smart, a philosophical kind of guy. And Peter Fonda in *The Wild Angels* is that way as well, the supercool leader of the gang."

With *The Wild Angels,* what Canfield labels "The Golden Age of the Bikersploitation film genre" was launched. *Hells Angels on Wheels* was unleashed in February 1967, starring Jack Nicholson as Poet, a gas station pump jockey who quits his job and is initiated into a Hells Angels chapter by the leader, Buddy (played by Adam Roarke, soon to become a star of the genre). Among the cast listed in the opening credits are "The Hells Angels of Oakland, San Francisco, Daly City, Richmond and the Nomads of Sacramento, California . . . and Sonny Barger, President of the Hells Angels." Barger is also credited as a technical adviser. "Barger said this was his favorite of the biker movies" Canfield says. "He said it portrayed them more like they really were." Canfield notes the authenticity in the final scene, when Poet, "disillusioned by the gang's unbridled brutality but entangled in a confusing free-love triangle with Buddy's 'mama' girlfriend," gets in a brawl with the leader. "It reminds me of Hunter S. Thompson getting a beatdown by the Hells Angels. He was accepted at first and then he began to question their ways."

John Cassavetes starred in *The Devil's Angels,* released in April 1967. In a clubhouse scene, there's a quick shot of a poster of Brando in *The Wild One*—someone drew a mustache and beard on his face. In July, Tom Laughlin directed and starred in *The Born Losers.* He went on to great success with the character Billy Jack. November saw the release of *The Glory Stompers.* Dennis Hopper plays a biker gang leader named Chino. These were only a few of dozens of biker flicks cranked out through the sixties and into the seventies. In 1969, Gray Frederickson was producing (along with Albert S. Ruddy and Brad Dexter) *Little Fauss and Big Halsy,* a comedy-drama about dirt bike racers, directed by Sidney J. Furie and starring Robert Redford and Michael J. Pollard (who played Pygmy in *The*

Wild Angels). "They were dirt bikers, but we talked about *The Wild One* a lot while we were doing it," he recalls. "Basically, Sidney Furie would say, 'This is not *The Wild One*!' It was about motorcycle dirt bike racing. 'This is not *The Wild One*! We're not shooting *The Wild One* here!'"

The highlight of the era arrived on May 12, 1969, when *Easy Rider* premiered at the Cannes Film Festival. The story of two bikers who complete a drug deal and travel across the country in search of the truth (but wind up dead) starred three heroes of bikersploitation: Dennis Hopper, Peter Fonda, and Jack Nicholson. The film was directed by Hopper and written by Hopper, Fonda, and Terry Southern. The Cannes jury awarded Hopper a special prize for "best picture by a new director," and the film was nominated for the Palme d'Or. Nicholson, as supporting actor, and Hopper, Fonda, and Southern for their screenplay, would be nominated for Academy Awards.

The lineage was clear. "The idea for *Easy Rider* came to me while I was in Toronto promoting *The Trip*," Peter Fonda said. "I'd taken a couple of aspirins and was lying on the bed looking at a picture of Marlon Brando in his *Wild One* get-up. And then it came to me: a modern western set on motorbikes! The next day, I called Dennis."

Fonda was the son of a Hollywood legend whose career was launched by Marlon Brando's mother. Hopper had appeared in *Rebel Without a Cause* with his friend, the Brando worshiper James Dean. Terry Southern had cowritten *Candy*. Jack Nicholson was a Corman regular who was not only a student of Brando's work, but in a couple of years he and the great actor would be sharing a private driveway high above Los Angeles on Mulholland Drive. And after years of biker flicks knocked out by low-budget exploitation producers like American International Pictures, *Easy Rider* was distributed by a major studio, Columbia Pictures, which had started it all with *The Wild One*.

"*Easy Rider* changed Hollywood," Canfield says. The film was embraced by critics, and more important, by the young audiences it was aimed at. Drugs, free love, hippies, rock music, sex, protest—and bikers, all the ingredients that had been thrown into the stew of biker flicks had emerged as art, and profitable art, at that. On a budget of less than $375,000, *Easy Rider* took in $60 million, and showed the suits that big money could be made on low-budget work by imaginative young artists. "The film shook and woke the antiquated Hollywood establishment," according to Canfield, "paving the way for the 'counterculture' New Hollywood style of the early 1970s filmmaking, forever changing the way the failing good-old-boy studio system operated."

And while the success of *Easy Rider* helped steer young filmmakers toward the A-list, the flow of low-budget independent B-movie biker flicks continued well into the 1970s. Most featured the usual cast of actors and bikers, but some starred unlikely riders, like Bette Davis and Ernest Borgnine in *Bunny O'Hare.*

The genre's popularity was revived in the era of videotape rentals, and by the passion of young fans turned filmmakers, like Quentin Tarantino. Biker films continued to be updated with the times, to varying success, with films including *Harley Davidson and the Marlboro Man* (1991), starring Mickey Rourke and Don Johnson; *Beyond the Law* (1993), starring Charlie Sheen and Michael Madsen; *Biker Boyz* (2003), with Laurence Fishburne; Ice Cube in *Torque* (2004); the comedy *Wild Hogs* (2007), with John Travolta, Tim Allen, and Martin Lawrence; *Ghost Rider* (2007) starring Nicolas Cage; and on television, beginning in 2008, Kurt Sutter's *Sons of Anarchy* and its 2018 spinoff *Mayans M.C.* All contain *The Wild One*'s DNA, but the one that best captured the wild, anarchic spirit of sixties bikersploitation was *Hell Ride*, in which a biker gang heads out to avenge a decades-old murder. The 2008 film was directed by and starred Larry Bishop, a veteran of classic biker flicks including *The Savage Seven, The Devil's 8, Angel Unchained,* and *Chrome and Hot Leather* (as well as Tarantino's *Kill Bill*). Tarantino, in the role of executive producer, made the film possible, and according to costar Michael Madsen, reedited it for release. Madsen, a longtime motorcycle rider and subject of the documentary *American Badass*, played "The Gent" in *Hell Ride.* The character stood out

The spirit of *The Wild One* lives on in films like *Hell Ride*, starring (from left) Michael Madsen, director Larry Bishop, and Eric Balfour. Executive producer: Quentin Tarantino. Dimension Films/Photofest © Dimension Films

because he rode a custom shovelhead Harley. He was also the one outlaw biker who was not wearing leather.

"It was my idea to dress up in a tuxedo," he says. "I figured if my character's name is The Gent, maybe I should have a tuxedo on, like I ran away from a wedding or something."

> One of the reasons I was so enthusiastic to do *Hell Ride* was because Dennis Hopper was in it. There I am, on screen with the guy from *Easy Rider*. I was friends with Dennis at the time from some low-budget film we had done before that, but to be in a motorcycle movie with him—and David Carradine and Vinnie Jones? I mean, wow, that's big talent. I think that *Hell Ride* is a very, very underestimated biker picture. I think it's a damn good movie, a mysterious, heavy-duty biker picture that never got a fair shake. And you can blame that on The Weinstein Company, because they sold it to DVD even before it was finished. So it never had a chance to even get out there. It's become a cult biker picture, as it should.

Madsen counts *Easy Rider* as among his favorite pictures of the genre. What else? "All I can say is I liked that stupid *C. C. & Company* with Joe Namath in it, and of course *The Wild One* is the first one. That's the one that sticks out in my mind. I've seen the movie; I got a poster of it. But you know, the funny thing about *The Wild One* is that Brando's sitting on a Triumph. Lee Marvin had the Harley."

Sixteen

Rebel with Causes

"He was a piece of work. I liked him. On *Godfather*, he was into American Indians," recalls Gray Frederickson, a producer on *The Godfather* trilogy (an Academy Award winner for producing *The Godfather: Part II*) and *Apocalypse Now*. "First though, he was into *India* Indians and the caste system in India, and how unfair it was for people born into lower classes. And then he kind of switched from India Indians to American Indians."

The plight of outcastes in India and his own position as an insider in Hollywood added up to Brando's opportunity to do more than appear in movies that reflected his social concerns. In 1955, he'd be handed the means to actually produce these films, tailor the messages, and, in his own naive way, "contribute in a telling way to the achievement of a peaceful world." Brando's passion to use his position to "make a difference" would perhaps be quixotic and beyond his emotional abilities, but would again have a lasting influence on generations of actors and "movie stars" to follow.

The opportunity came at a time when it seemed that Brando had long since outgrown his rebel image. *Désirée* had been released the previous November, and rather than move on to a film of social relevance, Brando took the money and ran, singing and dancing as Sky Masterson in *Guys and Dolls*. Production got underway on March 14 at Samuel Goldwyn Studios on Santa Monica Boulevard in West Hollywood. Sixteen days later, Brando was two miles away, at the Pantages Theatre on Hollywood Boulevard for the 27th Academy Awards, and he certainly did not look like the rebellious Johnny Strabler as he jogged to the stage after Bette Davis announced his name as Best Actor for his role in *On the Waterfront*. Cradling the statue in both hands, Brando was the picture of a man grateful for being accepted into the club. "It's much heavier than I imagined," he said to applause as he clutched the award in one hand while, in a Method move, rubbing down the back of his head with the other. "I guess I had something to say, and I can't remember what I was going to say for the life of me. Um, I don't think that ever in my life have so many people been so directly responsible for my being so very, very glad. It's a wonderful moment and a rare one and I'm certainly indebted. Thank you." After four consecutive nominations, Brando had won his first Academy Award. He was settling into a home in Los Angeles. The ground was shifting for him and the film industry, and months later he had the opportunity to take his career into his own hands—if he cared enough to.

With television, paradoxically still somewhat new but already in a "golden age," replacing motion pictures as America's shared entertainment experience, and talent agencies gaining more power through their representation of their most popular stars, the major Hollywood studios had all but lost their grip on the industry by 1955. While they churned out fewer films, with fewer big stars under their collective thumb, independent producers, who'd always been on the sidelines, pushing out cheap genre flicks or scouring the trades to find a performer who was on the outs and willing to accept a role in a low-budget quickie, moved in with bigger-budget, higher-quality fare. Simultaneously, the power of talent agents, who'd worked within and manipulated the system for decades, now burst into view in a dawn of "superagencies." Most prominent were the William Morris Agency, and, in Brando's case, the Music Corporation of America, known in shorthand as MCA. Bob Thomas of the Associated Press explained that "with the aggressive leadership of Jules Stein and Lew Wasserman, the agency was making deals which had been impossible during the absolute monarchies of the Harry Cohns and Louis B. Mayers. Studios now agreed to partnerships with stars they had once controlled. The stars selected their own properties, oversaw production and shared in the profits."

Brando was not a pioneer in this entry into the production side. As early as 1935, Constance Bennett had partnered in Bennett Pictures, while a dozen years later, her sister Joan formed Diana Pictures with director Fritz Lang and her husband, producer Walter Wanger; Cagney Productions and B. D. Productions were formed in 1942 by the powerful Warner Bros. contract players James Cagney and Bette Davis. By 1955, most of the big names had production companies: Humphrey Bogart with Santana Pictures, Alan Ladd's Jaguar Productions, Kirk Douglas's Bryna Productions, Marilyn Monroe Productions, Curtleigh, formed by married couple Tony Curtis and Janet Leigh, and Cary Grant with Grando, Granart, Granley, and Granox.

Marlon Brando, who in its "Top Exhibitoratings of 1954–1955" *Independent Film Journal* named as the "Top Money Actor" (above William Holden, James Stewart, and Bing Crosby), was offered his own shingle weeks after he took home the Academy Award. MCA convinced him that along with the artistic freedom, his own production company would provide a tax shelter, more profits, and control (on the downside, the actor as producer would have to shell out some of his own money on productions). The agency set him up with Paramount Pictures. Brando partnered with his father, Marlon Brando Sr., who'd been in charge of investing his money (most notably in a nine-thousand-acre cattle ranch in Nebraska) and his good friend, George Englund, a twenty-eight-year-old actor and would-be producer. He named the company Pennebaker, Inc., his mother's maiden name, in Dodie's honor. Paramount provided him office space on its Melrose Avenue lot, secretaries, and office staff. The studio promised to support Brando in whatever pictures he chose to make. All Brando need do was make pictures for Paramount.

When Pennebaker announced its initial slate of productions in early 1956, Brando's intentions were clear. The first picture would be a western, based on *To Tame a Land*, the latest novel by the frontier storyteller Louis L'Amour. It was not, Brando promised, to be your "typical" oater. "I want to make a frontal assault on the temple of cliches that have permeated the usual Hollywood western," he said. "Our early-day western heroes were not brave one hundred percent of the time, nor were they good one hundred percent of the time. I think Stanley Kramer started a good trend toward authentic realism in westerns with *High Noon*."

He also planned to take what could be seen as a revolutionary step. In his first public declaration of support for Native Americans, Brando promised that this cowboy-and-Indian drama would tilt toward the side of the American Indian. "Today the Indians are a broken race of people," he told the trades. "The white man took his culture away and destroyed his philosophy of life and morality. We challenged the precepts on which he based his religion and destroyed the very kernels of his existence."

He added: "There are certain concessions to commercial entertainment that must be made. After all, it is a business. Even Shakespeare had to insert bawdy humor in some of his plays to cater to the tastes of his audience. However, the last thing I'll ever be is a strictly commercial producer interested only in money. I never will be a quick-buck producer."

As the weeks passed, Brando proved that he was not a quick-buck producer nor a quick producer. A western would be his first film for Pennebaker, Inc., but it would not be *To Tame a Land*. The picture would not go into production for several years, and with a plot that had his character on a journey to kill a character named "Dad," was more influenced by sessions with Dr. Mittelmann than meetings with Native American activists.

In an attempt to start producing and turn Pennebaker, Inc. into a profitable entity, two more partners were brought on board. George Glass was a former partner of Stanley Kramer and an associate producer on *The Men*. Walter Seltzer was a producer and publicist. Both were anxious to get to work, but Brando was more concerned, as Gray Frederickson remembered accurately, with "India Indians." "How can you guys think of making movies at a time when there are millions of Indians dying of starvation?" he challenged his new teammates. Less concerned with the starving millions in India than their own ability to pay for groceries, Seltzer and Glass got in touch with a member of the Indian Film Commission. India's film industry was the world's second-largest, producing about two-thirds as many films as Hollywood, but because of language barriers and production quality, comparatively few were exported. The film commissioners saw Brando's participation as a way for their industry to grow in size and quality, so they responded with an offer of big money and first-class transportation and lodging for Brando to come over and star in one of their projects. According to his producing partners, Brando liked the idea—until he realized how much effort it would entail.

Brando's concern with Third World issues and his notion that he could eventually use his company to "make a difference" was evident in Pennebaker's second announced project, a drama based on the work of the United Nations Technical Assistance Program. "There is no more exciting, romantic and important work being done in the world today than that accomplished by UN technical assistance," Brando said of the program in which Western specialists in fields like medicine, agriculture, and education shared their knowledge with underdeveloped countries. "For sheer entertainment, their stories are unrivaled and will be told with all the magic and impact that motion pictures can provide."

While the subject did not seem the most colorful basis for a successful commercial film, the Pennebaker partners did throw a kidnapping plot into the mix, giving Louella Parsons the exclusive word that the "idea has to do with the mysterious disappearance of government researchers." In late January, Brando, George Englund, and Stewart Stern, who'd written the screenplay for *Rebel Without a Cause*, took off on a twenty-thousand-mile tour of Asia. The itinerary included Hong Kong, Singapore, Manila, and Bangkok, to scout locations and "study the government files for authentic data Stern will weave into a story."

"I found so much to stimulate me I couldn't begin to tell you in one conversation," Brando enthused on his return. "Americans don't even begin to understand the people of Asia. The average American couldn't tell you even three of the main bodies of land that comprise Indonesia, what the capital is. . . . American prestige is dwindling among those countries of Asia while the great masses of China and Russia are waiting to gobble them up. . . . The Asians are looking to us for signs of friendship. I hope my picture will help, but it must be entertainment. If it's not entertaining, I have accomplished nothing, and I may have done irreparable harm."

The Asia jaunt and his intentions to "communicate things I think are important" were foremost in Brando's mind when he took off for Tokyo for his next film role. *The Teahouse of the August Moon*, like *Guys and Dolls*, was based on a Broadway hit, and although Brando admitted he was "heavy-footed with comedy," was another comedic role. In what in later decades would be criticized as a prime example of "yellowface" casting, he played an Asian named Sakini, an interpreter for US occupation forces in Japan after the end of World War II. To get into character, Brando lost weight and experimented with makeup, including rubber eyelids, protruding teeth, a wig, and a coat of yellowish grease paint. Ultimately, the *New York Times'* Crowther would decide that the result "looks synthetic . . . and his manner of speaking broken English as though he had a wad of chewing gum clenched between his teeth . . . makes him hard to understand." But the filming gave Brando the opportunity to meet the press and expound on the United States' misguided actions in the Third World. (Brando returned to Japan in January 1957 to film *Sayonara*, another "message movie," which, because of script changes he insisted on, depicted racial intermarriage "as a natural outcome when people fell in love," and was another "example of the pictures I wanted to make, films that exerted a positive force.")

Englund and Stern, meanwhile, landed in New York to announce that the fruit of the trip would be a film called *Tiger on a Kite*, named for a phrase that "symbolizes the various countries breaking from the yoke of colonization." Stern said the story would be based on the adventures of the United Nations advisers: people like the agricultural expert from Nevada who, sent to share his expertise in Thailand, wound up uprooting and moving his entire family "to a land they knew about only through *Anna and the King of Siam*." The pair said that filming locations had been narrowed down to India, Ceylon, Thailand, or the Philippines. They made it clear that this was to be a dramatic, not documentary, film.

The most surprising reaction to the Pennebaker statements came from the studio. "Paramount is financing 100% a feature whose producer has no previous production credits and for which there is no story," *Variety* reported. "Other than Brando, no cast, yet, obviously since the characters haven't been drawn. . . . The fact that Brando is to star is a major factor, of course, but for a major studio to ante up for a production at nothing more than the 'idea' stage is unique."

Tiger on a Kite was never produced. Some of its ideas and spirit would be included in *The Ugly American*, the 1963 film starring Brando, written by Stern, and produced and directed by George Englund. The experience proved to be a factor in Brando's growing radicalization and his lessening interest in making movies other than to promote his causes.

"When I first heard about the UN's technical-assistance program and America's foreign aid, I had thought of them as wonderful examples of the haves helping the have-nots with compassion and charity," he told

Robert Lindsey. "But when I visited Third World countries for UNICEF, I had realized that the policies of the industrialized nations were not only selfish, self-serving, and misguided, but also weren't working. . . . Throughout Latin America and Asia . . . our government created dictators who robbed, cheated, and murdered their people with impunity, but as long as they were against communism, it let them get away with anything, including murder. Further, if we sent any aid to these countries, there were strings attached. It wasn't because we wanted to fight starvation, ignorance, disease and poverty; it was because of self-interest, greed and the myths about communism."

Pennebaker, Inc. did, finally, complete a motion picture, although it would take several years to produce and a couple more to release. The journey began when the company optioned *The Authentic Death of Hendry Jones*, a recent novel by Charles Neider that was a fictional take on the Billy the Kid story. Brando planned to star in the film. Stanley Kubrick, who impressed Brando with his work on *The Killing* and *Paths of Glory*, was brought on to direct. Brando and Kubrick worked together on the script in 1958, but as the process dragged on and the story veered further from the source material, the two did not get along. Kubrick was not happy with being fired, but publicly said it was his decision to drop out in order to prepare for his own film, *Lolita*. Brando decided to take over as director. Production on the picture that would be titled *One-Eyed Jacks* began in Monterey, Mexico, on December 2, 1958, and progressed slowly through the second day of June 1959, as the first-time director spent a lot of time encouraging his actors to use improvisational techniques he'd carried with him since his first classes with Stella Adler. More than time was used up during the six-month shooting schedule. Brando exposed more than a million feet of expensive VistaVision film (according to Bob Thomas, this was a "world record"—"the average movie used about 150,000 feet of film") and had forty thousand feet of film printed. After reshoots in October 1960, the price tag came to about $6 million. Brando put his heart and soul into editing the film and managed to get a cut of four hours and forty-two minutes before throwing his hands up. Paramount took over and released a two-hour-and-twenty-one-minute version on March 30, 1961.

Reviews for *One-Eyed Jacks* weren't bad, and the picture earned a small profit, but in the years following Brando's initial foray into independent production, the most substantial effect of Pennebaker, Inc.'s place on the Paramount lot was Brando's proximity to the commissary. It was there, grabbing lunch, that he not only bumped into Elvis Presley, but where, in November 1955, he first laid eyes on Anna Kashfi. She was a young actress completing her first movie, *The Mountain*, starring Spencer Tracy,

E. G. Marshall, and Robert Wagner. A stunning, dark, and slender beauty of twenty-one, she was born Joan O'Callaghan of British and Welsh parentage, raised in Calcutta, and was passing herself off as an exotic Indian model and actress. Brando was, it was said, "smitten." They began a relationship. After Kashfi announced that she was pregnant, she and Brando were married on October 11, 1957, in a place that had figured in several important moments in Brando's personal life: the living room of his aunt Betty Lindemeyer's house in Eagle Rock. Brando was thirty-three. Anna Kashfi was ten years younger. Their son, Christian Devi, was born on May 11, 1958. Christian was named for Brando's good friend and occasional lover Christian Marquand. Kashfi said "Devi" was in honor of the Indian man she claimed to be her father, though it was pointed out that "devi" was the Hindu word for "goddess." The marriage did not take. Kashfi was volatile. She could not accept Brando's lifestyle—mainly the other women who were in and out of his life.

The couple's marriage ended on April 22, 1959, but their painful saga did not. In the years to follow, Brando and his ex-wife would be in and out of court and great tabloid drama would play out in a tug-of-war over custody of Christian. The courtroom appearances, eruptions, and embarrassing testimony were gobbled up by the press and would often overshadow the important political and societal work Brando was trying to accomplish. The effects on young Christian were inestimable, and decades later, his own shocking actions would lead to tragedy and scandal that would put Brando back in the witness box and the headlines in the most embarrassing and legacy-threatening episode of his life.

Brando's "coming out" as an activist and the first hints of the radicalization that would subsume his career and influence generations of activist actors to come took place on May 2, 1960. The cause was not related to Indians, American or India's, nor the issues of Asia. It was the case of Caryl Chessman, a prisoner on California's Death Row.

At thirty-eight years old, Chessman was undoubtedly the most famous Death Row inmate in America, if not modern history. On the second day of May, he had been on Death Row at San Quentin prison for eleven years and three hundred and five days, had lived through eight stays of execution, and was counting on receiving yet another delay. Chessman had been a small-time crook and parolee from Folsom Prison when he was arrested in Los Angeles in 1948 and accused of being the Red Light Bandit, a criminal who carried a red light, similar to one used by police, in order to pull over or approach young couples in their cars in secluded areas. He would then rob them, drag the female from the vehicle, and force her to engage in oral sex. Chessman allegedly confessed to the crimes after a seventy-two-hour interrogation, and was charged with eighteen counts of robbery, kidnapping, and rape. He was tried, convicted, and sentenced to death in the gas chamber of the prison in Marin County, California. It was agreed that this was an unusual application of the death penalty, but applicable because he had dragged one victim more than twenty feet from the car, which counted as kidnapping with bodily harm—a capital crime in California.

"Chessman was a pain in the ass. He was a smartass," says Alan Bisbort, the Beatnik authority and author of *When You Read This, They Will Have Killed Me: The Life and Redemption of Caryl Chessman, Whose Execution Shocked America.*

> The reason he got the death penalty was that he swaggered into court—and he did have a genius IQ—and thought he was smarter than everyone and didn't want a lawyer. So he argued his own case. And *that* is a death sentence. And California happened to have on the books the residual law that was a result of the Lindbergh kidnapping, so his death sentences came for kidnapping, obviously not for murder, since no one died. I got this impression that he was sort of half Eddie Haskell and half—I don't know, *angel* or something. He was smart and he knew it, and if you weren't ready for it, he could rub you the wrong way. I mean, his behavior at his trial was inexcusable. It's like you want to shake him and go, "Do you realize if you fuck this up, you're going to San Quentin, you're going to *die?* What the fuck?!" And he's up there browbeating the woman who's testifying against him. If you were a woman and you'd been raped and your rapist is in court hectoring you? It's like, "*What are you thinking?*"

In San Quentin, Chessman shouted his innocence, claiming to have been a victim of mistaken identity or conspiracy. Acting as his own attorney, he filed dozens of appeals, and reached out to the public. He wrote four books while on Death Row. All of them became bestsellers. The first, *Cell 2455, Death Row,* a memoir, was published in 1954 and soon was turned into a movie starring William Campbell. The film was released in May 1955, six months before *Rebel Without a Cause,* and after James Dean's death that September, Columbia Pictures cashed in on the *Rebel* image.

"It wasn't a great film, but it wasn't horrible," Bisbort says. "Because Chessman was a car thief and he would go for joyrides, the one-sheet pictured a guy driving a sports car at high rates of speed, laughing with a gun in his hand—that whole *Rebel Without a Cause* thing. In fact, I saw an ad in a newspaper for the film, next to an ad for *Rebel Without a Cause.*"

This was the cause that Marlon Brando had taken on. He was first among celebrities who came out very publicly against the death penalty, especially in a case in which no victim was killed. "Brando had a social conscience," says Bisbort. "He became one of the major figurehead

The case of Caryl Chessman, the most famous death row inmate in America, was the first step in Brando's radicalization. Photofest

champions for saving the life of Caryl Chessmen and leading the anti-death penalty push. And this was a chancy thing for Brando to do."

The latest execution date was set for Monday morning at 10 a.m., Pacific time, on May 2. On May 1, Brando, actress Shirley MacLaine, and television personality Steve Allen visited Governor Edmund "Pat" Brown in Sacramento in an attempt to convince him to give Chessman more time by issuing a ninth stay of execution. In February, Brown had issued a sixty-day stay at the eleventh hour to give Chessman more time to file appeals. This time, he was noncommittal. "Chessman wasn't a nobody at that point," Bisbort says.

> He was a best-selling author around the world. In March he'd been on the cover of *Time* magazine. And Pat Brown realized his political future was hanging on this thing, so he just decided not to do anything. Other than, as a Catholic, he kept saying, "I'm a Roman Catholic. We do not believe in the death penalty," but he just didn't do anything. It's not like he called up and said, "Kill him." It's just that he didn't do it. He did not stand up when the time was right. This is May of 1960, and it's my theory that he was eyeing the August Democratic convention. He was hoping to be the nominee for president. And a young whippersnapper from Massachusetts, also a Catholic, was picked instead, and I think a lot of it had to do with fallout from Chessman. He bungled it because he wanted to play at both sides.

From Brown's office in Sacramento, Brando traveled to San Quentin prison, where more than a hundred people had already gathered to protest what was scheduled for later in the morning. He spent most of the night outside with the demonstrators. By daybreak, the small crowd had grown to about six hundred, spread out along the road to the prison, while across San Francisco Bay from the prison, a group of Quakers and other religious sympathizers had kept their own vigil throughout the night and into the morning, kneeling in the sand and praying quietly. Sheriff's deputies and prison guards keep a close watch as the demonstrators marched and chanted. The lawmen also keep an eye on a group of men on the surrounding hills. There were about twenty of them. They were not beatniks. They could be regarded as "counter-protesters." Most of them said they were from the nearby Alameda Naval Air station. They heckled the crowd in the valley below, and when things got too loud, ran down the hill to confront the anti-death penalty protesters.

Bisbort paints the picture:

> It's pretty astonishing. Here's one of the most popular, if not the most popular male movie star at that time, spending all night outside of a prison. If you've been up there, you know San Quentin is on this little promontory of land. I don't know if there were buses or if people walked there, but it's not an easy place to get to. So you had all these people cramming in there,

plus the cops and the media people—and you have this famous movie star out there. And a lot of people came over from Berkeley. Mario Savio and all these people were there and obviously, the Berkeley free speech movement wouldn't really get going until four years later, but these all were people who had been involved with the civil rights movement people, longtime anti-death penalty people. So he was immersed in a group of highly politicized people for that entire night. There was no way he would be walking around with everybody saying, "Can I have your autograph?" I have this image of him talking to groups of people who'd give him information and I really do think that an experience like that would have radicalized him.

According to the *San Francisco Examiner*, many of the protesters were "garbed in the beatnik uniform of beards and sandals." Brando, however, was not. Although one reporter said he appeared "white and drawn and needing a shave," the *Examiner* pointed out that the "dapper . . . Hollywood actor "sported "a blue French gabardine suit and white oxford cloth shirt."
"In May of 1960, Brando was established," says Bisbort.

He was talking about starring in *Mutiny on the Bounty*, and he's standing at San Quentin with the proto-hippies; these are the first of these young people with long hair. If you look at the photographs, they're just beginning to grow their hair out. And there's Brando, in a suit. He's out there, really well-dressed. There's a photo of him standing beside the San Quentin sign, talking to people in the crowd. He's standing with Jerry Brown, who was then a seminary student, and whose father was Pat Brown. What a weird situation. Jerry Brown was protesting the death penalty that his father was dragging his feet to protect.

Brando was among those who addressed the crowd that morning over the loudspeakers set up by the Marin County Group for Abolishment of Capital Punishment. "Capital punishment is not a deterrent to crime," he said, repeating that if Chessman had committed the crimes, "he should be observed and rehabilitated."
Meanwhile, the Supreme Court of California had met at 8 a.m. to consider Chessman's latest appeal. At 9:48 a.m., twelve minutes before execution time, the court refused to grant Chessman a stay of execution, which would have allowed his case to be appealed once again to the US Supreme Court. But eleven minutes later, one minute before the deadline, Judge Lewis E. Goodman of the US District Court in San Francisco approved the stay. His secretary was instructed to phone the prison and stop the deadly proceedings.
She dialed the wrong number.
The cyanide pellets dropped into the San Quentin gas chamber at 10:03 a.m. Caryl Chessman was pronounced dead at 10:12 a.m. Warden Fred

R. Dixon heard Chessman's last words. He said Chessman never lost his composure, and "asked me to specifically state that he was not the Red Light Bandit. He felt that the end was near, and he hoped he had contributed toward the end of capital punishment."

"They just didn't call it in on time," Bisbort says. "I have it from George Davis, God bless him, lived to ninety-eight. He was Chessman's lawyer at that time. He took me through the sequence of going to the federal judge's offices, pleading the case, and saying, 'We need to stop this,' and then the judge going, 'Okay.' I mean, it was straight out of a Hollywood film, where the judge told the secretary, 'Go ahead, call the warden,' and the secretary messes up the phone call. Misdials and then tries again and gets, 'Sorry. We just dropped the pellets.'"

Straight out of a Hollywood film? When word reached the demonstrators outside the prison that Chessman did not have more than nine lives after all, there was silence but for the barking of a dog, the sobbing of some women, and the wailing of a baby. The man in the blue French gabardine suit and white Oxford cloth shirt spoke again. "Chessman died as a matter of political expediency," Brando said, and blamed California lawmakers who supported capital punishment for "a shortsightedness that has done damage to the United States in world opinions."

Then he added a cinematic shock to the scene, announcing that he would portray Caryl Chessman in a motion picture. Brando had received permission from Chessman himself through an exchange of notes handled by attorney Davis shortly after midnight. Brando said Chessman was pleased someone wanted to turn his story into a movie and promised it would depict the evils of capital punishment. All profits, including his own salary, he said, would go to the fight to abolish capital punishment.

The attack came rather swiftly from the political right and death penalty advocates. From Hollywood the mouthpiece was the still powerful and fiercely conservative and vitriolic Hedda Hopper. The gossip columnist had never really gotten over the fact that Brando had refused to kiss the hem of her garment when he first arrived from Broadway. "It would take a derrick to get Shirley MacLaine, Steve Allen or Marlon Brando on the road to sell their pictures, yet they took time to go to Sacramento to plead for Caryl Chessman's life," she wrote in her syndicated column that week. "It was nauseating. It seems to me there should be a revision of our laws before any other case such as this drags on and makes a laughingstock of American justice." Later, she claimed that Shirley MacLaine and Steve Allen had agreed to roles in Brando's Chessman biopic. "So it was business, not sentiment, after all."

This wasn't the only chance the press had that week to needle Brando. A dejected Brando had stepped away from the microphone outside San

Quentin on Monday. On Wednesday, he was in Superior Court in Santa Monica, California, for a hearing over custody of his son with Anna Kashfi. Brando was complaining that his ex-wife was not delivering Christian to him on the occasions they'd agreed, and that when she did, the child would often be chauffeured by a private investigator who'd been hired to spy on Brando.

In court that day, Anna Kashfi did all she could to steal the headlines from Caryl Chessman. On the witness stand, under questioning from Brando's attorney, she suddenly exploded. "I don't like being shouted at!" she snapped.

"I don't care what you like, young lady," Judge Allen T. Lynch admonished.

"Well, isn't that too damn bad! I thought this was supposed to be a democracy!" She then tossed a pencil onto the counsel table where Brando sat, leaped from the witness stand and stomped out of the courtroom.

Her attorney caught up with her in the parking lot and convinced her to go back to the witness stand. She apologized, and after a recess the hearing continued. But during the recess, Kashfi made another display, confronting Brando in the courtroom. According to the Associated Press report, "Miss Kashfi, fists clenched, walked over to where Brando was sitting at the counsel table, and in a low voice told the actor that he is

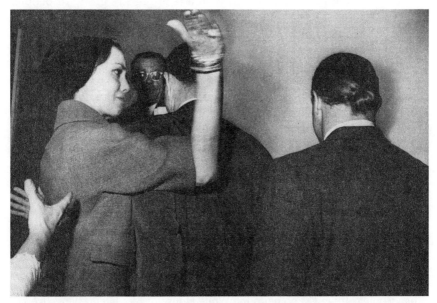

Brando's ex-wife (and mother of his son Christian) slaps him outside court. The divorce and custody battles and her theatrics often made headlines that overshadowed Brando's activism. Photofest

not a model former husband. Among her choice epithets: baboon, over-grown juvenile delinquent, slob. After the tirade, Brando just looked at her disdainfully."

The following day, Kashfi was back on the witness stand. Her behavior was calm, but her words were just as incendiary. "I feel Mr. Brando is an immoral man," she testified. "I don't want my child to grow up in this environment." She said that she was upset by newspaper reports of Brando's romances. "I believe the affairs of the bedroom should be kept private, and not flaunted in the newspapers. I do not want my child to grow up idolizing immorality." Mrs. Sydney Crecy, who'd worked as a childcare nurse in Kashfi's home, said she'd quit in January, and that the private detective had ordered her to report on Brando's behavior during visitations with Christian. "His conduct was that of a loving father," she testified. "The baby's crazy about him and he seems to be crazy about the baby. They are very close."

Brando did not get any extra visits with his son, but Kashfi was ordered to fire the private eye who'd gone undercover as a chauffeur. The fight would go on. As for Caryl Chessman? Brando never got around to making the film. But the setbacks did not stop him from pushing forward in his determination to change the world and set a new standard for Hollywood stars.

"At San Quentin, Brando was in with a really heady group of people. These weren't just willy-nilly beatniks smoking pot. These were people who took this seriously: Quakers, seminary students, pacifists, and beatnik poets," Bisbort says. "Theodore Hamm wrote in his book on the death penalty, '*Time* magazine's thumbnail sketch suggested the most vocal supporters of Chessmen by the end of the case were the students, writers, and artists who comprised the disparate voices of the early New Left.' There was a radical element in that."

Hamm also noted that Norman Mailer, in "Superman Comes to the Supermart," his essay on the 1960 Democratic Convention published in *Esquire* magazine, linked John F. Kennedy's appeal to "the private madnesses of the nation which had thousands—or was it hundreds of thousands—of people demonstrating in the long night before Chessman was killed, and a movie star, the greatest, Marlon the Brando out in the night with them."

"For Brando, an actor, let's put it this way: it was a hell of a lot braver then to do it than it is now," Bisbort adds.

I really do think this was the beginning. By November, a new young, very handsome couple was going to the White House. It was like a changeover, a real cultural changeover, and not just a political change, because you had eight years of sort of dusty, cobwebby Ike—nice guy but old hero, and then suddenly you have this Brando-handsome-type president and his gorgeous wife who knows several languages and a Catholic, to boot. You have this complete changeover. I think that was one of the beginnings you could point to. Brando's move into civil rights? I think it's all of a piece. I don't see a jarring disconnect, at all. It's all part of a humanist view of life, the sanctity of life. And there was a lot of overlap. If you were in the anti-death penalty movement, you were probably also taking part in civil rights. There was a level of awareness and what they called 'consciousness raising.' If your conscience was raised, it was raised on many fronts, not just anti-war but even the early environmental movement. Civil rights, gun violence, Native American rights, all that was part of the package.

Seventeen

The Sixties

> Some of the pictures I made during the sixties were successful; some weren't. Some, like *The Night of the Following Day*, I made only for the money; others, like *Candy*, I did because a friend asked me to and I didn't want to turn him down. . . . Some of the movies made a lot of money; some didn't. I was interested in other things, but I had to make a living and took what was available.

For Marlon Brando, the 1960s may have been his first "lost decade" when it came to making movies, but beginning with the night spent outside San Quentin prison, the years were the most active and influential when it came to what he believed was his true calling. The example of his activism in many interlinked causes, from civil rights to Native American rights, and to his first, and early, exposure to environmentalism, would not only set precedent for the activism of entertainment stars to follow, but influence popular culture, from the box office to Black Lives Matter—all the while, at the expense of his film career.

"No question, it was a risky thing and it got more risky as his career went on, when he got involved with the Black Panthers and Native Americans," Alan Bisbort says.

> Everybody just kind of rolled their eyes at that point like, "Oh yeah, Marlon Brando," like he had completely lost his marbles. It may have looked like that to Joe Middle America, but in retrospect it seems to me that Brando was ahead of his time as far as looking at these issues seriously. We're living in a time right now when I would love it if there was a Brando-level talent who would go out there and stand outside the US Capitol. Nobody else was doing it, and I don't know if there was a bigger star at that time than Marlon Brando.

As Brando was the first to admit—proclaim, even—his movie output in the decade was a mixed bag, and it could have gone in another direction. In 1959, around the time Brando was wrapping work on *The Fugitive Kind*, Sam Spiegel, producer of *On the Waterfront*, had another Oscar-bait role in hand: that of T. E. Lawrence in *Lawrence of Arabia*. Listed by the American Film Institute in 2007 as number seven on its list of "greatest American movies of all time" (*On the Waterfront* placed nineteenth; *The Godfather* was second only to *Citizen Kane*), the film would surely have elevated Brando's standing as a great actor even further, but he turned it down. Angry that Spiegel had announced his casting before he even knew about the offer, Brando allegedly stated, "I'll be damned if I spend two years of my life out in the desert on some fucking camel."

Instead, Brando chose to be out on the ocean on a replica of a tall ship and, beginning October 1960, wound up spending the greater part of nine months bouncing between French Polynesia, Hawaii, and the Metro-Goldwyn-Mayer and Hal Roach Studio lots in Culver City, California. And that was not his first choice.

"I know that Brando was very reluctant to sign on to film *Mutiny on the Bounty* because he told the press at the time that what he really wanted to do was make a film about the story of Caryl Chessman," Bisbort says. "And everybody rolled their eyes at that, I'm sure. Chessman gave an interview in which he said, 'I'd rather be a corpse than a snitch,' and I could see Brando mouthing that line in a film."

Bounty would leave its own mark. Brando's friend, the journalist Bob Thomas, wrote that it was

> unsurpassed in film history . . . as an exercise in human folly. No movie project has been marked by worse executive judgments, pettier personality squabbles, and more profligacy of creative and financial resources. Along with the concurrent *Cleopatra, Mutiny on the Bounty* signaled the almost total disintegration of the studio system as a source of power in the film industry. Marlon Brando was both the unwitting cause and the ultimate victim of the entire affair. . . . At times he tried to use his power to remedy the ills of the production; at other times he merely acted in a peevish childlike way. Inevitably, he was given the blame for all that went wrong.

Throughout those troubled months of production and into the sixties, Brando's behavior, romances, increasing number of children, and continued court and custody battles with Anna Kashfi would compete for headlines with his higher-minded pursuits, and leave him open to criticism and ridicule. While in Tahiti in June 1961, struggling through the *Bounty* shoot, he was forced to make a thirty-hour trip to Santa Monica for another court appearance over visitations with three-year-old Christian. On the witness stand, he announced his marriage to a longtime girlfriend, Maria "Movita" Castaneda, and the birth of their son, Miko. Having arrived from the set as Fletcher Christian, Brando had his hair pulled back in a British mariner's pigtail, foreshadowing his appearance in the same courthouse thirty years later, when, much heavier, but with his hair again

Arriving in Tahiti for location filming of *Mutiny on the Bounty*. Pictured with flight attendant Maxine Reynolds, director Lewis Milestone, and actress Tarita Teri'ipaia. Brando would marry Tarita and later buy and develop the Tetiaroa atoll. *Photofest*

tied back, he would plead for leniency and take the blame as a bad parent in Christian's murder trial.

When it came to activism and the issues closest to his heart, *Mutiny on the Bounty* did take Brando to Tahiti, the exotic location he'd discovered while daydreaming and riffling through pages of *National Geographic* in study hall at Shattuck Academy. During the *Bounty* shoot, he would find and marry another wife, twenty-year-old Tarita Teri'ipaia, with whom he would sire more children. He eventually would purchase his French Polynesian island. The Tetiaroa atoll would become a research lab for issues including coral reef and island preservation. Brando's work and plans are now carried out by several of his children with the Tetiaroa Society, whose stated mission is "to ensure island and coastal communities have a future as rich as their past—strengthening their resilience to global change, by restoring their ecosystems, and preserving their cultures."

The work in French Polynesia inspired worldwide environmental and ecological movements, and the activism of Hollywood figures including Leonardo DiCaprio, Ed Begley Jr., George Clooney, Daryl Hannah, Edward Norton, and Shailene Woodley. Brando opened a small eco-lodge, Tetiaroa Village, which attracted some of his Hollywood friends to the island. After his death, new owners transformed it into the eco-friendly Brando Resort (focused on sustainability, using solar power, coconut oil biofuel, and recyclable materials), which pioneered the boom in eco-tourism—and *luxury* eco-tourism.

Brando began work in the spring of 1962 on *The Ugly American*. Based on the bestselling book, the project was a long-delayed spin on Pennebaker, Inc.'s plans for a film based on the United Nations Technical Assistance Program. With Pennebaker being bought up by Universal, Brando was set on denouncing United States policy in Third World countries and depicting the corruption and failure of the US diplomatic corps in Asia. When the film opened in April 1963, *New York Times* critic Crowther cautioned that "the seminar nature of this drama about Cold War politics will discourage the unsophisticated," but concluded, "it is so extraordinary, and so well played in crucial roles, it should be seen." Brando, as a newly appointed ambassador to a new country in Southeast Asia, ended the film with a lecture to reporters—and the audience. "Unless we recognize their fight for independence to be part of our own, then we drive them to seek understanding in some other place. I'm saying we can't hope to win the Cold War unless we remember what we're for as well as what we're against. . . . I can't preach the American heritage and expect to be believed if I act out of impatience or sacrifice my principles for expediency. I've learned that the only time we're hated is when we stop trying to be what we started out to be two hundred years ago. I'm not blaming my country. I'm blaming the indifference that some of us show to its promises." The ambassador's speech is broadcast to the United States and is shown on a television set. Before Brando finishes speaking, the uninterested viewer switches it off.

In 1965, Brando starred in a film that addressed racism when he portrayed a Texas sheriff in Arthur Penn's *The Chase*. *The Appaloosa*, also filmed in 1965 and released in 1966, was a western in which Brando played a buffalo-hunting saddle tramp tracking down the Mexican bandit who stole his prized horse. Brando was responsible for casting Native Americans in background roles as white ranchers.

When in late 1966, he took on the role of the sexually repressed, closeted, and impotent US Army Major Weldon Penderton in John Huston's *Reflections in a Golden Eye*, Brando was the first major motion picture star and leading man to portray a homosexual (if one discounts his role in *The Wild One*—as many would).

There were other films and significant work that were clear steps toward his renaissance in 1972 with *The Godfather* and *Last Tango in Paris*. But his most important roles during the 1960s were offscreen. Just as there were highlights among his films, certain dates and scenes stand out.

July 12, 1963: Brando's civil rights activism began close to home and close to his work, when he spoke to a group of three hundred at the Beverly Hilton hotel. At the meeting of the arts division of the American Civil Liberties Union, Brando declared there was racism in the movie industry that needed to be addressed. "They speak of prejudice in motion pictures," he said. "It is there. A studio head said he wouldn't advocate any story with miscegenation in it. I've seen people refuse to hire Negroes. 'We will lose forty percent of the market,' they say. 'We have a moral obligation to the banker,' they claim.

"All of us are late in joining this movement. We can do something. We *must* do something. This is not a Negro movement, it's a democratic movement."

Brando threatened that he and other movie stars might "refuse to work unless there's a fair representation of Negroes" in the industry. Other speakers included Charlton Heston and Burt Lancaster. The audience included Paul Newman and Anthony Franciosa, who would accompany Brando as his civil rights activism ventured closer to the heart of the matter.

That month, civil rights demonstrations were being held in cities and towns across the country. There were marches in Charleston, South Carolina; pickets outside a department store in Danville, Virginia; sit-ins, hunger strikes, and other protests at White Castle hamburger joints in and around New York City; and a march against job discrimination at the site of the upcoming Sonny Liston–Floyd Patterson bout in Las Vegas. Days after his appearance at the Beverly Hilton, Brando announced that he'd join protests in Cambridge, Maryland, that Saturday, July 20, and the following day at a segregated amusement park in Baltimore. But on Wednesday, he was rushed by ambulance from his home in Coldwater Canyon to St. John's Hospital in Santa Monica. He'd been stricken with a kidney ailment—acute pyelonephritis, which had first knocked him out while he was in Tahiti and again on his recent Asian publicity tour for *The Ugly American*. Two days later, while Brando was in his hospital bed, sedated, a private eye finagled his way into the room and served him with papers in a paternity suit from a Filipina dancer who'd named Brando as the father of her four-month-old daughter. These are the types of events, personal tabloid fodder, that would distract attention from the "important" work Brando wanted to publicize. In this case, his illness was laughed off by critics and opponents of the Black cause who accused him of "faking" in order to avoid attending the demonstrations. Brando got in touch with the *Los Angeles Times* from the hospital and made it clear that nothing "will alter my plans to assist in the civil rights movement for the Negroes." The fact that NAACP leaders confirmed that Brando had volunteered his services for demonstrations in the South didn't stop the drumbeat, leading his doctor to make his confidential medical records public "because of the talk over the weekend that Brando was faking illness."

When Brando walked out of the hospital on Monday, he told reporters, "I meant everything I said about going to the South."

With his doctor insisting he remain under medical supervision for two more weeks and return to the hospital for more tests, Brando did attend a civil rights protest in the "south" on July 27—twenty miles south of Hollywood, down the 405 freeway to the city of Torrance. Wearing black slacks and a checkered sports jacket, Brando joined about 120 demonstrators in a march through the Southwood Riviera development, an all-white housing tract that had been the subject of picketing and sit-ins by the Congress of Racial Equality (CORE). About a hundred police officers were on standby. They warned the protesters they'd be arrested if they didn't keep moving. Two dozen people were arrested. Brando, who stopped and was warned more than once along the way, was not. During the two hours he was on the scene, he passed a group of small boys wearing white robes, carrying signs saying, "Down with CORE." One of the boys thrust a placard in his face. It read "Big Deal Brando—Hollywood Race-Mixer." Brando ignored the sign. When a homeowner ran up to him and complained that the reporters and photographers were destroying his lawn and shrubbery, Brandon replied softly, "I'm sure some of the flowers are being stepped on today, but so are some people's civil rights."

Assuring reporters that "we are here as devoted and peaceful representatives of goodwill . . . not as agitators, interlopers, or interferers," Brando and fellow actors Paul Newman, Anthony Franciosa, and Virgil Frye arrived on August 22 in Gadsden, Alabama. The city was the site of a long and ugly desegregation battle, where in recent weeks more than five hundred Black demonstrators had been arrested. Brando spoke at a rally in a Baptist church that night. "It is not going to be long before they will realize that clubbing you and beating you is not going to do any good," he said. "Civil rights is a wave that is going to sweep the country. We want to be part of it."

Black leaders in Gadsden wanted the stars to lead another a mass demonstration, but Brando had other plans. He said he wanted to broker a meeting between them and city officials; get everyone around a table, establish communications, and "try to close the gap between you and the hard-core segregationists." It wasn't going to happen. The next day, Mayor Leslie Gilliland accused the Hollywood crowd of "rabble rousing," refused to talk to them, and warned that if they violated the law, they'd go straight to jail.

As the actors headed out of town, Newman in particular expressed his disgust. "It's all right when we come down South to raise money for a hospital and it's perfectly all right when we're asked to donate our services for other humanitarian causes. They don't call us rabble-rousers then." Brando promised that the same group or others from Hollywood would be back to continue the fight.

Five days later, Brando was in Washington, D.C., in front of the Lincoln Memorial, witnessing and being part of a historic moment in the civil rights battle. The March on Washington for Jobs and Freedom had led here, an unprecedented, massive, dramatic protest, with a quarter million Blacks and white sympathizers, demanding an end to segregation and racial discrimination.

This was the rally in which, among many speakers, the Rev. Dr. Martin Luther King Jr., head of the Southern Christian Leadership Conference, stood out when he departed from his advance text and delivered his legendary "I have a dream" speech, "a dream deeply rooted in the American dream—one day this nation will rise up and live up to its creed, 'We hold these truths to be self-evident, that all men are created equal.'"

For Bud Brando, the activism that his mother had inspired and to which his illustrious acting career had taken second place seemed to have paid off. Twenty years earlier, on the road for the American League for a Free Palestine, he wrote to his parents, "Washington is strongly anti-Negro and I'm getting awfully mad." Now, at thirty-nine, he was looking out on a crowd of two hundred and fifty thousand, all with one purpose, one dream.

"At the March on Washington, I stood a few steps behind Dr. King when he gave his 'I Have a Dream' speech, and it still reverberates in my mind," Brando recalled. "He was a man I deeply admired. I've always thought that while a part of him regretted having to become so deeply involved in the cause of racial equality, another part of him drove him to it, though I'm convinced he knew he would have to sacrifice himself."

Brando, as a leader of the Hollywood stars in attendance, brought as much attention to the cause as did President John F. Kennedy, who initially did not support the march, but met with leaders afterward and proclaimed that "the cause of twenty million Negroes has been advanced." (A civil rights bill was never passed by Congress before Kennedy's assassination, but his arm-twisting successor, Lyndon Baines Johnson, got the Civil Rights Act passed on July 2, 1964.)

Following the march, Brando was featured in *Hollywood Roundtable*, a discussion filmed by the United States Information Agency, to share his thoughts about civil rights and what he'd witnessed that day. The conversation, which included his friend, James Baldwin, along with Charlton Heston, Harry Belafonte, Sidney Poitier, and Joseph Mankiewicz (director of *Julius Caesar* and *Guys and Dolls*), would be shown in schools, on local television, and in more than a hundred countries. Questioned by the moderator, broadcast journalist David Schoenbrun, Brando was one participant who extended the civil rights issue beyond the United States.

"Mr. Brando," Schoenbrun asked, "have you been on this road for a long time?"

"I don't know," Brando replied. "There was a time when nobody was on the road, really. But there was a time when Rosa Parks stood up on a bus in Montgomery, Alabama, and from that date the Montgomery bus boycott took place, and somewhere in the fifties, eighteen Negroes in a Georgia prison camp broke their legs with sledgehammers to bring attention to the condition that they were in, and slowly, bit by bit, I became involved in this issue. And I guess my springboard was listening to Martin Luther King speak about the distress in California."

"We all heard Mr. King say today that this was perhaps the greatest day for freedom in modern American history," Schoenbrun said. "Perhaps we could ask Mr. Brando to tell us what that means to him. Do you think then, if it's the greatest day for freedom, that this is the beginning of some tremendous change in our country? And if so, how do you see it developing?"

> Well, this is a revolution, of course, that's sweeping our country now. And if it ends up properly, perhaps Indians will be given some of their land back that they have rightful claims on by treaty. Certainly . . . all minorities—Jews, Filipinos, Chinese, Negroes, Hindustanis, Koreans, all people—will benefit. Today was an unprecedented event, in that it is the only time in history, I believe, in America when over two hundred thousand people have gathered to say with one voice and with one spirit, one cause. And I think that it's easy to oversimplify this problem. The problem seems to me a subtler one and it has to do with hatred. . . . And no matter where you look, whether it's in Franco's Spain or Chiang Kai-shek's government or in some of the South American countries, the distress that you see in Haiti today, gives evidence to the fact that we are all as human beings filled with anguish and hatred and fear. And I think that that is what we are expressly addressing ourselves here, today here, in this movement. I think it's one step closer to trying to understand the human heart, to try to understand what is it that has produced this; what excuses did we give ourselves to give the expression, to burning children with cattle prods and destroying people.

An unusual and defining moment at the Academy Awards ceremony in 1973 led Brando to be closely identified with the Native American rights movement. He made his first public, and very passionate, statement in defense of the cause on January 17, 1964, when he showed up, unannounced, in Washington, D.C., at a meeting of the executive council of the National Congress of American Indians. "Most people in this country don't know that US treaties with the American Indian have been broken," he said. "They don't know the Indian has been blackmailed into keeping quiet.

"The Bureau of Indian Affairs of the Interior Department has followed a nearly consistent policy to obliterate the Indians. The bureau hit its depths during President Eisenhower's administration. I was astounded by the policy of obliteration of Indian identification and culture; how little change there has been since the Battle of Wounded Knee."

Brando said that most white Americans "think of Indians as these people who sell trinkets in Albuquerque. So do many legislators in Washington. The Indian has five more years to win a battle of understanding or he faces extinction. People say that Indians are uneducated. Indians are *over*educated. They are overeducated in suffering and denial."

Brando promised to dedicate himself to the Indian movement through the production of films. "I want to make one film for Indians to see. I want the Navajo to see a volunteer white worker, sacrificing his spare time to help other Indians. I want Indians to see for themselves that there are people who do care. Many of your tribesmen don't know that." He also vowed to produce and act in "a movie that would tell the story of the misery of the American Indian today." He listened to their stories of discrimination, sorrow, and disappointment, and while in Washington, he brought his case to congressional representatives and reporters, as well as the recently widowed Jacqueline Kennedy and her sister Lee Radziwill in a well-publicized three-hour dinner.

Then he took action.

"I'm going to help the Indians in any way I can, even if I have to go to jail for it." Marlon Brando spoke those words on March 3, 1964, before climbing into a twelve-foot Indian dugout canoe on the Puyallup River in Pierce County, Washington. Five hundred Native Americans, dozens of reporters, press photographers, television cameramen, police, and gaming officials watched as the movie star, an Episcopalian canon from San Francisco, and Puyallup Indian chief Bob Satiacum paddled across the river and lowered an eight-fathom gillnet into the water. The crowd followed as they drifted for about two hundred yards. Brando, in a brown suede jacket, tight pants, leather slippers, and scarf, looked the part of the hero, although he made the chief nervous as he insisted on standing up on the shaky vessel. The trio hauled in two ten-pound steelhead trout, and as the hundreds of spectators cheered, paddled back to shore—where they were arrested.

Walter Neubrech, chief enforcement officer for the State Game Department, informed the men that they'd be charged with illegal fishing with a net capable of taking game fish. The Indian chief would not be booked, but Brando and the minister were placed in a Game Department car and driven to the Pierce County Jail. In what was described in the local press as "one of the strangest bookings in Pierce County history," the sheriff and prosecutor leaned over the booking table to shake Brando's hand.

Brando told reporters that he was there to enforce the Indians' treaty with the United States that guaranteed them fishing rights in their usual and accustomed fishing grounds, as well as furthering Indian treaty rights with the United States. He compared the treaty violations with the United States' situation in Panama, where there were riots protesting the US presence in the canal zone. The US government, he said, claimed the treaty with Panama couldn't be broken, yet abused American Indians' treaty rights. "We made treaties as a young, weak nation when the Iroquois confederation could have wiped us out. When we got stronger, we broke them. If these Indians don't fish, their children don't eat. The government has been trying to divide and conquer the Indians. The Indians' rights must be protected."

The press ate this up. They wrote of Brando's "return to the waterfront," and his "mutiny on the river." His star power had an effect, as did a bit of humor with the newsmen. Looking down at one reporter's notes, Brando asked, "How do you read these things? I know your editor wouldn't be able to." The reporter asked Brando his name. When Brando told him, the reporter said, "The actor?"

"Well, I was last night," Brando said. "But I'm not so sure now."

Brando continued making appearances on behalf of his causes while making movies. Working with the UNICEF emergency food program in March 1967, he bore witness to starvation and death in the famine- and drought-stricken state of Bihar in northeast India. Brando was appalled by the caste system's treatment of the lowly "untouchables." ("Looking back," he said, "in the United States we've always had our own untouchables—American Indians, Blacks, homosexuals. Who knows who will be next?") He said he was heartbroken by the plight of starving children. "The suffering moved me to make a forty-five-minute movie about it, which I filmed with a sixteen-millimeter camera. On my last day of filming, after photographing a child who had died right in front of me, I put my camera down and cried. I couldn't take any more. I knew that I had to get the scenes I had filmed to the American people and thought if I did so, the whole country would be appalled and do whatever it took to ameliorate this misery."

The assembled footage, known as *Untitled Famine Relief Fund-Raising Documentary*, for which Brando is credited on the IMDb website as cinematographer, was screened at UNICEF headquarters in New York on

April 11, 1967. Brando said he tried to get the footage shown on American television, but that CBS News and NBC News turned him down.

By this point, the radicalization of Marlon Brando was complete, as was his frustration with the progress of race relations following the March on Washington. There were the Watts riots in Los Angeles in 1965 and the "long, hot summer" of 1967, with race riots exploding in more than one hundred and fifty American cities. The rebellions against poverty, police brutality, and racism gave Brando new inspiration in early 1968 when it was time to prepare for his next screen role. He'd signed for two films. *The Arrangement* was a reunion with director Elia Kazan, based on Kazan's autobiographical novel. Brando was more excited about Gillo Pontecorvo's film about a British agent sent to manipulate a Caribbean slave revolt in the 1840s. Brando believed he had the right director—Pontecorvo had directed the acclaimed 1966 war film, *The Battle of Algiers*—and subject for his first truly political film since *The Ugly American*. Originally titled *Queimada*, the picture would be released in the States as *Burn!*, in reference to "Burn, baby burn!" the catchphrase of R&B disc jockey Magnificent Montague that became a rallying cry during the Watts riots.

In search of more parallels between Gillo Pontecorvo's film and the current-day Black struggle, Brando moved from the nonviolent realm of Martin Luther King and reached out to the revolutionaries who were fighting fire with fire—and guns with guns. The Black Panther Party for Self-Defense had been founded in 1966 to challenge the excessive force of the Oakland, California Police Department, and expanded into a Black Power organization advocating class struggle around the world. The group would attract the support of and raise thousands of dollars from well-meaning liberal celebrities. Tom Wolfe's essay "Radical Chic: That Party at Lenny's," published in *New York* magazine in June 1970, satirized a fundraising party for the Panthers, hosted by Leonard Bernstein in his posh New York City apartment and attended by his wealthy, elite friends. "Radical chic" (and later, "terrorist chic," along with "white guilt") would become part of the lexicon. Marlon Brando was a step ahead of the crowd in this respect as well. In his case, his association with Black Panther leaders Bobby Seale and Eldridge Cleaver, and his embrace of a militant group that was organizing weaponry and violence against the police—or "pigs"—was not only a remove from the work he was doing for Dr. King's organization, but dangerous, as well.

Brando's "research" for *Burn!* hit the headlines when he showed up at Berkeley Municipal Court, where Bobby Seale and his wife were facing gun charges after police raided their home. Brando told reporters he'd come up from Hollywood specifically to attend the hearing. He said he thought the Panthers were "earnest and dedicated people who are working for a life of dignity and respect for the Black man. I don't see myself in any participatory role, just an interested private citizen."

As he had first expressed in Gadsden, Alabama, five years earlier, Brando said he wanted to attend the hearing because of a "communications gap."

"Whenever a Black man enters a court there is a possibility of racism. It was frightening for me to find that Black people are having to arm themselves."

Bobby Seale was even more to the point. "There is no justice for the Black man in the White man's court," he said.

That was April 2, 1968. On April 4, Martin Luther King was gunned down, shot dead in Memphis, Tennessee. Brando's world was rocked. In the days to follow, he backed out of *The Arrangement*, despite the opportunity to work, after more than a decade, with the director he respected most. He also called off talks to star with Paul Newman in *Butch Cassidy and the Sundance Kid* at 20th Century-Fox. (*Burn!* remained in play.)

When Brando surfaced on April 12, it was again in Berkeley, at the Ephesian Church of God in Christ on Alcatraz Avenue, for the open-casket funeral of seventeen-year-old Bobby Hutton. Hutton was a member of the Black Panther party who'd been shot and killed by police in West Oakland two days after the murder of Dr. King.

Brando with Black Panther Captain Kenny Denmon at the funeral of seventeen-year-old Bobby Hutton in Berkeley, California, in April 1968—days after the assassination of Martin Luther King Jr. Everett Collection Historical / Alamy Stock Photo

More than twelve hundred people packed into the church for the services. Almost all were Black. Brando entered on the heels of eighty Black Panthers who walked two-by-two and stood during the two-hour service. After the burial, Brando stood with a group of Black Panthers and addressed a crowd of two thousand people.

"We just came from Bobby Hutton's funeral and I'm not going to stand up here and make a speech because you've been listening to White people for four hundred years," he said as he began a short speech. "They said they were going to do something. They haven't done a thing as far as I'm concerned, in reenfranchising the Black man. It's up to the individual to do something to force the government to give the Black man a decent place to live, a decent place to bring his children up in. That could have been my son lying there, and I'm going to do as much as I can. I'm gonna start right now to inform White people of what they don't know. The reverend said the White man can't 'cool it' because he's never 'dug it.' And I'm here to try to dig it, because I myself as a White man have got a long way to go and a lot to learn.

"I haven't been in your place. I haven't suffered the way you've suffered. I'm just beginning to learn the nature of that experience and somehow that has to be translated to the white community, now. Time's running out for everybody."

Brando's words—"That could have been my son lying there"—were prescient and sounded very similar to what President Barack Obama told reporters on July 19, 2013, when commenting on the acquittal of George Zimmerman, a neighborhood watch volunteer at a gated community in Sanford, Florida, who fatally shot Trayvon Martin, a Black seventeen-year-old (like Bobby Hutton) who was there to visit relatives: "When Trayvon Martin was first shot, I said that this could have been my son."

"I haven't suffered the way you've suffered," Brando said. "I'm just beginning to learn the nature of that experience and somehow that has to be translated to the White community, now."

Said Obama: "When you think about why, in the African-American community at least, there's a lot of pain, it's important to recognize that the African-American community is looking at this issue through a set of experiences and history that doesn't go away."

"I don't have to give you this man's qualifications as an actor. I think he is probably considered by other actors and people in the entertainment profession as probably *the* greatest actor of our times. I admire him for that. I also admire Marlon Brando for his conscience as an American and his moral commitment when he believes in something. Will you welcome, please, Mr. Marlon Brando."

Johnny Carson's introduction when Brando appeared on *The Tonight Show* in May 1968 showed his deference to a great star of the screen making a rare television appearance. It also signaled that this was going to be one of those "spinach" segments, in which intellectuals and authors were featured on TV programs in that era; interviews that taught, not necessarily entertained, audiences.

When Brando first sat down between Carson at his desk and sidekick Ed McMahon, he kept things light, as would frequent guests like Buddy Hackett or Orson Bean. He told a funny story of the last time he was on the show, when he rushed onstage after being served champagne in the green room. "I can hardly remember, but I remember vague things about it. I almost fell down as I came in, I was so dead drunk!"

"I remember you weren't as bad as you thought you were," Carson assured him, "and you came out and you saw the lights and the lights hit ya and . . . all of a sudden you sounded just like Stanley Kowalski from *Streetcar*: 'Man, these lights are kinda bright, aren't they?' It was a great interview. One of the highlights of our show."

The audience laughed. Brando was charming. Then Carson quickly got down to business. "It was in headlines in one of the papers yesterday, that you have stepped out of a motion picture that you were going to do with Elia Kazan, *The Arrangement*, for a very important reason and I thought you might like to mention why and then we'll, we'll pick up from there."

What followed was an extraordinary, emotional presentation by Brando that was even more predictive than his words after Bobby Hutton's funeral. Warning of what was to come, he seemed to set the template for modern-day White actors who use their platforms to discuss issues like White privilege and systemic racism.

> Yeah, it was a very tough decision to make because I can't think of a director that's better than Gadg Kazan. To me, he is the best director, and I've looked forward during the intervening years since I worked with him last, to working with him again. It's of course the story of the year, perhaps the last two years, and I was wanting to do it more than anything. And King got shot. And I sat in front of the television set and I wondered what it meant to me that he's dead and that he died, and his last act was trying to get a fifteen-cent wage increase for garbagemen, and that he was hauled to his grave by two mules on a rickety cart, and that on his tombstone was written "Free at last, free at last, thank God almighty, free at last." And in his last speech on television, as I watched the news reports come over, it shows his last words the night before. And he said that he'd been to the mountain and that he'd seen the promised land and he said, "I don't know if I'm gonna get there with ya, but it doesn't matter about me, 'cause I know we're gonna get there. Mine eyes have seen the glory of the coming of the Lord." And he was shot dead the next day. And I thought somehow this has got to matter,

somewhere. And if we don't, all the citizens, do something that is a person-to-person contribution, I don't think that we're really gonna have any place to come home to if we do get a job. I felt that it was—that there was just nothing that I could do in terms of what I know and what I see and what I feel. I couldn't think of any other alternative rather than to make my time, my energies, and my money fully available to do what I can as an individual to rectify the situation we're in. . . . I think that nothing's really gonna change unless I do it, unless the trombone player does it, unless the guy sitting and watching the television with a beer can does something about it.

Like one of the authors featured on the show, Brando promoted a recently published paperback. *The Report of the National Advisory Commission on Civil Disorders* detailed the findings of the Kerner Commission, appointed by President Johnson to investigate the causes of the 1967 riots.

It tells in chapter and verse the situation we're in, why we're in it, and why the Black people can't get up off their knees. And it points very specifically to the White man and his feeling about the Black man. It points to racism and discrimination in its most subtle forms, in its most cruel and blatant form, and that's where it is. That's the Bible. . . . It isn't enough to talk anymore. It isn't enough to shake our fingers. We have to do something, we have to get up our money, we have to give our time, we have to give our hearts, and we must then be involved in a person-to-person program. Fundamentally because now that King is dead, many people I think, and—

He turned to Carson. "—You've certainly felt it, too, that there is the vacuum formed—"

Carson interjected: "And I think a lot of people are worried that maybe the militants might rush in and try to fill that vacuum."

"Well, that's where it's going to go and I think that we've got one chance," Brando said. "I was talking with [AFL/CIO leader and civil rights activist] Walter Reuther on the way to King's funeral, in the march, and Walter Reuther said that we've got one last chance as White people to straighten things around in this country. And if we don't do it soon and if we don't do it massively, then there's going to be—it's going to be Armageddon. It's going to be guns; it's going to be thousands of people killed. It will be internment camps. We will have reduced ourselves as a nation and our stature as a people, importantly."

Brando then made his pitch: for viewers to donate 1 percent of their annual salary to the Southern Christian Leadership Conference, to help carry on Martin Luther King's philosophy and works. Brando named some celebrities and industry people who'd already committed to doing so. He said that he was contributing 10 percent of his own earnings.

"I think truly it is time to stand up and be counted in this country, where you stand rather than just talking about it," Carson said, "because it's pretty strange. If we cannot learn to live together in this country, I don't know how in hell's sake we are ever gonna learn to live with anybody else in the world. . . . I would prefer not to do this, but I'm doing it only as a help. Because anything that will get this thing going, I would be delighted. I would be happy to give you a check, and I told you about this before the show, for 1 percent of my income for the year, for exactly what you want. And I hope it does some good."

Brando accepted the check, smiled, and shook Carson's hand. "Beautiful, John," he said.

Brando made his most widely seen political statement on March 27, 1973, when he did not show up at the Dorothy Chandler Pavilion in downtown Los Angeles for the forty-fifth Academy Awards. Roger Moore and Liv Ullman were presenting the prize for Best Actor, and when Ullman read out, "Marlon Brando in *The Godfather*," there was some shock and amusement when a young woman rose from her seat in the audience. Wearing a beaded buckskin dress and moccasins, her long black hair in traditional Native American beaded ties, she walked onto the stage, and held up a hand, as if to push away the statuette Moore was offering.

Then she stepped to the microphone. "Hello. My name is Sacheen Littlefeather," she said. "I'm Apache and I am president of the National Native American Affirmative Image Committee. I'm representing Marlon Brando this evening and he has asked me to tell you in a very long speech, which I cannot share with you presently because of time but I will be glad to share with the press afterwards, that he very regretfully cannot accept this very generous award. And the reasons for this being are the treatment of American Indians today by the film industry—" She was interrupted by a mix of boos and applause. "Excuse me," she said, and continued. "—and on television in movie reruns, and also with recent happenings at Wounded Knee. I beg at this time that I have not intruded upon this evening and that we will in the future, our hearts and our understandings will meet with love and generosity. Thank you on behalf of Marlon Brando."

The speech by the twenty-six-year-old activist was met with applause, but backstage there was reportedly an uproar. John Wayne, Hollywood's legendary "Indian fighter," was said to be infuriated. There were jokes at Littlefeather's and Brando's expense later in the broadcast.

Brando addressed the controversy on *The Dick Cavett Show* on June 12, eleven weeks after the Oscars broadcast. He admitted that he was disappointed at the response to his statement but said he would not have done anything differently.

"Since the American Indian hasn't been able to . . . have his voice heard anywhere in the history of the United States, I felt that it was a marvelous opportunity for an Indian to be able to voice his opinion to eighty-five million people," he said. "And I felt that he had a right to, in view of what Hollywood has done to him. And I was embarrassed for Sacheen. She wasn't able to say what she intended to say, and I was distressed that people should have booed and whistled and stomped. Even though perhaps it was directed at myself, they should have at least had the courtesy to listen to her. But I think she did very well. And I was very glad that she did have what opportunities she had to say what she did."

Brando said he understood that the Hollywood elite didn't want their evening interrupted and that perhaps they had a point. "But I don't think that people generally realize what the motion picture industry has done to the American Indian—as a matter of fact, all ethnic groups, all minorities, all non Whites. . . . And people actually don't realize how deeply these people are injured by seeing themselves represented. Not so much the adults, because they're already inured to that kind of pain and pressure, but children, Indian children seeing Indians represented as savage, as ugly, as nasty, vicious, treacherous, drunken, they grow up only with a negative image of themselves and it lasts a lifetime."

"He took a stand," says Larry Karaszewski, the screenwriter, producer, director—and a former vice president of the Academy of Motion Picture Arts and Sciences.

People had turned down the Oscars, notably George C. Scott [in 1971], but they had turned down the Oscars in the sense that actors shouldn't compete. There was much more thought about the machinations of awards for performance, and the term *best actor*. Brando took it a step further. He wanted to make a statement. He wanted to make a statement about the way Native Americans have been betrayed—and betrayed in motion picture history. And that's why it landed so hard. It was more than just a political statement. It was a political statement about Hollywood, to the most powerful people in Hollywood at the time. So I think that's why it always was considered to be such a bigger moment. When George C. Scott turned it down, it was just, "Mr. Scott turned it down and he's not here tonight." The actual act of having Sacheen get up there and turn down the award made it much more of a spectacle. The entire world was watching.

It may have been, as Karaszewski suggests, "the right time period, when actors felt that they had to use their forum for a political cause," but it is evident that Brando had launched the modern tradition of political speechifying at the Oscars. In 1975, Bert Schneider, accepting the Best Documentary award for the Vietnam war documentary *Hearts and Minds*, read a telegram from the North Vietnamese delegation to the Paris peace talks. In 1978, when Vanessa Redgrave won Best Supporting Actress for *Julia* (starring political firebrand Jane Fonda), she used her acceptance speech to call out "Zionist hoodlums" who'd burned her in effigy because of her support of the Palestine Liberation Organization. In years to follow, stars like Tim Robbins, Susan Sarandon, Halle Berry, Michael Moore, Sean Penn, Meryl Streep, Common, Leonardo DiCaprio, Spike Lee, and Joaquin Phoenix, among others, have used the Oscars stage to blurt their political views. "That didn't happen in earlier days," Karaszewski observes. "Before in Hollywood, if they were going to get political, it would be, 'Let's support our troops.'"

Sacheen Littlefeather claimed that her appearance at the Academy Awards led her to be attacked, harassed, and blacklisted. In August 2022, the Academy apologized. (Littlefeather died in November 2022, and weeks later, her sisters revealed that she was not Native American, but of Mexican heritage, a claim that she denied for decades. By then, the controversy was irrelevant.)

"Many members of the Academy respect what Brando was trying to do that night, so it's no longer considered an outlier," Karaszewski says. "I think at the time, people thought, 'Brando is being Brando. What is he doing?' Nowadays, time has caught up to where obviously the betrayal of the Native American in motion picture history is kind of shameful and Marlon was merely trying to point that out. So I think it's gone from ridicule to the point where people acknowledge that he was probably doing the right thing."

Once again, Marlon Brando proved to be ahead of his time. After decades of protests that its name and logo were offensive and racist, the Cleveland Indians of Major League Baseball, underwent a name change to the Cleveland Guardians in November 2021. The Atlanta Braves, and their "tomahawk chop," in which fans celebrate by making a chopping motion with the forearm and open palm, live on.

Eighteen

The Godfather

Pop culture and film historian Gary Shapiro is talking about Marlon Brando's effect on film acting.

In 1927, when sound came in, movies had to basically start over. Every movie made before 1927 was instantly an antique and got put on the shelf, and nobody looked at them again until the 1960s or '70s. And they had to start all over, because the camera couldn't move. In the earliest films like *The Great Train Robbery*, the camera is still, like it's in the front row of an audience looking at a stage play. Eventually, the camera learned to move and directors like King Vidor really had that camera moving around, but when sound came in and the camera was making noise, the director couldn't pull the performance out of the actors the way he used to. He couldn't talk to them anymore, so everything started over. And when the actors started to talk, they had to learn how to talk, and they got actors who could speak. And an actor like Clark Gable became a star, and Clark Gable always delivered his lines. When young people in my film appreciation class watch Clark Gable, they say, "Well, it's like he's saying his lines," which of course he is, but he says them in a wonderful way. But all actors in those movies talk while other actors listen, and then the other actors talk. And a kind of American film acting developed, and actors who excelled in it could say their lines, had character, were good actors and were believable.

But then you see a movie like *The Men*. I believe that *The Men* is the greatest example of the impact that Brando had as an actor, because it's kind of like watching a silent movie with one "talking actor" in it. That is, after *The Men*, all acting in film became as antiquated as silent film acting. Brando, in contrast to everyone else in the film, is real, and everyone else in the film is an actor saying their lines. Teresa Wright? I think she's one of the greatest actresses in the history of movies, and I love Jack Webb, and I love Everett Sloane. Those are all people who I think are really fine actors. They say their lines. And here's this guy who's *not* saying his lines. He's a veteran who was crippled and thought he was going to die. Then he was afraid he wasn't going to die and now he doesn't know where his life is going, *and he cries!* When does an actor cry onscreen before *The Men*? Never! There's not a single scene of an actor crying—and he just cries. And when she puts her head on his chest and she won't go, he's just crying. That's just an amazing moment in the history of motion pictures. Acting would never be the same.

Larry Karaszewski, the screenwriter, producer, and director, agrees.

You can definitely see [the difference in] acting in film before Brando and after Brando. And in all honesty, I'm not sure which I like better, in the sense that there's that classic kind of Hollywood acting, that movie star acting. And in all fairness, it's absolutely wonderful, whether it's Bogart or Cary Grant or Clark Gable. It's not like they're not being real—I mean, Humphrey Bogart plays very real, like a real person—but you don't have that "inner thing" that's going on with Brando. Brando showed other actors that acting was not necessarily about being the movie star as much as it is about finding some kind of truth. It's like Bob Dylan and music. Before Bob Dylan, you weren't a singer-songwriter, you were Frank Sinatra or Doris Day. You were a singer of songs; you were a singer. And after Bob Dylan, unless you were singing your truth, you weren't considered upper tier. There are so few just pure singers that come after Dylan who've left a mark. Obviously, there are the Celine Dions, but with the people who seem to have changed the world, whether it's Bruce Springsteen or Kanye West, you're seeing their inner workings in the song. I feel like that's what Brando did to acting. Like there were so many "new Dylans," there are so many "new Brandos." Whether it was Paul Newman or Al Pacino, the world is always looking for the next Brando.

Just as the "new Brando" label was not a boost for Brando's contemporaries like Newman and James Dean, the "old Brando" haunted the actor himself a decade after his first Academy Award (following his fourth nomination), a time in which the conventional wisdom had it that Brando had become flabby, physically and artistically. Critics and colleagues alike considered the films he chose to be beneath his abilities, and his muscle-flexing in changing scripts and ignoring direction detrimental. By choosing political activism over acting ambition, it was agreed, he'd torpedoed a once-magnificent career.

The Hollywood gossip mill, entertainment reporters, and some critics had been chastising and sniping at Brando since the late 1950s, if only as payback for the lack of deference he displayed at their altars. But by the mid-sixties, serious critics, even friends, were vocal in their criticism. Pauline Kael, writing in *The Atlantic* in March 1966, compared Brando's perceived slump with the decline of the American motion picture industry ("American movies have never been worse. . . . American enthusiasm is fed largely by foreign films, memories, and innocence"), lamenting that "Brando, our most powerful young screen actor, the only one who suggested tragic force, the major protagonist of contemporary American themes in the fifties, is already a self-parodying comedian."

Kael pointed to his recent films, including *Mutiny on the Bounty*, in which he "played the fop with such relish that audiences shared in the joke; it was like a Dead End Kid playing Congreve," and *Morituri*, where "his principal charm is his apparent delight in his own cleverness." Brando the rebel had been cut down to size, she wrote, by accepting "trashy assignments. When he appears on the screen, there is a special quality of recognition in the audience: we know he's too big for the role. . . . What he needed was not more docility, but more strength, the confidence to work with young talent, to try difficult roles. But he's no longer a contender, no longer a protagonist who challenges anything serious. Brando has become a comic."

Kael dismissed film critic Hollis Alpert's earlier attack on Brando for not returning to the stage—"as if the theater were the citadel of art. *What* theater?" She could leave that latest hit to one of Brando's oldest friends. Billy Redfield, the actor who was part of Brando's original Broadway crowd, was the friend who'd been very disappointed when Brando chose a secondary role in *Arms and the Man*, rather than starring in *Hamlet*, on their 1953 summer stock jaunt—which turned out to be Brando's last turn on any stage. In 1964, Redfield played Guildenstern to Richard Burton's Hamlet on Broadway, and he wrote a book about the experience. *Letters from an Actor* was excerpted in the *New York Times* on January 15, 1967, ten days after the London premiere of Brando's latest film, *A Countess from Hong Kong*, directed by Charlie Chaplin (Crowther in the *Times*: "It is awful"), and focused on his old friend, Bud. Redfield's cutting remarks might have been described by Brando's Mark Antony as the "unkindest of all," for, using Burton as the standard, Redfield insisted that Brando was not a "great" actor because he had not played the great Shakespearean roles on stage, nor returned to legitimate theater since 1949.

> Brando remains the only American actor to be seriously thought of as Hamlet during the last three decades. We who saw him in his first, shocking days believed in him not only as an actor, but also as an artistic, spiritual, and specifically American leader. . . . His Kowalski on stage (forget the film) generated true mystery and overwhelming excitement. . . . Even Laurence Olivier, hugely accomplished though he was, could not produce such incendiary effects. . . . But by 1953 he no longer cared—which is the last stop on the streetcar. To try may be to die but not to care is to never be born. . . . Scofield, Finney, Burton, Richardson, Guinness, and Olivier are our remaining first-rank actors. Brando is nothing of the kind. He is a movie star. A little more than kind (Rock Hudson) and less than kin (Spencer Tracy). . . . The money he commands is irresistible, while important roles alarm him. As an actor, Brando must be either forgotten or fondly remembered.

By the time the selection appeared in the *Times*, Brando had completed a groundbreaking dramatic role in *Reflections in a Golden Eye*, directed by John Huston. He considered Redfield's criticism to be a betrayal and the end of their friendship, and rather than take up the challenge, took on two roles in 1967 that would do little to burnish his fading reputation. (Brando may have lived to regret passing up *Hamlet*. In 2011, Johnny Depp said he recalled a "conversation with Marlon. He said, 'Why don't you play Hamlet? You should play Hamlet.' I said, 'I don't know. Hamlet's kind of the cliche thing.' He said, 'No, man, do it before you're too old to do it.' He said, 'I never got the chance. I never did it.'")

Admittedly, because he needed the money, Brando agreed to play a kidnapper in the low-budget thriller *The Night of the Following Day*. Roger Ebert of the *Chicago Sun-Times* noted that the movie's final image is a freezeframe of Brando, "smiling the same curious smile he used in the last shot of *The Wild One*, the movie that made him famous. This is probably not a coincidence. *Night of the Following Day* seems designed to resurrect the old Brando image of an inarticulate tough." According to director Hubert Cornfield, the freeze was a necessity. Brando didn't want the film to end with that shot of his face, so he kept making funny faces into the camera before the cinematographer could settle in on a shot.

Candy was different. It was a sex satire based on the novel by Terry Southern and Mason Hoffenberg and directed by Brando's friend and former lover, Christian Marquand. Part of the appeal to Brando was that this was to be a cameo role in a sexy, Swinging Sixties psychedelic farce, and once he signed on, Marquand was able to cast James Coburn, John Huston, Walter Matthau, Ringo Starr—and Richard Burton. Brando most likely took the role as payback. Marquand had been instrumental in Brando's purchase of Tetiaroa, the French Polynesian atoll, by ending the opposition of the Tahitian Territorial Assembly. The assembly was led by Jacques-Denis Drollet, whose son, Dag, would become the lover of Brando's daughter Cheyenne. (In May 1990, Dag would be shot dead by Brando's troubled son Christian—Cheyenne's half-brother and Marquand's namesake.)

Whatever the intentions, Brando's role as Grindl, a guru with a temple in the back of a traveling eighteen-wheeler, was seen by many critics as the nadir in Brando's already checkered career. Renata Adler, in the *New York Times*, said she didn't dig the film—"One line, 'It's not funny, Livia. It's not a funny situation,' seems to sum the whole thing up"—but found Brando to be "less unendurable, because one is glad to see him on the screen, in anything, again."

What wasn't remarked upon in Adler's critique, or in many others in the decade, was what Pauline Kael acknowledged: "Brando accepts the trash, but unlike the monochromatic, 'always dependable' Gable, he has too much energy or inventiveness or contempt just to go through the motions."

The 1960s may have been the decade when Brando began to write off film acting as inconsequential, but, from his odd take on Fletcher Christian in *Mutiny on the Bounty* to his unexpected flair for broad comedy in *Bedtime Story* (a performance that took more than a little from Jerry Lewis and would be the model for Steve Martin in the remake, *Dirty Rotten Scoundrels*), Brando never "phoned it in." Even in the "trash," his commitment to each of the characters, and his choices in portrayal, were precursors to some of the more openly eccentric roles he took beginning in the mid-1970s with *The Missouri Breaks*. They also continued to have a tremendous influence on young filmgoers and a new generation of "new Brandos."

"*Mutiny on the Bounty* is an example," says Shapiro.

> I think it's an amazing performance. He's foppish, really. And he's not manly in any way in that movie. If you compare it to Clark Gable's performance in the original version of the film, Gable is very manly. He's shirtless and extremely masculine. His interpretation of Fletcher Christian is as a swashbuckler. And I liked it when Brando would play a Gregory Peck kind of role, like in *The Ugly American*, where he turns that kind of role on its head by just being so real. An adventure picture like *Morituri* turns a Paul Newman or Clint Eastwood kind of role on its head by being Marlon Brando in that scene—like "What would Brando do here? What if this was really happening to a real person?"

In *The Night of the Following Day*, Brando wore a short blonde wig. For *Candy*, he had long, stringy hair. Buff in a tight T-shirt in *Night*, shirtless in *Candy*, he was in fine shape in both films, as fit and sculpted as he'd ever been, and amid his political activities, on the way to make one last, great, and influential stand in films and popular culture.

The two films to follow, the first of Brando's films to be released in the United States in the 1970s, showed an actor primed to reclaim the title not only of contender, but king—and not the cinematic king Kael had mocked as "a 'king' like Gable, going from one meaningless picture to another, performing the rituals of manly toughness, embracing the studio stable, to be revered, finally, because he was the company actor who never gave anybody any trouble."

Burn! was released in Italy as *Queimada* in the last month of 1969 and opened in the United States on October 21, 1970. "Mr. Brando is worth watching under almost any circumstances," Vincent Canby wrote in the *New York Times*, "and you should enjoy seeing him here, using that Fletcher Christian accent and, towards the end of the film, looking very much like the late Ernest Hemingway, a tired and tragic hero whom life has somehow double-crossed."

The film was considered by Brando to be "the best acting I have ever done"—and by Karaszewski as "one of my favorite films of all time"—but its production was, like *Mutiny on the Bounty* earlier in the decade, troubled and over budget. As was the case with most of Brando's recent films, it wasn't a big moneymaker, leading Brando to be labeled in the industry with that cliché, "box office poison." In November 1970, he was moved to accept what could be considered a meager sum of $50,000 for a month's work on *The Nightcomers*, a low-budget psychological horror film, to be shot in England. Around the same time, he was talking with director Francis Ford Coppola and producer Albert S. Ruddy about starring in *The Godfather*, based on the bestselling novel about a Mafia crime family. He even agreed to take a screen test for the role of Don Corleone in late 1970, but by the early weeks of 1971, the suits at Paramount were still wavering about taking a chance on the former star. "Think of all the people they considered, including Sinatra, to play the part of Don Corleone," Shapiro says. "Even Olivier was considered. They didn't want Brando at all. Box office poison!"

Brando set off for England.

Directed by Michael Winner and filmed outside Cambridge, *The Nightcomers* was conceived as a prequel to Henry James's gothic novel *The Turn of the Screw*. Brando, with a lilting Irish brogue he copped from workers at a pub, played the caretaker on an isolated estate where he controls two orphaned children and their governess. A scene with the kids, in which he blackens his teeth and pulls faces to make them laugh, would be echoed in his death scene in *The Godfather*. The sex scenes with the governess, played by Stephanie Beacham, were kinky, full of ropes and bondage and nudity, and were by far the most sexually explicit that Brando would display on screen. Cinematically—and politically—they were a preview of what was ahead in *Last Tango in Paris*.

The *Nightcomers* sex scenes also showed off the physical condition that Brando was in at age forty-six when he returned from the UK and went into production as the old Don in *The Godfather*. "He transformed," Gray Frederickson recalls. "I mean, he was buff when he showed up. He had a washboard stomach, and was trim and thin, and looked young—he looked about thirty. And we had to go through an hour of makeup every morning to pad him up and make him look older and fat."

Brando may have been "poison" at the box office, but his influence on younger actors had already become clear with the new wave of American cinema that was ushered in in 1967. Gene Hackman in *Bonnie and Clyde* and Dustin Hoffman in *The Graduate* had emerged as pretenders to the throne. In 1969, Jack Nicholson, who broke through with *Easy Rider*, said, "I'm part of the first generation that idolized Marlon Brando."

"Dustin Hoffman, Gene Hackman, and I would meet once a week at a drugstore in New York City years ago," Robert Duvall, who'd worked with Brando on *The Chase*, recalled. "If we mentioned Brando's name once, we would mention it twenty times because he was an inspiration to a lot of young actors."

Now, Duvall would be portraying Brando's consigliere in *The Godfather*, and the actors who'd been cast as the children of Don Corleone—Al Pacino, James Caan, John Cazale, and Talia Shire—would be among the great actors to come into their own in the 1970s, under Brando's thrall. "They were very much in awe of him," Frederickson remembers. "Absolutely! He was *Marlon Brando!*"

It's been recorded that for all the difficulties during production, Brando, and his very broad sense of humor, kept things light on the set. Frederickson speaks about the evening, after a preproduction dinner, that Caan accepted a dare from Duvall and stuck his bare ass out a car window and "mooned" Brando, who was in a car nearby. Brando responded in kind, and throughout the shoot, "mooning" became a competition among the actors. "They were all mooning each other!" Frederickson recalls. "They were laughing and carrying on. They had a great time. It was a great atmosphere on the set." Brando was ultimately declared the "winner,"

Brando's Academy Award-winning role in *The Godfather*: Francis Ford Coppola's picture established a new generation of Brando-influenced actors. Zoetrope Studios/ Photofest © Zoetrope Studios

after he outdid all the others before hundreds of extras on the grounds of a Staten Island mansion while filming the wedding that opens the picture. "He stood up on the stage there on the last day of the wedding and mooned the whole crowd! I remember they were all applauding and cheering," says Frederickson. "Of course, they finally said, 'He beat us all' when he mooned the whole world in *Last Tango in Paris*!"

The younger cast members were also exposed to Brando's somewhat unusual working habits, which included the use of cue cards posted around the set, a technique that was first obvious onscreen in *The Young Lions* in 1957. "He was such a pro," Frederickson says. "He couldn't remember lines, but that didn't matter. He'd figure out a way to do it. We had lines taped everywhere. We had lines on people. He had lines everywhere he looked. And I'd heard, I wasn't there, when he did *On the Waterfront*, he's always looking up. He's looking at the roof of the car 'cause the lines are written up there." Some wrote it off to laziness, but Brando insisted "that not memorizing increased the illusion of reality and spontaneity, a step beyond the groping for words and so-called mumbling that some critics complained about in *A Streetcar Named Desire*. Everything about acting demands the illusion of spontaneity."

"Listen, that's the way he works," Duvall told *Entertainment Weekly* fifty years later. "You can do that for spontaneity to keep it fresh, to be always searching. He was revolutionary in his way of being very natural, but within pulses still being able to keep it alive emotionally.

"It wasn't laziness. Brando could learn the lines. He sometimes had contempt for the work that he was doing, but it was his method, to constantly struggle for what to say," says Karaszewski, who's worked with Brando-influenced actors, including Danny DeVito, Johnny Depp, Edward Norton, and Courtney Love (who has said she believes Brando may be her grandfather).

> Brando got put down in later years for not learning his lines or having all his lines written down somewhere. As opposed to knocking him for that, I feel that what he was trying desperately to do was to make sure that the character he was playing onscreen had some kind of thought process going on. Sometimes I watch a movie and it's just actors doing lines back and forth, even if they're great actors. And I don't think that's a problem. I'm not saying that actors should improvise or do things that aren't in the script. I'm a screenwriter, so I want to protect that screenplay, but you can sometimes feel the way actors are just reciting lines. Brando wanted to always be struggling with those lines, and that made them more real. That's why he has that cat in (the opening scene of) *The Godfather*, because if he didn't have that cat, he would just be reciting his lines, he would just be playing the scene. He wanted this animal that could not be controlled in his lap, so he had to deal with that, and so as he's talking to the person, that's almost secondary. And good actors do that quite a bit.

Karaszewski says he saw a reflection of Brando on the set of *Big Eyes,* the film he scripted with writing partner Scott Alexander, and produced with Alexander, Lynette Howell Taylor, and director Tim Burton.

I remember watching Christoph Waltz in one of his big scenes with Amy Adams. I was watching him, take after take, eating a lot of bread because they were at a restaurant, and he didn't want to be just talking to Amy. He was in a restaurant, so he was buttering his bread and he was chewing on it, and with half the lines he'd have bites of bread in his mouth. And I was like, "Oh my God, he's doing the Brando thing." He's doing the thing where his character hasn't eaten since lunch and his character is just as interested in buttering that bread as he is in telling Margaret Keane that he's in love with her or about his art world. And I feel that's the kind of thing that Brando brought to the screen.

Writer and film critic Vincent Cotroneo adds that

Brando was a big proponent of authenticity, and natural human conversations wouldn't be as mechanical as Aaron Sorkin's writing—which is great, but so not human. It's theater. Brando was all about being real, and in the human mind, words appear, but not like they're being read on a teleprompter. There's a difference between reading a speech and saying something on the fly, and in the moment, you need to process what you're about to say. Brando was really good at that—taking in what he heard, analyzing it, and then delivering it with the right tone after giving the audience that bit of suspense. It's hard to put suspense in general, everyday dialogue but he was able to do it very, very well. And it gives more for the camera to cover. Looking around, it's not like he's looking for dialogue. He's looking for the words to appear in his mind, according to the character, just as it would in everyday conversation.

Brando followed *The Godfather* with *Last Tango in Paris*. He arrived in the city in February 1972 to portray a middle-aged grief-stricken, recently widowed American businessman, dealing with the suicide of his French wife, and who embarks on a clandestine, anonymous sexual affair in a vacant apartment with a twenty-year-old Parisian woman played by nineteen-year-old Maria Schneider. Brando says that the young director Bernardo Bertolucci did not speak much English and that they had to communicate "in French and sign language." Bertolucci also had Brando write most of his own dialogue and encouraged him to improvise.

In constructing and delivering several scenes and monologues, Brando made use of Stella Adler's method of applying his imagination, but also mixed in his own experience and traumas—perhaps too much. As has been discussed, *Last Tango* was notorious for its X rating—and influential in its uninhibited depictions of sex, rape, male domination, and

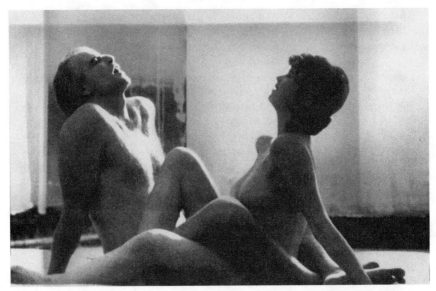

***Last Tango in Paris* confronted taboos of male sexuality, and challenged Brando as an actor in ways he refused to repeat.** United Artists/Photofest © United Artists

submission—but in recent decades it has been appreciated more for the intensity of the acting that led to Academy Award nominations for Brando and director Bertolucci. The scene that remains most devastating is not the one in the apartment in which Brando's character Paul uses butter as a lubricant when he rapes Schneider's Jeanne, but the one in which Paul speaks to his wife, who is dead.

"In that scene, when he sits in the hotel room with his wife's body, he emotes in a way that's uncomfortable to watch, it's so harsh and real," Gary Shapiro says. "And this mixture of love and misogyny and grief, it's just one of the most painful and real things you'd ever seen in film. It's an amazing thing and I think it was very painful for him to do. When you watch it, and I've watched it repeatedly, I think it's a great, great, great work of art, an amazing performance. I don't think I've ever seen anything like it on film and I don't think anybody ever has."

According to Brando, *Last Tango* was indeed just as painful to perform as it was to watch. He had to not only show the pain that his character felt, but needed to experience it as well, in every take, from every camera angle. This time, by revealing so much of his real life while experiencing the unfathomable pain of his character, Brando said, "I felt I had violated my innermost self. . . . *Last Tango in Paris* required a lot of emotional arm wrestling with myself, and when it was finished, I decided that I wasn't ever again going to destroy myself emotionally to make a movie."

"And he never did," Shapiro says. "I mean, he did *Superman.*"

Nineteen

"Doing Brando"

"It bugs me that you, over the years, have acted so little," Dick Cavett confided to Brando, four months after the release of *Last Tango in Paris*. "And it seems like there must be about fourteen great plays and great films that you ought to do and oughta make, and I worry that this feeling that you—that acting is not a noble profession for a man, maybe is what's kept you from it. I can now move on to something else if you like, but does that observation bug you at all?"

"No."

Cavett, the erudite and witty host, had been stepping gingerly around subjects his reluctant guest might not want to address, when he asked, "Why do you downgrade acting as a profession?"

"I think we couldn't survive a second if we weren't able to act," Brando eventually replied. "Acting is a survival mechanism, and it's a social unguent, and it's a lubricant. And we act to save our lives, actually, every day. People lie, constantly, every day by not saying something that they think or saying something that they don't think or showing something that they don't feel."

"Are there roles you wish you'd played, that you crave acting?"

"No," Brando said. "It's been a good living. I mean, if you were in the lumber business and you went on *The Dick Cavett Show* and somebody says, 'Well, how do you like the lumber business, Ralph?' It is a business. It's no more than that, and those who pretend that it's an art I think are misguided. And acting is a craft and it's a profession, not unlike being an electrician, plumbing, or an economist. It's a way of getting on and providing food and shelter for yourself and family."

After filming Last *Tango in Paris* in early 1972, Brando kept true to his word that "I wasn't ever again going to destroy myself emotionally to make a movie." It was nearly three years before he signed on to his next film. *The Missouri Breaks* was a western directed by Arthur Penn and starring Jack Nicholson, who since 1971, had been Brando's neighbor, sharing a gate, a driveway, and, it is said, women. With this picture, all the eccentric shadings that Brando had added to his films in the sixties burst forth in full bloom—as did his expanding girth. As Lee Clayton, a sociopathic "regulator"—hired gun—he is a sexually-ambiguous, lilac-scented, oversized dandy who makes his entrance hidden behind an approaching horse (before poking his head out from underneath), slips in and out of the Irish brogue from *The Nightcomers*, and for reasons that at this point no one bothered to explain, appears in one scene in drag. When the film opened in May 1976, Vincent Canby was not amused by an "out-of-control" performance that turned a potentially elegiac western into "camp. . . . There's no grandeur to Mr. Brando's character. Nor much mystery. He behaves like an actor in armed revolt." Which, in many ways, he was. "Brando said it in interviews many times," Larry Karaszewski reminds the author, "that acting is silly." This new attitude, an existential weariness and hopelessness brought on by his experience filming *Last Tango*, was made clear to his friends and colleagues on August 31, 1976, when Brando arrived in the Philippines to film his role in director Francis Ford Coppola's already trouble-plagued epic, *Apocalypse Now*.

"He shows up and he's three hundred pounds!" producer Gray Frederickson recalls. "Francis says, 'What the fuck am I gonna do with him?' We had to hide him in the shadows and put black pajamas on him because he was so huge!" Brando had written that it was his idea to cover his character, Colonel Kurtz, in the shadows. "It was necessity. He was too fat!" Frederickson insists. "And I think he came with a shaved head. Francis was very upset with Brando when he showed up. He had not read the script. Nor had he read the book, *Heart of Darkness* [upon which the script was based], so he really didn't know who the character was—or anything! Instead of motor homes, we had houseboats, and Francis would go down to the houseboat in the morning and sit there and go through the lines and explain each scene to Brando."

The *Apocalypse Now* approach to filming was put to use when Brando was featured in the first of the cameo roles that would define much of the rest of his acting career. Brando reached out to David Wolper Productions in December 1978, seeking a role in *Roots: The Next Generation*, the sequel to *Roots*, the monumental television miniseries based on Alex Haley's novel about his family line from slavery to freedom. Brando wanted in because he was impressed that the viewing public had responded to the "fresh perspective of history." He told the producers he "didn't want to play a nice guy," and so he was cast as George Lincoln Rockwell, founder in 1959 of the American Nazi Party. The scene would reenact Rockwell's interview by Haley (played by James Earl Jones) for *Playboy* magazine, and cinematographer Joseph M. Wilcots saw on first meeting that it would take some ingenuity to make Brando, who "was a huge, huge guy . . . like over three hundred pounds," resemble the real-life Nazi.

> I said, "One of the things that I'm gonna do for you is I'm gonna take two hundred pounds off of you." And he says, "That'll be a trick." And I said, "No. You see that fireplace? That's gonna be the key source . . . for your light, and then most of the light will end up on the flag, on the background. . . . You will have to play peekaboo through the shadows." . . . I knew that he was anxious about his weight and concerned about it, and when he heard me say, "You'll play peekaboo through the shadows," he liked that.

There would be far fewer roles in the decades to come, but in the period between *Apocalypse Now* and the *Roots* sequel, Brando set the course for a controversial era in cinematic history—and post-pandemic cinema—when he signed on for *Superman*, a movie based on a comic book character. He took the role "for the money"—and why wouldn't he? In exchange for a handful of scenes as Jor-El, Superman's biological father on the planet Krypton, producers Alexander and Ilya Salkind guaranteed him top billing and $3.7 million, plus a cut of the domestic and international grosses of *Superman* and *Superman II* (his scenes for both would be filmed simultaneously). The deal made Brando, who, for *Mutiny on the Bounty*, was the first actor to be paid $1 million for a film, Hollywood's highest-paid actor yet.

Brando arrived for twelve days of work at Shepperton Studios outside London on March 23, 1977. For a combined fifteen minutes of screen and voiceover time, he would ultimately rake in around $15 million and have a huge effect on the future of Hollywood filmmaking. He is the one who made comic book, or "superhero" movies "safe" for respected actors.

"Brando was hired on *Superman* to give it class," Karaszewski says. "There was a sense that superhero movies were silly, superhero movies were for kids, and Marlon Brando at the time was the God of movie acting and of movie stars, and I think the Salkinds threw so much money at him for so little work that he couldn't say 'no.' And when he said 'yes,' all of a sudden the idea of *Superman* with Marlon Brando became a thing, where Gene Hackman would sign up. This is no longer a silly kid's thing. This will be a world-class piece of cinema."

Christopher Reeve would star in four *Superman* movies. Many more pictures featuring Superman and other DC comics superheroes would follow, most notably *Batman* in 1979, which starred Jack Nicholson as The Joker. The DC franchise would be rivaled only by Marvel Studios, which in 2008 launched the Marvel Cinematic Universe, which has attracted major actors, including Robert Downey Jr., Samuel L. Jackson, Scarlett Johansson, Benedict Cumberbatch, William Hurt, Willem Dafoe, Tim Roth, and Brie Larson, among dozens of others.

The number and success of superhero movies in the past decade led filmmaker Quentin Tarantino to complain in 2022 about the "Marvelization of Hollywood," which he claimed is making the "movie star" obsolete. "You have all these actors who have become famous playing these characters. But they're not movie stars. Right? Captain America is the star. Or Thor is the star. . . . It's these franchise characters that become a star. My only axe to grind against them is they're the only things that seem to be made, and they're the only things that seem to generate any kind of excitement. . . . They are the entire representation of this era of movies right now, and there's not really much room for anything else."

Undeniably, the success can be traced back to Brando signing on to *Superman.*

"There are big markers in terms of the Marvelization of Hollywood, but that's probably the first gigantic one—even though it's DC," Karaszewski says. "It was the moment that the Superman movie is for real, that it's going to be the biggest movie of the year."

"Comic book films were not considered commercial at the time," says the critic Vincent Cotroneo.

There was still a bit of camp to them, and with the original *Superman* and *Batman* series, it was more for fun. Brando brought a bit of sophistication to that role, and a bit of elegance. Even though he was doing it for reasons that would ultimately benefit him in the long run, he still did an amazing job as Jor-El. I think that was still the best interpretation of Superman's father shown onscreen, animated or not, so far. Whether or not he read the comic books, we'll leave that to interpretation, but he did an amazing job of being the catalyst for Kal-El's journey. Yeah, his planet was destroyed, but Brando's character is the reason why Kal-El becomes Superman. His words of wisdom—"You will go far, my son"—were powerful and meaningful, and ultimately, Kal-El is out to fulfill what his father had envisioned for him. He's going to do great things, and he did. The film is campy. Superman's flying off in the distance, smiling into the camera and winking, but it comes from a place of sincerity and fulfilling that vision of hope, which is what Marlon Brando's character Jor-El ultimately wanted. And I think that's why they brought Brando back in *Superman Returns*, the remake/sequel with Brandon Routh. [Director Bryan Singer combined footage of Brando from the 1977 shoot with computer-generated imagery.] They use Marlon Brando's image not only to connect the thread line of the series but because his presence was so powerful and his line delivery was so perfect. And for what? Less than ten minutes of screen time in a nearly two-and-a-half-hour film. That says a lot.

"Brando was always saying, 'I'm doing it for the money,' and then he would invent incredible characters in these films," says Stephen Rutledge, the historian and writer. "I think he had an enormous impact on actors who came after him."

Brando may have set the course for the huge paychecks that would attract him in the future, but *Superman* was also a harbinger of how he'd work in his final decades. Brando would not appear in many more films in the twenty-five years of life that were left after *Apocalypse Now* had its premiere at the Cannes Film Festival. Most of his appearances were in cameo roles, some finely crafted, and some, simply over-the-top.

"Brando made a lot of movies for the check, there's no there's no doubt about it," Karaszewski says. "And *Superman* is one of the beginnings of that. It was clearly just the check."

Brando's first film of the 1980s was a role in *The Formula*, working opposite George C. Scott, the only other actor to reject a Best Actor Oscar. For three scenes as a seventy-year-old oil baron, the fifty-five-year-old Brando was paid $3 million. He arrived on set with the top of his head shaved. He arranged several long strands of hair in a combover, and got further into character with false upper teeth, nose plugs, and a hearing aid, which doubled as a device through which an assistant fed him his lines.

The Formula took in $8.5 million on a $13 million budget. It was not a hit. Brando was not recognizable from his earlier starring roles, and this was his last role before a self-imposed "retirement" that lasted until 1988. But as it happened, this pause in his career coincided with the dawn of the VCR era, offering a chance for his greatest work to be studied and his lesser-known work to be scrutinized. The first home video recorders and players went on sale in the 1970s, and by the early 1980s, many films were available for sale—and soon, for rental. *The Wild One, On the Waterfront,* and *The Godfather* were soon in shops on VHS and Beta tape, and a generation of young actors and filmmakers, too young, or not yet alive to see them in theaters, could now watch, freeze, rewind, and study them, over and over again.

"Method acting is ultimately the search for truth, and Brando paved the way for actors to find the truth in their own ways, whether it's Heath Ledger locking himself in a hotel room to be The Joker or Daniel Day-Lewis bringing Abraham Lincoln home with him," Cotroneo says.

> I think it's very subjective to the actors themselves, but I think Brando gave them the opportunities and the tools to search for their truth and how to bring that to the camera. And also how important line delivery is, taking that time to understand that you are throwing a fishing line out to the audience and that's ultimately where their engagement lies. And he was, I think, the first one to really throw that line through the screen and connect to the audience on an emotional level. It's not easy to do. And I think all that comes down to the way that his body was just as important to the roles as his eyes. That's where a lot of actors could cite that inspiration: how he used every part of his body and just the right time, whether he was exploding on that Dogs of War speech in *Julius Caesar,* or those very subtle movements in *The*

Godfather. When he did explode in that film, it was very powerful because you see the simmering, building up, and then when he just yells at Johnny Fontane, "You can act like a man!" it was like, "Wow! He had this rage in him all the time?"

Frederickson could see the influence in the spring of 1982. He was in Oklahoma, working with Francis Ford Coppola on *The Outsiders* with a cast of young actors that included Matt Dillon, Patrick Swayze, Ralph Macchio, Emilio Estevez, C. Thomas Howell, Diane Lane, and Tom Cruise. "Yeah, he had an effect. Matt Dillon, specifically, was Brando. He was mumbling or something, and Francis said, 'He's channeling Brando today.'"

"*The Outsiders* was very, very Brando-inspired, in detail," Rutledge says. "I've worked with Matt Dillon, in *Drugstore Cowboy* and *Singles*, as an actor. He is, in real-life, on set, extraordinarily nice and polite and professional. And he certainly did have that vibe, complete with the leather jacket."

Politics and his activism brought Brando back to films in 1988, when he returned to England to play a famous South African lawyer in *A Dry White Season*. The apartheid drama was directed by Euzhan Palcy, the first Black woman to helm a mainstream Hollywood picture. Brando was attracted by the political message and "the Black perspective." He offered to do the role for free, and donated his scale salary of about four thousand dollars to an anti-apartheid group. Roger Ebert wrote that his scenes were "not a star turn, but an effective performance in which we see a lawyer with a brilliant mind, who uses it cynically and comically because that is his form of protest." The scenes led to an Academy Award nomination for Best Supporting Actor, and Brando began the final stretch of his career.

By this point, Karaszewski says,

> Almost all the movies Brando appeared in were financed because they got Brando, and because they got Brando, they could get whoever the hottest actors in the world were to be with him. Every young actor wanted to play opposite Brando. It became this thing where if you got Marlon Brando in a movie, you could get Johnny Depp, you could get Ed Norton and Robert De Niro. And when you went to the movies, you were always looking for what Brando's going to do in this. And when something like *The Island of Dr. Moreau* came along, you'd just be like, "Holy shit! Oh, my God! Look what he did!" That's an almost unwatchable movie, except for Brando. He's so funny and good, and him acting with the little person, it's one of the most jaw-dropping things in in movie history.

The Island of Dr. Moreau, filmed in Australia in 1995, paired Brando with Val Kilmer (and with the two-foot four-inch-tall actor Nelson de la Rosa as a miniature version of Brando's Dr. Moreau). De Niro and Edward Norton worked with Brando in 2000, in the heist drama, *The Score*.

"There's this history of famous actors, and I do think it sort of begins with Brando, because Brando had such an enormous effect on the psychology of men in in America," Norton told Joe Rogan in 2019.

> And if you look at what I would call "the great generation of American actors"—Dustin Hoffman, Robert De Niro, Robert Duvall, Gene Hackman, Al Pacino, Morgan Freeman, Meryl Streep—that's all like the post-Brando generation. All of those people, literally all of them wanted to become actors because of Marlon Brando. He so rewrote the idea of what it was, what it could be. It was like what Bob Dylan did in the culture; he just rewrote the game. He changed the idea of the type of person that male actors wanted to be. Suddenly . . . they wanted to be visceral, not polished. They wanted to be muscular. They wanted to be masculine. They wanted to be intense. When you think back on Jimmy Stewart, Cary Grant, that is not what movie stars were aspiring to. They were aspiring to . . . a kind of a polish.

There are many "new Brandos" on stage and screen today. One of the more unlikely is an actor who got his start as a standup comedian in New York City in the late 1970s. Andrew Clay Silverstein was born in Brooklyn in 1957. He first showed up in comedy clubs with an impression of Jerry Lewis's nerdy Julius Kelp from *The Nutty Professor* that transformed into John Travolta as Danny Zuko in *Grease*, and ultimately, a character he called "The Diceman." Clay moved to Los Angeles in 1980 and found work as an actor, beginning with the comedy slasher movie, *Wacko*, and an episode of the television series *M*A*S*H*. As Andrew "Dice" Clay, he appeared in films like *Pretty in Pink* and *Casual Sex?*, and television series including Michael Mann's *Crime Story*. All the while, he was gaining success as a standup comic, with his persona as the Diceman.

The Diceman had devolved into a polarizing, deliberately offensive, racist, homophobic, and misogynist character cloaked in an outrageously studded leather jacket and pocketful of obscene nursery rhymes. By the end of the decade, the Diceman had overshadowed not only Clay's acting credits, but most all others in the comedy field. He had top-selling comedy albums and several HBO specials, and, while his crude act got him "banned for life" from MTV, he was performing in massive arenas across the country. In 1990, he was the first comedian to sell out two consecutive nights at Madison Square Garden in New York City. He also starred in the film, *The Adventures of Ford Fairlane*.

And throughout his rise, Andrew Clay's intolerant Diceman was relying in part on its direct, albeit twisted, lineage to Marlon Brando and Johnny Strabler in *The Wild One*.

The writer and intellectual Joyce Carol Oates saw the connection when she stepped into the controversy, brushing off Clay as "an entertainer" who was "merely symptomatic of our era, when ethnic and racial hatreds suddenly seem to abound." The Diceman act was a "campy homage" to Elvis "and very likely to the Marlon Brando of *The Wild One*."

Clay would confirm as much in his autobiography, *The Filthy Truth*, but with a crucial alteration. "Marlon Brando wore leather in *The Wild One*. James Dean was a leather guy. Elvis was all about leather. . . . Starting with Brando and James Dean and going through Elvis and Travolta and Pacino and Stallone, these were macho guys with soft hearts. But a couple of things changed when I got to LA." In creating the Diceman character, Clay removed the heart.

"He modeled the leather-jacket, motorcycle-punk aesthetic on Marlon Brando from *The Wild One*," Tim Grierson wrote in *Mel* magazine, "but Brando always wore his masculinity like a burden, as if he was wrestling with the limits of what it meant to be a man. Clay transformed that turmoil into an uncomplicated cartoon, Dice exaggeratingly lighting his cigarettes and wearing a championship belt in the most uber-macho way possible."

"I always loved Brando," Clay tells the author.

If you don't love Brando's work, you're a fool. He's one of the greatest actors ever. The Brando thing always came into play because I always would believe: *Become what you are doing*. I figured, "Well, if I'm gonna do this, I'll just become the biggest there ever was," so the confidence was very real. There was no self-deprecation, which every comic through the decades would have. There were no apologies with Dice. The reason Dice ever happened was because I didn't believe in going to an acting school once a week when I could get on a stage every single night, seven days a week, and create my own method of acting. But when I would do a film role or a TV thing, I get to step away from Dice onstage and become whatever the part calls for.

Amid backlash and protests, "The Diceman" burned out. A kinder, gentler, and likable version of Andrew Dice Clay showed up in December 1995, when he starred in *Bless This House*, a CBS sitcom based on *The Honeymooners*. Cathy Moriarty, Academy Award nominee for Martin Scorsese's *Raging Bull*, played his wife. Clay's persona softened as well, as he carried on a more low-key comedy and acting career over the next decade-and-a-half. In 2011, he received good notices playing himself on the HBO series *Entourage*. The following year, he landed a role in a Woody Allen film.

Blue Jasmine was Allen's take on, tribute to, or critique of *A Streetcar Named Desire* (set in San Francisco, a city also known for its streetcars). Cate Blanchett was in the Blanche DuBois role as Jasmine, a troubled, recently impoverished socialite who moves in with her younger, working-class sister, Ginger, in her humble apartment in San Francisco. As Ginger, Sally Hawkins was a riff on Stella. Clay played Augie, Ginger's ex-husband, and in some ways split the Stanley Kowalski role with Bobby Cannavale, as Ginger's working-class boyfriend. (In one scene, Clay wears a white "wife beater" T-shirt—as Brando did onstage in *Streetcar*). Like Stanley Kowalski, Augie does not get along with the intruder, suspects Jasmine of monetary chicanery, and in one standout scene, confronts her in the street.

Clay says he rewrote the confrontation scene in very Brandoesque fashion, just as he's done with almost every role he's played (and always with the approval of directors, including Michael Mann of *Crime Story* and Martin Scorsese during the HBO series *Vinyl*). "I worked on that scene for three days in my hotel room," he recalls. "I brought my son Max with me, to sort of direct me. I told my son, who was eighteen at the time, 'You know me better than Woody, so I'll listen to Woody. But you'll give me notes after he does.' We show up on the set and here comes Woody, where we're waiting to film, on location. I go, 'Look, nothing against your writing. You're a great talent, but I saw the part going way deeper than what was written. So I just rewrote the whole thing.' Woody was shocked." Allen asked Clay to act out the scene for him.

> So I do it and he goes, "Okay." So now we're filming. I've got two sons. I'm divorced at this point from their mother, and the scene is really heartfelt. And now they're done with Cate and they're turning the camera around to get my shot, and I come over to my son and I go, "Whaddaya think?"—about what am I gonna do in this scene. And he goes, "Just talk to mom." That was his only direction. So I do this monologue and I think I wind up in tears, and when Woody yells "Cut," there was dead silence on that street corner. I mean from the cameraman to everybody. It took Woody about five minutes before he even came over to me, but here comes Woody with another producer and he goes, "Andrew, that . . . that was perfect. That was brilliant. I mean we can do it again, just for safety if you want, but we got it."

Blanchett had played Blanche DuBois in the Sydney Theatre Company's production of *Streetcar* in 2009. She would win a Best Actress Oscar for *Blue Jasmine*. And in a cast that also included Michael Stuhlbarg, Peter Sarsgaard, and Alec Baldwin (who'd played Kowalski on Broadway), Andrew Dice Clay received accolades. Karen Kemmerle in the *Tribeca News* called his performance "one of the year's most devastating and honest. Clay never plays Augie as a fool or an idiot, simply as a working-class man who trusts the wrong people. . . . It is only fitting that he is the one to bring Jasmine's world crashing down. . . . Clay never raises his voice or his fists (as we, the audience, expect he might). He simply tells Jasmine exactly what he thinks of her and her ex-husband with a matter-of-fact delivery and essentially steals the scene from Blanchett."

"When I did *Blue Jasmine*, they were saying, 'He's like Marlon Brando,' and I go, 'I'm not like Marlon Brando. *At all*,'" Clay insists, while admitting that Brando had always been an influence,

one hundred percent. I don't even think he understood how major he was. When you're that guy, you don't realize how far that reaches, so I think he was just playing the parts. Maybe when he got older, because he really got eccentric, but as an actor, I think in his younger years, he was just doing what he did, and it came from inside. He knew the Method, but it was him. It's ultimately the person. It's gotta be in you to come out of you. I actually watch the beginning of *The Godfather* at least three times a month, where he's sitting at the desk, petting the cat. I just love that opening scene so much. I don't know if it was the calmness of how he was petting the cat—try to hold a cat some time. The only way you're holding a cat is if that cat wants to be in your lap at that time. He's petting the cat so gently that when he put it on the desk, the cat just stayed. He just had this inner sense as to what needed to be when he played a part.

As an actor, Andrew Dice Clay came to embrace the sensitivity and self-doubt that Brando had brought to the original leather jacket rebel and, willing to show himself as a "human being," continued to stand out in television and movie roles, most memorably in 2018, in *A Star Is Born*, directed by Bradley Cooper.

"Bradley Cooper was another one," Clay says.

This was a really big-budget film, so I asked him at the very beginning, after we did the readthrough, "Can I change it up a little?" And he goes, "I'm expecting all of you [to do that]." We met on a Friday, spent three and a half hours in his office. I didn't even know if he had a part in mind for me. Saturday, he had me meet Stefani, who's Lady Gaga, at a music studio, and he gave us some improv scenes. One was very fun and one got very deep. And the next thing you know, she's got her head on my chest and tears are falling off my face. And I'm not seeing Lady Gaga, I'm seeing her as the part, as my daughter. And Bradley Cooper's on the floor drinking coffee, and he jumps up, he goes, "I knew it! I just knew it!" On Monday, he calls me to offer me the part of her dad.

Of all the contemporary actors working under Brando's influence, the one who'd most deserve the title of "the new Brando," carrying on his art and legacy, just might be Johnny Depp. Depp not only shared scenes with Brando in two films, but directed and befriended him. Few of Hollywood's leading men have taken the chances, shown their feminine side, and been as unafraid to lose themselves in eccentric and unrecognizable Brandoesque characterizations.

Depp was twenty-one when he filmed his first starring role, in the sex comedy *Private Resort* (with costar "Andrew Clay"). Like Brando, he was already a star—in Depp's case, a reluctant teen idol from the Fox television series *21 Jump Street*–when, in his fifth motion picture, he played a motorcycle-riding rebel in black leather.

Cry-Baby, released in 1990, was a musical romantic comedy, set in Baltimore in the 1950s, and written and directed by John Waters, the veteran auteur of transgressive, queer, shock, "bad taste" cinema who'd moved into the mainstream in the eighties with *Polyester* and *Hairspray*. Depp played the eponymous hero, a very sensitive bad boy with an ability to shed a single tear. Nathan Rabin, in an editorial on the *Rotten Tomatoes* website, wrote that Depp "accomplishes the seemingly impossible feat of matching the charisma of Elvis Presley back in his *Jailhouse Rock* days, when his androgynous sexiness posed an implicit challenge to an uptight nation that was both aroused and confused by the swiveling of his hips. . . . Depp is the one who is relentlessly sexualized, who is treated as eye candy as much as a flesh-and-blood human being. The camera doesn't just love him; it obsesses over him in a way that would probably result in a restraining order if it were human."

The sexual ambiguity in Waters's work, like that of Tennessee Williams, was coded with queer sensibility. "Everyone in the film is so performative that this is effectively a queer cast—or the closest Waters could get to a queer cast in Hollywood in the early 90s," Billy Stevenson wrote in *CinemaTelevisionMusic*. "Waters's 50s are already full of sly homoerotic moments, and not simply in a revisionist spirit but in a wonderfully frank tribute to how much homoerotic pleasure even or especially the most strait-laced and clean-cut 50s spectacles could provide to those who knew how and where to look."

Edward Scissorhands, Tim Burton's take on the Frankenstein story, opened in December 1990, with Depp as a humanoid whose arms ended in scissor blades, a sensitive, misunderstood creature who is adopted by a White suburban family in the film and was adopted by queer audiences who identified with the loneliness and isolation of Depp's character. (In 2018, the film was reimagined in Los Angeles as a stage musical with a queer love story).

Depp's cinematic adventurism continued through the nineties. A highly praised role was in 1994's *Ed Wood*, written by Scott Alexander and Larry Karaszewski, in which Depp starred as the hapless low-budget filmmaker and crossdresser. "Johnny was very influenced by Marlon Brando," Karaszewski says. "I think he loved Brando. He clearly had such respect for Marlon as an artist and as a person."

When Johnny Depp took the witness stand in his 2022 defamation trial, some saw a reflection of his friend Marlon Brando. Author's collection

Depp recounts how he got the chance to work with Brando after he wrapped *Ed Wood*.

He was the absolute opposite of everything that they told me he was gonna be, which is some testy guy who wants to know that he's in control. And that's not at all what the man was. No matter what he did, going to work, whatever, the most important thing on his mind was justice. Equality and justice. Just justice. Marlon and I met over the phone, because I wanted to do *Don Juan DeMarco* with him. We spoke for three hours on the telephone. I was in New York; he was in Los Angeles. I went back the next week; he invited me for dinner. We sat and we talked, and we connected on many levels, especially the fact that no one wants to be a novelty. But one of the things that happened was I asked him about a quote by William Saroyan—it's the preface of *The Time of Your Life*, the play. . . . It's something that had touched me in a large way . . . the way to live your life, a real road map how to live your life. And so I asked him about it, and he said, yeah, he knew, and he said, "How well do you know it?" So I began to recite it, because at that time I had memorized it . . . and I got to a certain point and he finished it, verbatim. And I was somewhat stupefied. I said, "That's incredible." I pulled out my wallet. I said, "I've carried this this dog-eared thing that I'd ripped out of a book. I've carried this for years in my wallet." And he said, "Hang on a second." And got up and he grabbed a frame that was just by his bed . . . and he showed it to me, and he had a very similar dog-eared, folded, well-used version of the same thing that he had carried in his wallet through all those years. So he understood me very well instantly, and I understood him, and I was very lucky to become so close with the man.

In the time of your life, live—so that in that good time there shall be no ugliness or death for yourself or for any life your life touches. Seek goodness everywhere, and when it is found, bring it out of its hiding place and let it be free and unashamed.

—from Preface, *The Time of Your Life* by William Saroyan

Larry Karaszewski recalls the day he and his writing partner met with Depp on the set of *Don Juan DeMarco* and got to witness how Brando worked with directors and young actors in the last stages of his career.

If you remember that movie, Brando is Johnny Depp's psychiatrist and Johnny Depp thinks he's Don Juan DeMarco. This was one of the psychiatric sessions, so it was almost exclusively a monologue by Johnny, and Brando was just reacting at the end. And what showed much respect for Brando was that Johnny wasn't even on camera. It was the turnaround. It was just a shot of Marlon Brando sitting at a desk, and Johnny, off camera, just sat there and did this five-minute monologue, just totally off his head, totally acting 100 percent—he was acting with Marlon Brando! A lot of actors of that caliber don't come in for the off-camera stuff, but Johnny was giving his all, off-camera to Brando. And what happened consistently, take after take, was Johnny would finish this huge five-minute monologue off the top of his head and Brando would be sitting there, nodding his head, in his own world, and he'd say—[Karaszewski pauses a few seconds]—"Line!" [He laughs.] And they would give him his line, and then Brando would futz with it and deliver the line. But it actually even went one step further, where the line was supposed to be, something like, "I have to leave right now. We'll talk again tomorrow" or something. And Brando kept on changing it to some version of "I'll see you later tonight," or he kept on changing the timeline, and the director would have to interfere and say, "No, no, no. You understand, you're going straight from this scene to a party." So it became this incredibly frustrating experience just to get Brando to say the very simplistic line that he had. I was witnessing Brando acting, but there was no meat to the scene whatsoever, and he was treating it like it had no meat. He was treating it as just a ridiculous process and almost at a certain point we were wondering whether he was just giving everybody a hard time just to give everybody a hard time.

Depp worked with Brando again in 1996 when he starred in and directed *The Brave*, the story of a Native American who is so desperate to provide for his family that he agrees to be killed in a snuff film for fifty thousand dollars. It was an independent film with a tragic history, originally set to be directed in 1993 by Aziz Ghazal, until Ghazal bludgeoned his thirteen-year-old daughter and estranged wife to death before killing himself. Once Depp picked up the film, he wound up spending millions of his own money to complete it. After a disastrous reception at the Cannes Film Festival in 1997, he refused to release it in the United States. "What I will say about that film and about Marlon in particular is that it's one of the best performances he's given since *Last Tango*," Depp told Larry King in 2011. "It's one of the performances where he dug down deep and gave of himself so much."

"Marlon reinvented acting," said Depp. "He revolutionized acting. It was not about behavior in the sense as it was just about being in a moment. And he was a dangerous element. He was a dangerous element, and he remained a dangerous element all the way through, man, until his last breath. I worshipped him. And I still do."

So it is fitting that throughout his career, Depp continued to make film choices that went against expectations, challenging himself as an actor and choosing parts in which he would be subsumed by characters. After many unconventional films and a fame that far exceeded his box office record, Depp became a superstar in 2003 by going full Brando in *The Curse of the Black Pearl*, the first installment of Disney's blockbuster *Pirates of the Caribbean* series. Brando's foppish Fletcher Christian in *Mutiny on the Bounty* had nothing on Depp's Captain Jack Sparrow, the tipsy, mincing, lisping pirate with Keith Richards kohl. Yet even in a franchise based on a theme park ride, Depp's outrageous take on the pirate would not have been possible had his hero not gone there first.

In the digital, streaming age of the twenty-four-hour news cycle and social media postings, the closeness and similarities to Brando would also be found beyond the world of cinema. The press, the media, the ones who Brando confused and played with at the start of his career, who sought revenge once he settled in as a Hollywood figure, and who stalked him once he made himself less available, would treat Depp in much the same way. They would celebrate his success, but find even more delight in his scandals.

For Brando, the reckoning came in 1957, when the impish writer Truman Capote, on assignment for *The New Yorker* magazine, visited him during the filming of *Sayonara* in Kyoto, Japan. Against the advice of the director, producer, and others around him, Brando agreed to be interviewed by Capote, alone in his suite at the Miyako Hotel. Capote, the boyish, brilliant, wicked writer, showed up with a bottle of vodka, which was soon depleted, and with the help of a serving of his own family secrets, managed to get Brando to let down the guard he had in place for more than a decade in the public eye. When *The Duke in His Domain* was published in November, Brando was horrified. He'd talked about his love affairs, directors, other actors, his years of psychoanalysis, and, for the first time, growing up with an alcoholic mother. It was a bitter lesson.

"The little bastard spent half the night telling me all his problems," he said. "I figured the least I could do was tell him a few of mine."

Depp got the treatment from a writer for *Rolling Stone* in June 2018. He was fifty-five. He was in the midst of legal entanglements with his former business managers and his ex-wife Amber Heard, whom he'd married in 2015 and who filed for divorce fifteen months later, alleging domestic abuse. Depp's attorney and close friend arranged what was expected to be a much-needed positive interview with the pop culture magazine to discuss the "injustice being done to Depp's reputation and bottom line." Stephen Rodrick visited Depp in his mansion in London and came away with a story that *Rolling Stone* headlined "The Trouble with Johnny Depp," and subtitled "Multimillion-dollar lawsuits, a haze of booze and hash, a marriage gone very wrong and a lifestyle he can't afford—inside the trials of Johnny Depp."

> Depp has long built his life by imitating his legends—buying an island like Brando, becoming an expert on quaaludes like Hunter S. Thompson. . . . It's estimated that Depp has made $650 million on films that netted $3.6 billion. Almost all of it is gone. . . . There were whispers that Depp's recreational drug and alcohol use were crippling him. . . . Over the past 18 months there were reports he couldn't remember his lines and had to have them fed to him through an earpiece.

In 2022, Depp sued Heard for defamation after she put her name to a ghostwritten op-ed piece in the *Washington Post* in which she referred to herself as "a public figure representing domestic abuse." Although Depp's name was not cited, readers may have assumed he was the domestic abuser referred to in the article. The case went to trial in 2022, livestreamed and broadcast live across the globe, the latest celebrity courtroom drama in a genre that began thirty-one years earlier with the trial of Brando's son Christian for the murder of Dag Drollet.

The "highlight" of the defamation trial was Depp's turn on the witness stand. And when his testimony began, there were gasps among those who knew him, knew Brando, or were aficionados of celebrity trials.

Gray Frederickson, the Academy Award-winning producer who'd worked with Brando on three films, was speaking with the author in May 2022, when talk turned to the current national media obsession. "Johnny Depp," Frederickson said. "Someone said the other day, 'Did you see Johnny Depp's court testimony? He was doing Brando!'" He laughed. "Ponytail and all! Don't you think he was? The manner of speaking and the little whispering voice, it was all Brando. He was doing Brando!"

Twenty

Lying for a Living

June 12, 1973, is a date that can't be overlooked when considering the legacy and influence of Marlon Brando. This was the day Brando arrived in New York City and taped that appearance on *The Dick Cavett Show,* four months after the release of *Last Tango in Paris;* eleven weeks after he'd dispatched Sacheen Littlefeather to decline, before a television audience of eighty-five million, his Academy Award for Best Actor. The Cavett show on the ABC television network was the forum in which Brando explained his reasoning behind the stunt, spoke eloquently about Native American rights, pointed out the casual racism on films and on television, and once again dismissed the notion that acting was a great art.

For Cavett, the interview was a coup, and as it would turn out, a historic visual document. More than fifty years later, the episode is still being studied. Clips on YouTube have generated millions of views. Young people continue to learn about Hollywood and American history from the actor who was the greatest of the twentieth century.

There's a footnote to that appearance that brings in another aspect of Marlon Brando's influence on popular culture today. After the taping, he and Cavett went out for dinner together. At around 9:30 that evening, the two of them were walking down the curved Doyers Street in Chinatown, seeking a restaurant. Being celebrities in the big city, both men wore sunglasses at night, and continued their conversation, ignoring the man maneuvering around and in front of them, clicking away with the camera he held. Ron Galella was New York City's leading paparazzo and celebrity chaser, somewhat famous, or at least infamous, in his own right, for the thousands of photographs he'd taken of Jacqueline Kennedy Onassis. Galella was such a pest, stalking or ambushing the former First Lady in public, that Jackie O got a restraining order to keep him at least one hundred and fifty feet away (a judge eventually reduced that to twenty-five feet). Now, Galella was less than an arm's length from his subjects. He'd hounded Brando earlier in the day when the actor landed at the heliport. Brando was wearing sunglasses there as well, and when Galella shouted a request that he remove the shades for a better picture, Brando ignored him. Backing up ahead of Cavett and Brando, Galella asked again. "At first, Brando was nice and friendly," Galella told columnist Earl Wilson.

> I took about six pictures of them and walked ahead of them. Finally, Brando said, "Why are you continuing to take the same picture?" I said, "For variety, I'd like both of you to have your glasses off." This time, he said, "No, I won't." Then he whipped his right arm at me and hit me square in the center of the jaw, breaking the top of the jawbone. He was coming at me, and he said, "You want more?" I was gushing blood and I didn't look back. I went to Bellevue Hospital. They gave me nine stitches, putting my jawbone in place with a brace.

I can't understand Brando," the forty-two-year-old photographer claimed. "He talks about how people mistreat the Indians. Look how he mistreats the photographers."

The next day, Brando was admitted to the Hospital for Special Surgery with an infected hand. Galella eventually sued. He reached a settlement with Brando out of court. In 1974, Galella's assistant took a photo of the photographer following close behind Brando. Galella is wielding a camera . . . and wearing a football helmet.

Actors like Sean Penn, Alec Baldwin, and Shia LaBeouf may have taken note. The attention of the gnat-like paparazzi and requests to remove your sunglasses to smile for a picture in the street were annoyances to Brando that he never quite accepted as part of the job. So for the most part, he ignored the press, toyed with them, and as the press expanded into the "media," made himself less available, which only made him more a figure of fascination as well as a target.

In the 1990s, the tabloidization of popular culture began to consume the media and American life. The celebrity-industrial complex expanded beyond the supermarket scandal sheets like the *National Enquirer* and *Globe* to magazines like *People, US Weekly,* and *Entertainment Weekly;* tabloid television shows like *A Current Affair, Hard Copy,* and *Entertainment Tonight;* gavel-to-gavel television coverage of courtroom trials; the syndication of Howard Stern's radio program; and a celebritization of "reality stars" and criminals alike. Marlon Brando, the great actor, the influential Hollywood rebel, was, like many others, tossed into the mix.

For Brando, it began tragically, with a gunshot in his TV room on the night of May 16, 1990. Brando's son Christian argued with twenty-six-year-old Dag Drollet, boyfriend of Christian's pregnant, twenty-year-old half-sister, Cheyenne. Christian accused Dag of abusing Cheyenne. Then he put a bullet in Drollet's head. Christian, thirty-two, was charged with

murder. His father, one of Hollywood's most protected and private figures, was suddenly in the harshest spotlight of all.

But even in his grief, Marlon Brando knew how to play the media. After
a hearing on May 22, he walked out of the West Los Angeles Municipal
Courthouse and straight toward a pack of reporters and cameramen.
"The messenger of misery has come to my house, and has also come to the
house of Mr. Jack Drollet in Tahiti," he said. "To those people who have
known these kinds of tragic circumstances in the world, no explanation
is necessary. To those people who do not know the nature of this acute
misery that both our families suffer, no explanation is possible. . . . We
must just be strong, and I think that the family, with love and supporting
each other, will prevail."

Most of the newsdogs in the pack were silent, as if they couldn't believe
what they'd snared. There he was, the Great White Whale, in their sights,
standing there to answer their questions. The rat-a-tat peppering that
would be expected from the talking heads did not occur. Most of them
simply stared. At least one reporter later received a dressing down from
his editor and was handed a list of questions to fire at Brando when, and
if, he surfaced again.

Brando did. On days he showed up at court, he briefed the pack afterward. He gave out select bits of personal information and told them what
he wanted them to hear. Meanwhile, he'd gotten Cheyenne out of the
country, back to Tahiti. Without her testimony, and with Robert Shapiro,
the future O. J. Simpson "dream team" attorney representing Christian,
prosecutors offered to make a deal. In January, Christian pleaded guilty
to involuntary manslaughter.

All eyes were on Marlon Brando at the sentencing hearing on February
28, 1991. He was dressed in black, hair pulled into a small ponytail, when
he stuffed his three-hundred-pound bulk into the witness box and made
a plea for leniency. Brando blamed himself for his son's problems. He
dug deep. He wept. He gave what Dag Drollet's father called "the performance of his life." It was, at least, the performance that many saw as the
model for Johnny Depp, caught on the stand, "doing Brando."

Christian Brando was sentenced to ten years in prison. He was released
in 1996, and died of pneumonia in 2008. Cheyenne had given birth to a
son in June 1990. She hanged herself in Tahiti in 1995.

In July 1990, while the shooting scandal was still generating fresh headlines, Brando's latest movie arrived in theaters. In *The Freshman*, Brando
plays a mobster named Carmine Sabatini, who happens to be a dead
ringer for Don Vito Corleone from *The Godfather*. The film was well-
received. *Variety* praised Brando's comedy performance as "sublime";

Janet Maslin of the *New York Times* said he was "an unexpectedly deft comic actor." (Stephen Rutledge calls *The Freshman* "my particular favorite. Because he has such a great sense of humor about himself. And it's so sly. It's not quite a parody. He seems invested in the character and it's funny and meta. I just always thought it was such a sweet performance.")

Brando had time for another half-dozen movies and a few short films in what was left of his life. He grabbed the next offer shortly after Christian's plea bargain, a cool $5 million for a cameo as Torquemada in *Christopher Columbus: Discovery*. This was another role "for the paycheck." He had legal bills to pay. He'd take a few more cameos along with more substantial roles in films like *Don Juan DeMarco* and *The Island of Dr. Moreau*. But in that tabloid decade, to the average American sitting at home with the television remote, Brando was the fat guy who used to be the Godfather, recognized from his appearance on Larry King's CNN talk show in 1994. The ninety-minute conversation went live from Brando's house and ended with a song and kiss on the lips. Larry Karaszewski says the episode is

> one of my favorite Brando things that I actually watch. Sometimes, instead of putting on *A Streetcar Named Desire*, I'll put on the Larry King interview. I have it on a VHS tape labeled "King versus Brando" or something. It's a complete hoot. At one point I had friend who could do a pretty good Brando, and I was like, "Should we do a stage version? Should we just do midnight at a local theater every Saturday night? People can come and we'll have one person be Larry King and you'd be Brando." Because it really is a tug-of-war. Brando is being more open because he's trying to promote his book, but there's still that weird gleam in his eye. And he's so entertaining.

Brando fell deeper into the tabloid stew thanks to his old friend and neighbor Quincy Jones, who'd introduced him to Michael Jackson. Jones had produced Jackson's blockbuster album, *Thriller*, and was instrumental in landing Brando's son Miko a job in the Jackson organization. Brando's friendship with Jackson led him to New York City for a bizarre appearance at Madison Square Garden in September 2001. The *Michael Jackson 30th Anniversary Celebration* was a pair of concerts, filmed for a CBS television special celebrating Jackson's thirty years as a solo artist. Jackson, his brothers, and other entertainers performed, and celebrities, including Elizabeth Taylor, Macaulay Culkin, and Liza Minnelli, paid tribute to the self-proclaimed "King of Pop." On September 7, after an energetic opening number by Whitney Houston, Usher, and Mya, the lights came up to reveal Brando onstage, sitting on a leather chair, wearing a suit and dark glasses, and playing with his watch. After an uncomfortable delay, he removed his shades, picked up a microphone, and began what David

Segal in the *Washington Post* called "a grumpy, half-comprehensible lecture about the 'hundreds, if not thousands of children' being starved and hacked to death in some foreign land. Michael Jackson, he gravely intoned, is one of the few souls out there trying to help. . . . All cheer in the room vanished, replaced first by startled quiet, followed shortly by anger and a hail of boos. 'Stella!' hooted a wag."

The second show was taped on September 10. The following morning, terrorists crashed two jetliners into the twin towers of the World Trade Center—and an urban legend was born. *Vanity Fair* floated the story that amid the chaos and terror, and with all flights grounded, Jackson, Brando, and Taylor crammed themselves into a car—just the three of them—and hit the highway in an escape from New York. They allegedly made it as far as Ohio.

Days like these added up, and would seem to overshadow Brando's accomplishments and influence in the twenty-first century. "I don't think he ever let it get lost," the actor Michael Madsen insists.

> I think he never let the media get to him. He had too much integrity to ever let it get to him. Because the more that you try to avoid the fucking media, the more that they become fascinated with trying to get you and trying to reveal you and trying to kill you. Marlon protected himself. He sat down with Larry King, but you could tell he was just kind of bored and he decided to talk to Larry for a while. But nobody was going to get to him, and he wasn't going to let them get to him. He was smart enough with his money that he could afford to have his privacy. And when you're that big of an actor . . . [he pauses]. Can you imagine what it would be like to be called "the greatest actor who ever lived"? That's quite a fucking crown to wear. There really isn't anybody like that anymore.

Madsen is in a better position than most to comment on Brando and his influence. Early in his career, he was close friends with Christian Brando, spent time at the Brando house, and met Christian's father several times. In August 2001, Madsen costarred with Marlon Brando in the short film/music video for Jackson's song, "You Rock My World." It was Brando's final film performance.

"I think it's a foregone conclusion that the guy just had a gift for presenting himself," Madsen says. "I don't think he was acting as much as he was being himself in a given situation, portraying different qualities of his own personality or his own presence, in the name of different types of characters that he played. I do the same thing, and that's where I got the idea of doing it—of not acting, of just being present in the moment and just doing what was going on with the characters in the story. I figured that out from watching him."

Marlon Brando died on July 1, 2004, at the UCLA Medical Center. The cause was respiratory failure. He was eighty years old, and as news spread across the globe, announcements of his death acknowledged the passing of a great man, a once-in-a-generation talent—and rebel.

Brando was, according to his *New York Times* obituary, "the rebellious prodigy who electrified a generation and forever transformed the art of screen acting, yet whose erratic career, obstinate eccentricities and recurring tragedies prevented him from fully realizing the promise of his early genius." The *Los Angeles Times* hailed "a two-time Academy Award winner who spent much of his career shunning the Hollywood establishment yet earned its enduring admiration through muscular, naturalistic performances that transformed the craft of acting and led peers and critics alike to hail him as the finest actor of his time."

Brando's body was cremated. Some of his ashes were shipped to Tahiti. His son Miko and other family members took the remainder to Death Valley in the Mojave Desert and sprinkled them along with the ashes of Wally Cox. Brando had kept his dear friend's cremains for more than thirty years. He'd been given the box of ashes by Cox's widow, on the promise he'd scatter them in the hills where Wally liked to hike. Instead, he stashed them in a drawer in his home; sometimes kept them under the front seat of his car. Brando kept his friend close. He said he often took out the ashes and spoke to them.

There in Death Valley, like the stereotypical dust in the wind, Brando was gone. But his influence did not blow away with his ashes.

In December 2015, the fashion industry was buzzing when twenty-year-old model Gigi Hadid was featured on the cover of *Vogue* magazine, wearing a black leather biker jacket, Breton top, and a peaked cap. "She probably doesn't know it, bless her, but the stylist has dressed her up like a '50s teen—part James Dean (the Breton), but mostly Marlon Brando in 1953's *The Wild One*." wrote Lauren Cochrane, senior fashion writer for *The Guardian*. "As the leader of 'a gang of hot riding hot-heads,' Brando's character, Johnny Strabler, wears biker leathers and a peaked cap throughout. . . . And so, the peaked cap and biker jacket has come to stand for classic youthful rebellion—edgy, on the prowl—for more than sixty years. Brando might be long gone, but his image—the original rebel—is still hanging around like the best kind of bad influence."

Seven years later, in April 2023, a photo of the eighty-nine-year-old actress Joan Collins wearing an Yves Saint Laurent motorcycle jacket was published on the *Daily Mail* website under the headline, "A month shy of 90, Dame Joan Collins is still a Wild One." "Yesterday," the article commented, "Dame Joan looked like she'd stepped off the set of the classic

Marlon Brando film, *The Wild One*, as she showed off her trim figure by matching the vintage jacket with a pair of tight black trousers."

There may be more influence still to be shared. In November and December 2001, at age seventy-seven, Marlon Brando led a series of acting classes. It was the first time the greatest actor of his generation had shared his knowledge and philosophy—if you don't count the lessons he'd given Quincy Jones III (a.k.a. Snoopy) in the 1980s, to repay his dad for introducing Miko to Michael Jackson. "He's got a kimono on and a ponytail," Quincy Jones recalled. "The funniest thing you ever saw in your life. He said, 'Knowledge on acting is very important for television and movies, but it's ten times more important when you've been out with one woman all night till five-thirty in the morning and you have to go home to your wife. And that's what makes it important.' Snoopy looking at him like he's crazy. He's seventeen years old—he doesn't know what he's talking about."

Benjamin Svetkey revealed the story of Brando's lost acting seminar in *The Hollywood Reporter*. Looking for a quick way to make millions of dollars to maintain his home on Mulholland Drive and private atoll in French Polynesia, Brando had been convinced to produce a series of DVDs about acting that could be sold on a home shopping channel like QVC. He rented a soundstage at Ben Kitay Studios on North Cahuenga Boulevard in Hollywood, had a wooden stage constructed, invited some acting students and famous friends, and presented a ten-day event he named "Lying for a Living." The British director Tony Kaye and a nine-man camera crew were hired to film everything, beginning with the teacher's very memorable entrance.

"Brando appeared wearing a blond wig, blue mascara, a black gown with an orange scarf and a bodice stuffed with gigantic falsies," Svetkey wrote. "Waving a single rose in one hand, he sashayed through the warehouse, plunked his 300-pound frame onto a thronelike chair on a makeshift stage and began fussily applying lipstick. 'I am furious! Furious!' Brando told the group in a matronly English accent, launching into an improvised monologue that ended, ten minutes later, with the actor turning around, lifting his gown, and mooning the crowd."

Brando's students included actors Nick Nolte, Sean Penn, Robin Williams, Whoopi Goldberg, Jon Voight, Peter Coyote, Harry Dean Stanton, and Edward James Olmos. Michael Jackson stopped by. It was, Svetkey wrote, "a wild ten-day symposium—as much a 1960s-style 'happening' as it was an acting course." A troupe of little people improvised with Samoan wrestlers; a homeless man was invited in for lessons; Philippe Petit, the French tightrope walker who'd walked between the Twin Towers, did stunts on a high-wire while a jazz pianist played; and students stripped naked in front of the class. "Was he serious about the class? As serious as a heart attack," Edward James Olmos said. "Brando had never taught an acting class before—this was the only time in his whole life. This was going to be his legacy to the acting community."

Early on, Tony Kaye—himself something of a performance artist and pot-stirrer—caused a commotion by showing up dressed as Osama bin Laden (only weeks after 9/11). A few days later, Brando asked Kaye to leave after he shouted "Cut!" and interrupted an improv scene. Kaye took half the young acting students with him (he'd brought them). Students from the Sanford Meisner Center in North Hollywood took their place. Phil Lander, now a successful Hollywood television producer, was among them.

> Marlon was very intimidating. I didn't see him in drag, but he was seated on a throne. He was very old—this was near the end of his life—very white-haired. But he was a massive, massive man. I don't remember him giving any acting advice. It was more his opinions on acting rather than acting techniques. He said straight up that he never memorized lines, and that he would put his lines on coffee cups, the backs of books, or wherever the hell his eyes would go. It's because he wanted to stay emotionally pure and in the moment. He was very big on being in the emotional moment. He wanted the emotion to carry him from one beat to the next. His point was that that acting is bullshit! And that's what the name of the class was! It was "Lying for a Living." And it was very interesting to see that philosophy coming from the greatest actor of all time. I was very new to the acting game and reading these acting books, taking the Meisner class, and learning about intentions and listening—all these acting techniques. And he is so far beyond that. He's throwing all that out and he's saying technique is nothing. It's bullshit! It's just lying. It's conviction and it's the emotion—the moment is everything! Everything had to be pure and in the moment.

When the symposium was completed and the film compiled, Brando attempted to edit the material, but he never finished. He died, and hundreds of hours of digital film—what Svetkey calls "in essence, Marlon Brando's brain preserved on magnetic tape"—were handed over to producer Mike Medavoy, the executor of Brando's estate. Medavoy refuses to show the footage.

He says there are no plans to ever release it.

Selected Bibliography

BOOKS

Adler, Stella, *The Art of Acting*. Howard Kissel, ed. New York: Applause, 2000.

Amburn, Ellis. *Subterranean Kerouac: The Hidden Life of Jack Kerouac*. New York: St. Martin's Griffin, 1999.

Anger, Kenneth. *Hollywood Babylon*. New York: Simon & Schuster, 1975.

Balcerzak, Scott. *Beyond Method: Stella Adler and the Male Actor*. Detroit: Wayne State University Press, 2018.

Barger, Ralph "Sonny," Keith Zimmerman, and Kent Zimmerman. *Hell's Angel: The Life and Times of Sonny Barger and the Hell's Angels Motorcycle Club*. New York: William Morrow, 2000.

Bisbort, Alan. *Beatniks: A Guide to an American Subculture*. Westport, CT: Greenwood Press, 2010.

———. *When You Read This, They Will Have Killed Me: The Life and Redemption of Caryl Chessman, Whose Execution Shocked America*. New York: Carrol and Graf, 2006.

Blevins, Winfred. *The Dictionary of the American West*. New York: Facts on File Books, 1993.

Bosworth, Patricia. *Marlon Brando*. New York: Viking, 2001.

Brando, Marlon, and Robert Lindsey. *Brando: Songs My Mother Taught Me*. New York: Random House, 1994.

Broughton, Sarah. *Brando's Bride*. Cardigan, Wales: Parthian Books, 2019.

Butler, Isaac. *The Method: How the Twentieth Century Learned to Act*. New York: Bloomsbury Publishing, 2002.

Carey, Gary. *Marlon Brando: The Only Contender*. New York: St. Martin's Press, 1985.

Clarke, Gerald. *Capote: A Biography*. New York: Simon & Schuster, 1988.

Clay, Andrew Dice, and David Ritz. *The Filthy Truth*. New York: Simon & Schuster, 2014.

Clayson, Alan, and Pauline Sutcliffe. *Backbeat: Stuart Sutcliffe: The Lost Beatle*. London: Pan, 1994.

Clurman, Harold. *All People Are Famous*. New York: Harcourt Brace Jovanovich, 1974.

———. *The Collected Works*. New York: Applause, 2000.

Cotkin, George. *Feast of Access: A Cultural History of the New Sensibility*. New York: Oxford University Press, 2015.

Dalton, David. *James Dean: The Mutant King*. San Francisco: Straight Arrow Books, 1974.

Dawson, Jim. *Rock Around the Clock: The Record That Started the Rock*. San Francisco: Backbeat Books, 2005.

Dennis, Jefferey P. *The Myth of the Queer Criminal*. New York: Routledge, 2017.

Doherty, Thomas. *Teenagers and Teenpics: The Juvenilization of American Movies in the 1950s*. Philadelphia: Temple University Press, 2010.

Downing, David. *Marlon Brando*. New York: Stein and Day, 1984.

Foley, Greg, and Andrew Luecke. *COOL: Style, Sound, and Subversion*. New York: Rizzoli, 2017.

Gabbard, Krin. *Black Magic: White Hollywood and African American Culture*. New Brunswick, NJ: Rutgers University Press, 2004

Geczy, Adam, and Vicki Karaminas. *Fashion and Masculinities in Popular Culture*. New York: Routledge, 2019

Gilbert, James. *A Cycle of Outrage: America's Reaction to the Juvenile Delinquent in the 1950s*. New York: Oxford University Press, 1988.

Goldman, Albert. *Elvis*. New York: McGraw-Hill, 1981.

Gopnik, Blake. *Warhol*. New York: Ecco, 2020.

Gould, Jonathan. *Can't Buy Me Love: The Beatles, Britain, and America*. New York: Crown, 2008.

Graham, Sheilah. *The Rest of the Story*. New York: Coward-McCann, 1964.

Graziano, Rocky, and Rowland Barber. *Somebody Up There Likes Me*. New York: Simon & Schuster, 1955.

Green, Jonathon. *Green's Dictionary of Slang*. Edinburgh: Chambers, 2017.

Guralnick, Peter. *Last Train to Memphis: The Rise of Elvis Presley*. Boston: Little, Brown and Company, 1994.

———. *Careless Love: The Unmaking of Elvis Presley*. Boston: Little, Brown and Company, 1999.

Hamm, Theodore. *Rebel and a Cause: Caryl Chessman and the Politics of the Death Penalty in Postwar California, 1948–1974*. Berkeley: University of California Press, 2001.

Harrington, Anne. *Mind Fixers*. New York: Norton, 2019.

Hayes, Bill. *The Original Wild Ones: Tales of The Boozefighters Motorcycle Club*. St. Paul, MN: Motorbooks, 2005.

Higham, Charles. *Brando: The Unauthorized Biography*. New York: Dutton, 1987.

Hoberman, J. *An Army of Phantoms: American Movies and the Making of the Cold War*. New York: The New Press, 2011.

Howlett, John. *James Dean: Rebel Life*. London: Plexus Publishing, 2016.

Hooven, F. Valentine III. *Tom of Finland: His Life and Times*. New York: St. Martin's Press, 1993.

Humphries, Patrick. *Elvis The #1 Hits: The Secret History of the Classics*. Kansas City: Andrews McMeel, 2003.

Jones, Dylan. *Elvis Has Left the Building: The Death of the King and The Rise of Punk Rock*. New York: Overlook Press, 2014.

Kazan, Elia. *Elia Kazan: A Life*. New York: Alfred A. Knopf, 1988.

———. *Kazan on Directing.* New York: Alfred A. Knopf, 2009.

———. *The Selected Letters of Elia Kazan.* Edited by Albert J. Devlin and Marline J. Devlin. New York: Alfred A. Knopf, 2014.

Kearns, Burt. *Tabloid Baby.* Nashville: Celebrity Books, 1999.

Kemper, Tom. *Hidden Talent: The Emergence of Hollywood Agents.* Berkeley: University of California Press, 2010.

Klein, George, and Chuck Crisafulli. *Elvis: My Best Man: Radio Days, Rock 'n' Roll Night, and My Lifelong Friendship with Elvis Presley.* New York: Crown Archetype, 2010.

Knight, Anna Ariadne. *Screening the Hollywood Rebels in 1950s Britain.* Manchester: Manchester University Press, 2021.

Lanza. Joseph. *Phallic Frenzy: Ken Russell and His Films.* Chicago: Chicago Review Press, 1994.

Levy, Shawn. *Paul Newman: A Life.* New York: Crown Archetype, 2009.

Lewisohn, Mark. *Tune In: The Beatles: All These Years.* New York: Crown Archetype, 2013.

Lhamon, W. T. *Deliberate Speed: The Origins of a Cultural Style in the American 1950s.* Cambridge, MA: Harvard University Press, 2002.

McDonald, Paul. *Hollywood Stardom.* Malden, MA: Wiley Blackwell, 2012.

McGilligan, Patrick. *Backstory 1: Interviews with Screenwriters of Hollywood's Golden Age.* Berkeley: University of California Press, 1988.

———. *Backstory 2: Interviews with Screenwriters of the 1940s and 1950s.* Berkeley: University of California Press, 1991.

McNeil, Legs, and Gillian McCain. *Please Kill Me.* New York: Grove Press, 1996.

Mailer, Norman. *The Naked and the Dead.* New York: Rinehart and Company, Inc., 1948.

Mann, William J. *The Contender: The Story of Marlon Brando.* New York: Harper, 2019.

Manso, Peter. *Brando: The Biography.* New York: Hyperion, 1994.

Mapplethorpe, Robert. *Certain People: A Book of Portraits.* Pasadena, CA: Twelvetrees Press, 1985.

Melnick, Monte A., and Frank Meyer. *On the Road with the Ramones (Bonus Edition).* London: Music Sales, 2019.

Miles, Barry. *Paul McCartney: Many Years from Now.* New York: Henry Holt & Company, 1997

Mizruchi, Susan L. *Brando's Smile: His Life, Thought, and Work.* New York: W. W. Norton & Company, 2014.

Norman, Philip. *John Lennon: The Life.* New York: Ecco, 2008.

Porter, Darwin. *Brando Unzipped.* New York: Blood Moon Productions, 2006.

———. *Paul Newman: The Man Behind the Baby Blues.* New York: Blood Moon Productions, 2009.

Porter, Darwin, and Danforth Prince. *James Dean: Tomorrow Never Comes.* New York: Blood Moon Productions, 2016.

Ramone, Johnny. *Commando: The Autobiography of Johnny Ramone.* New York: Abrams, 2012.

Redfield, William. *Letters from an Actor.* New York: Viking Press, 1967.

Robb, Brian J. *Johnny Depp: A Modern Rebel.* London: Plexus Publishing, 1995, 2004.

Rombes, Nicholas. *The Ramones' Ramones*. New York: Continuum, 2005.

Samuel, Lawrence R. *Shrink: A Cultural History of Psychoanalysis in America*. Lincoln: University of Nebraska Press, 2013

Saroyan, William. *The Time of Your Life*. 1939; New York: Methuen Drama, 2008.

Smith, Patrick S. *Andy Warhol's Art and Films*. Ann Arbor, MI: UMI Research Press, 1986.

Stuart, Johnny. *Rockers! Kings of the Road*. London: Plexus Publishing, 1996.

Sutcliffe, Pauline, and Thompson, Douglas. *The Beatles' Shadow: Stuart Sutcliffe and His Lonely Hearts*. London: Sidgwick & Jackson, 2001.

Thomas, Bob. *Brando: Portrait of the Rebel as An Artist*. London: W. H. Allen, 1973.

Thompson, Hunter S. *Hell's Angels: The Strange and Terrible Saga of the Outlaw Motorcycle Gangs*. New York: Random House, 1967.

Trevelyan, John. *What the Censor Saw*. London: Michael Joseph, 1973.

Vizzard, Jack. *See No Evil: Life Inside a Hollywood Censor*. New York: Simon & Schuster, 1970.

Williams, Tennessee. *A Streetcar Named Desire (1947)*. New York: Penguin, 2009.

Worth, Fred L., and Steve D. Tamerius. *Elvis: His Life from A to Z*. Chicago: Contemporary Books, 1988.

ARTICLES, VIDEOS

Anderson, Ariston. "Jean Paul Gautier Reflects on How Cinema Shaped His Career." *The Hollywood Reporter*, August 1, 2017.

Baker, Danny. "The Village People." *New Musical Express*, February 1979.

Camboli, Luca, Roberto Mazzagatti, and Michele Augusto Riva. "The Napoleon Delusion: 200 Years Later—Psychiatry in the Arts." *British Journal of Psychiatry* 220, no. 2 (February 2022).

Canfield, Edwin Lee. "*The Wild Angels*: The B-Movie That Inspired the Movie that Changed Hollywood." *New Horizine: A Zine about Roger Corman*, 2023.

Cochrane, Lauren. "From Marlon Brando to Gigi Hadid: The Return of Rebel Headgear." *The Guardian*, December 10, 2015.

Conley, Erin. "Theater Review: *Scissorhands*—A Musical Inspired by the Film at Rockwell Table & Stage." *On Stage and Screen*, December 15, 2018.

Dickson, Andrew. "The Best Shakespeare Films—Ranked!" *The Guardian*, February 8, 2019.

Dulaney, William L. "A Brief History of 'Outlaw' Motorcycle Clubs." *International Journal of Motorcycle Studies*, November 2005.

Eggert, Brian. "The Wild One." *Deep Focus Review*, September 21, 2019

Fearon, Fay. "How to Dress Like Marlon Brando." *British GQ*, April 3, 2020.

Goodman, Elyssa. "Soldier, Sailor, Stable Boy, Spy: 100 Years of Tom of Finland's Legacy." *InsideHook*, July 27, 2020.

Grierson, Tim. "Misleading Men: The Diceman Cometh." *Mel Magazine*, June 21, 2016.

Groopman, Jerome. "The Troubled History of Psychiatry." *The New Yorker*, May 27, 2019.

Heath, Chris. "Quincy Jones Has a Story about That." *GQ*, January 29, 2018.

Holmstrom, John. *PUNK* 1, no. 1, January 1976.

Johnstone, Iain. "Film 82 Special." BBC-1, 1982.

Jones, Sam. "Rocky's Shorts and Madonna's Bra on Display in Madrid in Gaultier Show." *The Guardian*, February 18, 2022.

Kael, Pauline. "Marlon Brando: An American Hero." *The Atlantic*, March 1966

Kemmerle, Karen. "Can We Talk about Andrew Dice Clay in *Blue Jasmine*?" *Tribeca Festival/Tribeca News*, December 18, 2013

Koch, Joe. "Marlon Brando: The Original Punk." *PUNK* 1, no. 1, January 1976.

Lenker, Maureen Lee. "Robert Duvall Reflects on *The Godfather* Mooning Contest, Working with Marlon Brando." *Entertainment Weekly*, March 18, 2022.

Lewis, Richard. "America's New Trinity of Love: Dean, Brando, Presley" (song). *Kerouac; Kicks Joy Darkness*. Rykodisc, 1997.

Love, Damien. "The Miracle Worker: An Interview with Arthur Penn." *Bright Lights Film Journal*, July 31, 2009.

Mailer, Norman. "Superman Comes to the Supermart." *Esquire*. November 1, 1960.

Marchese, David. "In Conversation: Quincy Jones." *Vulture, New York Magazine*, February 7, 2018.

Medoff, Rafael. "Ben Hecht's "A Flag Is Born": A Play That Changed History." The David S. Wyman Institute for Holocaust Studies, 2017. http://new.wyman institute.org/2004/04/special-feature-ben-hechts-a-flag-is-born-a-play-that -changed-history/.

Miculec, Sven. "*Easy Rider*: A Revolutionary Road-Trip Film that Heralded a New Era in Filmmaking." *Cinephilia & Beyond*, 2017. https://cinephiliabeyond.org/ easy-rider-revolutionary-road-trip-film-heralded-new-era-filmmaking/.

Mitchell, Mitch. "A Brief History of the Teddy Boys." *Revolutionary Socialism in the 21st Century*, February 19, 2019.

Nichols, Dave. "Birth of Bikers: How Motorcycle Culture Got Its Start." HighSeas- Rally.com, 2020. https://highseasrally.com/news/2020/06/birth-of-bikers -part-1/.

Ólafsdóttir, Ásta Karen. "Heteronormative Villains and Queer Heroes: Queer Representation in the Films of John Waters." University of Iceland School of Humanities, May 2014.

Paxton, John, and Ben Maddow (uncredited). *The Wild One* (screenplay, 1953). Daily Script. https://www.dailyscript.com/scripts/Wild%20One,%20The.txt.

Rabb, John. "Macho Comes to Music." *Washington Post*, June 24, 1979.

Rabin, Nathan. "Why John Waters' *Cry-Baby* Deserves More Attention." Rotten Tomatoes, July 19, 2016. https://editorial.rottentomatoes.com/article/ why-john-waters-cry-baby-deserves-more-attention/.

Robinson, Christopher. "Dragging Themselves through the Negro Streets at Dawn: The Influence of African American Culture on the Beats." Presented to the Liberty University faculty, April 1, 2009.

Rooney, Frank. "Cyclists Raid." *Harper's*, January 1951.

Ruffalo, Mark L. "The Psychoanalytic Tradition in American Psychiatry." *Psychiatric Times*, January 23, 2018.

Shedd, Matt. "Marlon Brando's Jazz-Culture Cool in a Musical Era before Elvis." *No Depression*, April 19, 2011. https://www.nodepression.com/marlon-brandos-jazz-culture-cool-in-a-muical-era-before-elvis/

Simmons, Jerold. "Violent Youth: The Censoring and Public Reception of *The Wild One* and *The Blackboard Jungle*." *Film History: An International Journal* 20, no. 3 (2008): 381–91.

Stevenson, Billy. "John Waters: *Cry-Baby* 1990." *CinemaTelevisionMusic*, June 27, 2017.

Strauss, Neil. "Obituary: Glenn Hughes, 50, the Biker of the Village People Band." *New York Times*, March 17, 2001.

Svetkey, Benjamin. "Marlon Brando's Real Last Tango: The Never-Told Story of His Secret A-List Acting School." *Hollywood Reporter*, June 11, 2015.

Thompson, Hunter S. "The Motorcycle Gangs: Losers and Outsiders." *The Nation*, May 17, 1965.

van Rheede Toas, John (a.k.a. Rockin Nidge). "The Clapham Common Murder 1953." The Edwardian Teddy Boy. https://www.edwardianteddyboy.com/page6.html.

Vogel, Carol. "Warhol's Presley and Brando Head to Auction." *New York Times*, September 4, 2014.

Walker, Beverly. "Interview: Gene Hackman, the Last Honest Man in Hollywood." *Film Comment*, November–December 1988.

Ward, Nathan. "How Rocky Graziano Became Boxing's Greatest Muse." *Deadspin*, January 18, 2016.

White, Armond. "Gaying the Oscars." *OUT*, February 20, 2015.

———. "How *Last Tango in Paris* Defined the Gay-Straight Sexual Revolution." *OUT*, December 7, 2016.

———. "The Power of *Women in Love*: How Alan Bates and Oliver Reed Fired Up Film Eroticism." *OUT*, June 11, 2018.

Wolfe, Tom. "Radical Chic: That Party at Lenny's." *New York*, June 8, 1970.

ADDITIONAL RESEARCH MATERIAL

Andy Warhol/Double Marlon Post-War & Contemporary Art. Christie's Auction, 2008.

Bonus Episode #153: Oscar Injustices. Gilbert Gottfried's Amazing Colossal Podcast with Frank Santopadre, 2018. https://www.gilbertpodcast.com/?s=153&id=4056.

Cyclist's Holiday: "He and Friends Terrorize a Town." *Life*, July 21, 1947.

Interview with Edward Norton. *The Joe Rogan Experience*, episode 1375, October 31, 2019.

"Interview with Joseph M. Wilcots." Interviews: An Oral History of Television 2002, Television Academy Foundation. https://interviews.televisionacademy.com/interviews/joseph-m-wilcots.

John Lennon: The Art College Days. National Museums, Liverpool.

Johnny Depp Special. *Larry King Live*, October 16, 2011.

Marlon, Andy Warhol 1928–1927. Christie's Auction, 2014. https://www.christies .com/en/lot/lot-5074049.

Marlon Brando films. IMDb.

Marlon Brando interview. *The Dick Cavett Show*, June 12, 1973.

Marlon Brando interview. *The Tonight Show*, starring Johnny Carson, May 11, 1968.

Marlon Brando on the Caryl Chessman Execution. Broadcast on KPFA, December 12, 1968. Pacifica Radio Archives. https://www.pacificaradioarchives.org/ recording/bb1597.

Marlon Brando Special. *Larry King Live*, 1994.

Meet Marlon Brando. Albert and David Maysles (directors). Maysles Films, 1966.

Paul Newman Interviews 1973, 1982, 1987. YouTube.

"The Ploughboys Murder." FullyBooked, 2017. https://fullybooked2017.com/ 2017/04/06/the-ploughboys-murder/.

Scorpio Rising. Kenneth Anger. Puck Films, 1963.

"Street Fashion: The Wild One' Tamed." *New York Times*, November 22, 1987.

"Top Exhibitoratings of 1954–1955, Top Money Actors." *Independent Film Journal* 36, no. 9 (November 12, 1955).

The Wild One. Laszlo Benedek, director. 1953.

Index

Academy Awards, xi, 37, 39, 106, 130, 145, 184, 187–88, 218–20, 236
Academy of Motion Picture Arts and Sciences, 219
Adams, Amy, 229
Adams, Marjorie, 103–4, 118
Adams, Nick, 129
Adler, Ellen, 100
Adler, Luther, 5, 9
Adler, Jacob P., 5
Adler, Renata, 224
Adler, Stella, 5–6, 9–10, 21, 23–24, 69, 100, 105, 115–16, 192, 229
The Adventures of Ford Fairlane, 237
The African Queen, 37
Alexander, Scott, 229, 241
Allan in Wonderland, 113
Allen, Steve, 196, 198
Allen, Tim, 185
Allen, Woody, 238–39
All People Are Famous, 100
Alpert, Hollis, 223
AlUla Arts Festival, 164
American Badass, 185
American Film Institute, 204
American International Pictures (AIP), 178, 181
American League for A Free Palestine, 9–11
American Nazi Party, 232
Anderson, Maxwell, 6
Andrews Sisters, 63
Angel of Death. See Eagle Rampant
Angel Unchained, 185

Anger, Kenneth, 142, 158, 162–63
Anna and the King of Siam, 191
Antigone, 8
Apocalypse Now, 232–33, 235
The Appaloosa, 206
Arms and the Man, 103–4, 223
Arkoff, Samuel Z., 178
Arnold, Eve, 117
The Arrangement, 213–14, 216
The Asphalt Jungle, 42
Atkinson, Brooks, 23, 115, 119
Atlanta Braves, 220
The Authentic Death of Hendry Jones, 192
Avalon, Frankie, 178

Bacon, James, 79, 109, 111–12, 122
Baer, Max, Jr., 178
Baldwin, Alec, 239, 248
Baldwin, James, 141, 143–44, 209
Balfour, Eric, 185
Bambi, 80
Bangs, Lester, 166
Bankhead, Tallulah, 10, 21, 23
Barger, Sonny, 132, 179, 183
Barker, Travis, 165
Barrymore, John, 23, 37, 126
Bates, Alan, 136
Batman, 233–34
The Battle of Algiers, 213
The Battler, 119
Baxter, Cynthia, 61
Beacham, Stephanie, 226
Bean, Orson, 216

Acknowledgments

Much credit for the genesis of this appraisal of Marlon Brando's accomplishments and influence goes to Lee Sobel, the Johnny Strabler of his own gang of rebel writers, both a leader and visionary who loves books as much as he revels in and guides popular culture. Lee is the rare literary agent who is both entrepreneur and artist, and the one who gave me the sage advice to, for once, write about someone people have heard of. For that guidance alone, he's to be commended. For everything else, he is thanked. Many thanks also to the legendary editor John Cerullo, who selected this project for Rowman & Littlefield, for his taste, support, and for being so cool. And gratitude to the team at Rowman & Littlefield, including Barbara Claire, Melissa McClellan, Chris Chappell, Emily Jeffers, Gary Hamel, and Lori Pierelli for the care, time, and assistance that elevated this project.

This book would not have been possible without the love, support, and patience of Alison Holloway. Legs McNeil was a valuable sounding board, editorial adviser, and friend, and Jeff Abraham, my "pardner" in pop culture. Special thanks to Michael Madsen, Larry Karaszewski, David Del Valle, and Alan Bisbort, who have always been more than generous with their time and insights. Invaluable to this project as well were Edwin Lee Canfield, Dick Cavett, Andrew Dice Clay, Vincent Cotroneo, John Holmstrom, Phil Lander, Andrew D. Luecke, Monte A. Melnick, Gary Shapiro, Andy Shernoff, and Douglas Thompson.

Most helpful was the work of others who'd preceded me in exploring Brando-related territories, including Kenneth Anger, Jeffery P. Dennis, Elyssa Goodman, Blake Gopnik, Peter Guralnik, Bill Hayes, F. Valentine Hooven III, Elia Kazan, Anna Ariadne Knight, Joseph Lanza, Shawn Levy, Mark Lewisohn, Robert Lindsey, Paul McCartney, Patrick McGilligan, Peter Manso, William J. Mann, Barry Miles, Susan L. Mizruchi, Philip Norman, Dave Persails, Darwin Porter, Danforth Prince, Matthew Rettunmund, Jerold Simmons, Johnny Stuart, Benjamin Svetkey, Bob Thomas, and Armond White. Their work, and the work of others, should be sought out (and can be found in the Bibliography). Thanks also to Alexis Arakelian, Robert Bader, Robert Bellissimo, AJ Benza, Peter Brennan, Doug Bruckner, Mike Catalano, Jon Crowley, Derek Davidson, Donato Di Camillo, Bud Elder, Dana Gould, Frank Grimes, Tom Hearn, C. Courtney Joyner, Sally Jade Holloway Kearns, Sam Kearns, Sacheen Littlefeather, Matt Lubich, Gillian McCain, Jeff Mantor of the Larry Edmunds Book Shop, Jason Ney, Ray Richmond, Alex Rosas, Albert S. Ruddy, Frank Santopadre, Jon Sotzing, Brent Sweer, Hanna Zoey Tur, Raquel Vasquez, Elli Wohlgelernter, and Brian, Alfie, Billy, and Clarence.

Much appreciation is given to Gray Frederickson, a good man who accomplished great things; a colleague, mentor, and friend who is and will be sorely missed. Working and sharing film credit with Gray and Al Ruddy was a highlight of whatever it is I can look back on and call a career.

And all thanks to Marlon Brando for his inspiration, life, and work that will live on through this century and beyond.

The Tonight Show Starring Johnny Carson courtesy of Carson Entertainment Group.

The Dick Cavett Show courtesy of Daphne Productions.